GORDON CRAIG'S
MOSCOW *HAMLET*

Craig's sketch of Hamlet being wooed by his daimon Death, during the soliloquy "To be or not to be." The inscription reads, "With affection and much admiration to Stanislavsky from Craig. EGC 1909." (N.N. Chushkin, *Gamlet-Kachalov* [Moscow: Iskusstvo, 1966].)

GORDON CRAIG'S MOSCOW *HAMLET*

A Reconstruction

Laurence Senelick

Contributions in Drama and Theatre Studies, Number 4

GREENWOOD PRESS
WESTPORT, CONNECTICUT • LONDON, ENGLAND

Library of Congress Cataloging in Publication Data

Senelick, Laurence.
  Gordon Craig's Moscow Hamlet.

  (Contributions in drama and theatre studies,
ISSN 0163-3821 ; no. 4)
  Bibliography: p.
  Includes index.
  1. Shakespeare, William, 1564-1616.   Hamlet.
2. Shakespeare, William, 1564-1616 — Stage history —
Russian S. F. S. R. — Moscow.   3. Shakespeare, William,
1564-1616—Stage history—1800-1950.   4. Craig, Edward
Gordon, 1872-1966.   5. Moskovskiĭ khudozhestvennyĭ
akademicheskiĭ teatr.   6. Stanislavsky, Konstantin,
1863-1938.   I. Title.   II. Series.
  PR2807.S44   792.9'2   81-20310

ISBN 0-313-22495-1 (lib. bdg.)   AACR2

Library of Congress Catalog Card Number: 81-20310
ISBN: 0-313-22495-1
ISSN: 0163-3821

First published in 1982

Greenwood Press
A division of Congressional Information Service, Inc.
88 Post Road West
Westport, Connecticut 06881

Printed in the United States of America

10 9 8 7 6 5 4 3 2 1

For Teddy Craig

... these artists were not striving after a "good production" but after something much greater: after a "mystery," "complete truth" — they were truly unattainable boundaries, heights which were above the clouds.

Grigory Kozintsev

CONTENTS

ILLUSTRATIONS

PREFACE

In 1935, Gordon Craig returned to Russia for the first time in twenty-three years, to attend a theatre festival. He was fascinated by the Jewish Theatre *King Lear* with Mikhoels in the lead; excited by Meyerhold's productions; delighted to see that the actors he had known as promising beginners were now the leading movers and doers; startled to find that the elegant Nemirovich-Danchenko dwelt in the same mansion as before but now had to answer his own door; and suspicious that Stanislavsky pleaded illness to avoid meeting him. He also met a young scholar named Nikolay Chushkin, who was anxious to garner information about the legendary production of *Hamlet* staged at the Moscow Art Theatre in 1912 from the survivors of the experiment. Craig professed disinterest in the past and explained that his ideas about *Hamlet* had changed. But when Chushkin followed up his solicitations with a letter to Florence the next month, Craig replied formally:

> I my self cannot reconstruct all the happenings on the stage of the Art Theatre of Moscow during the performance of "Hamlet". And whenever I attempt to do so, it is like returning to a plate of cold food that has been in a pantry for several years . . . one turns from it, not towards it.
>
> The historian, on the other hand, is excited by the idea of these things, which are so hidden; and the only excuse for the historian, so far as I can see, is that thinking of these old things which he has not seen and cannot see, will awaken his *imagination* (and I sometimes think there is no imagination so vivid as that of the historian) and enable him to create a performance of "Hamlet" or "Lear" or "Macbeth" such as never took place. But then, why does the historian mix this beautiful fantasy of his with dates and names?[1]

Chushkin was sufficiently undiscouraged by this reply to publish (if only in the 1960s) a book on Kachalov's performance as the Prince of Denmark, using all the testimony he had gathered from participants and eye-witnesses. And Craig continued to be questioned by interviewers. With the years his judgment on the Moscow Art *Hamlet* became harsher and harsher: by the end of his life he mourned that the whole enterprise had been like "taking God Almighty into a music-hall."[2]

Any attempt at reconstruction is complicated by contradictory reports of the production that appeared at the time, and the myth-making capacities of the individuals involved. In Russia, the Moscow Art *Hamlet* was considered a qualified failure or, at best, a *succès d'estime*; in Western Europe, it quickly won a reputation for brilliance. Stanislavsky's *My Life in Art*, published in America in 1923, revealed many of the production's problems, and in doing so, raised Craig's ire. Later commentators promulgated myths which, over time, took on a veneer of authority, and even a lavish catalogue on Craig and *Hamlet* for a major exhibition in 1975 erred by misdating events and retailing misinformation.

How is the historian first to justify the reconstruction of a long-defunct theatrical production, then to defend himself from Craig's characterization that he "imagines" past events, and finally to provide as accurate an account as possible?

To confront these questions in order: it is undeniable that the Moscow *Hamlet* was one of the seminal occurrences in the modern theatre. Craig, indisputably a leading theorist and ideologue of the new stagecraft, was given the opportunity to carry out his ideas within the framework of a well-equipped, dedicated theatre with a cultivated staff and public. Stanislavsky, another major figure in the development of twentieth century stage practice, whose innovations differed from Craig's in direction but not in intent, lent himself wholeheartedly to the enterprise. Participating at one level or another were persons who were also to make their mark on the theatre of their time: among them, Leopold Sulerzhitsky, Evgeny Vakhtangov, Alisa Koonen, Mikhail Chekhov, Sam Hume, Ryszard Bołeslawski. Whatever its shortcomings, the production consolidated Craig's reputation, disseminated his ideas, and revolutionized the staging of Shakespeare in this century. The Moscow *Hamlet* is therefore not an isolated creative spasm, but a ganglion in which the nerves of some of the most important art movements of our time came together.

Insofar as the production stimulated the imagination of those who saw it, the historian may stimulate the imagination of his own time by describing it. The accusations levelled against Craig (most memorably by Lee Simonson) that he was unpractical and incapable of realizing his fantasies mean little when weighed against the influence his unrealized ideas, provocative manifestos and evocative drawings had on other, more practical men. The principles behind his *Hamlet*, his variations on the theme of Shakespeare, and Stanislavsky's brainstorms that Craig's presence sparked, retain their power to inspire and beguile.

There are two further justifications for this study, I believe: one grand, and one much less so. It is instructive to see two of the great figures of modern theatre pool their brains and talents to realize one of the master-works of world drama; studying their approaches, one can only learn more of them and of it. And at the same time, it is reassuring to discover that the usual petty squabbles, the familiar misunderstandings, the outbursts of temper and temperament, the cross-purposes and frustrations that charac-terize so much work in the theatre, on whatever level, are present even at such a lofty endeavor. This is not intended as debunking. Rather, such exposure should bring us closer to understanding remarkable men who have too often been veiled by the shroud of mystique, and should re-engage present-day workers in the theatre who find themselves constantly confounded by compromise.

To bring this production to life, the historian must first pare away the accretions of tradition and myth. And to accomplish this, I have had recourse to a documentary approach, allowing the principal actors in this event to speak in their own words and the contemporary commentators to register their reactions as they occurred at the time. Luckily, all the participants kept elaborate records. The Moscow Art Theatre had a tradition of recording every stage in a production's development for the sake of the archives, and Craig himself was a jackdaw who tagged, annotated and filed away every scrap of paper that came his way. The production was an abiding source of interest to the press. As a result, it is one of the most thoroughly documented productions in the history of the theatre, and I am enabled to tell the tale through contemporary letters, rehearsal notes, reviews and diaries, much of this data previously unpublished, a great deal of it never before in English.

In dealing with original source material, the scholar always owes a tremendous debt to those whose task it is to preserve and administer the documents. For their cooperation and assistance I am beholden to:

H.E. Robert Craig, Senior Administrator of the Edward Gordon Craig C.H. Estate, for authorization to publish any Craig material that seemed to me relevant;

Mlle Cécile Giteau of the Fonds Rondel, Bibliothèque de l'Arsénal; and Mme Lalais and the staff of the Bibliothéque Nationale, Paris, for permission to consult and copy the Craig correspondence, notebooks containing rehearsal records and conversations, Craig's personally annotated script of *Hamlet*, and his drawings and models, and for efficiently providing me with microfilms and photographs;

George Nash, former Curator of the Enthoven Collection, Victoria and Albert Museum, London, and his staff, for making wise suggestions, pointing me towards material that would otherwise have eluded me, and lending encouragement to the project;

Ellen Dunlap and David Farmer, Librarians of the Humanities Research Center, University of Texas at Austin, who assisted my consultation of the Craig collection there, including his Daybooks and correspondence, and granted permission to quote and reproduce material;

Brooke Whiting, Curator of Rare Books, University of California, Los Angeles, for sending me photostatic copies of the Russian reviews of Craig's *Hamlet*, to be found among the Craigiana there;

Arnold Rood, most urbane of Craigophiles, who lent me relevant items in his collection and proved a continuing support;

Jeanne Newlin, Curator, and Martha Mahard, Assistant Curator, of the

Harvard Theatre Collection, for letting me make it a home away from home;

The Dance Collection of the New York Public Library at Lincoln Center, Astor, Lenox and Tilden Foundations, for permission to reproduce excerpts from Isadora Duncan's letters;

The Librarian and staff of the Society for Cultural Relations with the USSR, London, who permitted me free access to their stacks and the scarce volumes to be found there;

The Society for Theatre Research, which bestowed on me the honor of making public some of my work as the Edward Gordon Craig Memorial Lecture at the annual conference of the International Federation for Theatre Research in Toronto in 1979;

James Arnott, editor of *Theatre Research International* and Simon Trussler, editor of *Theatre Quarterly*, for publishing early versions of this study in their journals;

Michael McDowell, who typed the various stages of the manuscript on a wondrous word-processor and reminded me when I was repeating myself;

and in particular, Edward Craig, who shared with me his treasures, his reminiscences, his advice and his enthusiasm since the project's very inception, and to whom this study is dedicated.

In publishing these documents, I have taken two editorial liberties: the dates are given in accordance with the Gregorian calendar. Those who want to ascertain the Julian dates, still used in Russia at the time, need only subtract thirteen days. I have regularized the spelling of Russian names (Craig used idiosyncratic Germanized forms such as Stanislawsky, Wanja, Mosqvin and so on) and of Sulerzhitsky's erratic English. The notes and bibliography use a more exact transliteration than does the narrative.

Laurence Senelick

GORDON CRAIG'S
MOSCOW *HAMLET*

INTRODUCTION

If a "Who's Who" of the leading figures in world theatre had been issued in 1909, it is unlikely that the names of either Gordon Craig or Konstantin Stanislavsky would have appeared in it. The fame of the Moscow Art Theatre had not yet become a byword in the West, while Craig's pictures and manifestos circulated chiefly among a small circle of *aficionados*. Had the compiler of such a biographical dictionary chosen to include these two men, however, these facts would have been available to him:

Gordon Craig had been born "The Feather of England," at Stevenage, England, on January 16, 1872, the illegitimate son of the actress Ellen Terry and Edward William Godwin, architect and scenic designer. After a limited education at Bradford College and Heidelberg, Craig became an actor. He had made his first stage appearance at the age of 6 in *Olivia* at the Court Theatre and frequently supported his mother in minor roles, adopting the name Edward Henry Gordon Craig in 1888. After touring the provinces in such parts as Macbeth, Hamlet, Cassio, Mercutio, Petruchio, Charles Surface, Armand in *La Dame aux caméllias* and Cavaradossi in *Tosca*, he made his first experiment in directing in 1893 at Uxbridge with Musset's *On ne badine pas avec l'amour*. He starred in *Hamlet* at the Olympic Theatre in 1897 with Ben Greet's company, but gave up acting because, he claimed, he no longer believed in the theatre as it was constituted at the time.

Craig's dissatisfaction with conventional theatrical modes was made clear in the series of plays he designed and directed between 1900 and 1903: *Dido and Aeneas* for the Purcell Opera Society, *The Masque of Love* at the Coronet Theatre, *Acis and Galatea* at Great Queen Street Hall and *Bethlehem* at the Imperial Institute. Each was characterized by geometric patterns of action, presentational setting, symbolic movement and properties meant to convey a mood rather than a specific period, and unusual lighting effects. Critical opinion had been for the most part unsympathetic, and the effect on the public was negligible, owing to the remoteness of the theatres and the brevity of the runs: *Dido*, for instance, saw only three performances and *The Masque of Love*, one. When his mother took the Imperial Theatre, Westminster, to provide him with greater opportunity, Craig experimented with a more grandiose deployment of line and color, but the enterprise was commercially unsuccessful and folded after two months.

Meanwhile, Craig had been making a name for himself as a draftsman; his woodcut illustrations and even his homegrown magazine *The Page* had won him a wider public than any of his realized work in the theatre. The Bohemian world of London appreciated this enthusiastic, good-looking young man with no curb to his tongue and considerable personal charm; his outlandish garb, his innumerable love-affairs, his flamboyant manner became legendary. Such friends as Max Beerbohm and Will Rothenstein believed firmly in Craig's genius and chose to excuse the outbursts of temperament that accompanied it.

Craig too believed firmly in his genius and tried to found a school in which to promulgate his ideas. Failing that, he accepted an invitation from the German director Otto Brahm to stage the Hofmannsthal version of *Venice Preserved* at the Lessing Theatre. This project earned him fame in Germany and led him to publish a series of essays, *The Art of the Theatre*, which contained his first fully articulated theories. They were far from original and echoed Adolphe Appia whenever they expressed the need for three-dimensional scenery to harmonize with a three-dimensional actor, the use of light as a plastic element in stage design, and the indispensable unity of impression that a production required. The originality of Craig's pamphlet lay in its style, contagiously perfervid; it constituted a manifesto for theatrical revolutionaries. Moreover, he enunciated with maximal force a doctrine that had been taking shape in the work of Antoine, Stanislavsky, Brahm and Lugné-Poë: the subordination of all elements of stage art to a master-mind who was to coordinate the whole. Believing the theatre to be choked by words, Craig reduced the text of a play to equal status with music and lighting, dance and movement, setting and costumes, all of which were ordered and blended by the only begettor, the director.

While in Germany Craig had begun his tempestuous liaison with Isadora Duncan, then at the crest of her popularity; in addition to a child, this relationship engendered Craig's increasing interest in abstract movement as another element in the stage picture. It was Isadora who would be the agent responsible for bringing Craig and Stanislavsky together; but first she persuaded the Italian star Eleonora Duse to commission designs for Hofmannsthal's *Elektra*. Although this project was eventually scrapped, Craig did produce a *Rosmersholm* for Duse in Florence in 1906. But his growing impatience with the compromises entailed by collaboration and the practical exigencies of the theatre caused him to break with Duse when the sets were altered for a revival in Nice.

Craig was developing a reputation as an *enfant terrible*, impossible to work with, childishly demanding and lazy; he himself rejected the offers that came to him from Max Reinhardt and Herbert Beerbohm Tree, presumably afraid that his brain-children would be kidnapped by such strong-minded individuals. He cherished the notion of a school and a theatre of his own where his work could be carried out in a pristine manner. In 1908 he rented the Arena Goldoni in Florence and began to publish his journal *The Mask*. The very first number included the essay on "Actor and Ueber-marionette" which, by its demands that actors be totally subservient to the director's will, created a stir and helped to confirm Craig's reputation as an authoritarian dreamer.

The backgrounds of Craig and Stanislavsky were disparate, and what they most had in common was an indulged childhood protected from life's harsh realities, and a passionate love for the theatre, which stood for a sur-rogate world. But whereas Craig the lovechild had grown up behind the scenes of the bohemian, magical Victorian playhouse, Stanislavsky had enjoyed a sheltered bourgeois upbringing. He had been born Konstantin Sergeevich Alekseev on January 5, 1863, in Moscow, the son of the owner of a textile mill. Although he was descended from a French actress on his mother's side, his circle was composed of those enlightened merchants and businessmen who chose to be patrons of the arts in a society where political and social involvement was curtailed. Amateur theatricals, private per-formances of farces and operettas in which he starred brought the hand-some young man to consider the stage as a career, and he adopted the Polish name Stanislavsky to avoid offense to his family. His training was scanty: some singing lessons with the tenor Fyodor Kommissarzhevsky and brief enrollment in a school run by the actress Fyodotova, herself a pupil of the "grandfather of realistic acting," Mikhail Shchepkin.

In 1885 Stanislavsky became one of five directors of the Russian Musical Society, and in 1888, with Kommissarzhevsky and Fyodotova's husband, he founded the Artistic and Literary Society, a dedicated amateur group. With time, many talented individuals became associated with the Society and its reputation in Moscow literary and dramatic circles took on prestige; Stanislavsky, who usually played the male leads, gradually came to be con-sidered one of the finest actors in Russia. He was eternally dissatisfied with his own work, and eternally sought new ways to perfect it. For him, art was a religion, to be served unselfishly and singlemindedly. The theatre, he was to assert, was a temple.

In 1897 came the momentous meeting with Vladimir Ivanovich Nemirovich-Danchenko. Nemirovich, the son of a cavalry officer of reduced means, had worked his way up in the world as a literary man, a popular playwright, husband of a baroness, and a pedagogue at the Moscow Conservatory. Like Stanislavsky, he was dissatisfied with the contemporary theatre and longed for a more intellectually appealing, better disciplined stage. Between them, the two men drew up an elaborate charter and founded such a theatre; its principles included the preponderance of the director in artistic decisions, the dedication of the actor to ensemble playing, and the painstaking prepa-ration of each production, beginning with lengthy "table rehearsals," in which the ideas and meaning of a play would be elicited. Stanislavsky, who selected the best members of his Art and Literary Society for admission, was to have the veto in matters theatrical; Nemirovich, who invited his prize graduates from the Conservatory, was to have the literary veto.

The Moscow Art and Publicly Accessible Theatre (as it was first called) opened on October 14, 1898, with Aleksey Tolstoy's blank-verse chronicle play *Tsar Fyodor Ioannovich*. It had a resounding success, due primarily to the archaeological accuracy of the décor, the impressive handling of crowd scenes and the sensitive acting of Ivan Moskvin in the title role. But it soon became apparent that the popular audience the founders had hoped for was not forthcoming, and so, accepting the inevitable, they raised their prices, dropped "Publicly Accessible" from the masthead, and strove to attract a cultured, socially aware, middle-class public.

The rest of the first season was a qualified failure, for the theatre had not yet found a consistent acting style and the Saxe-Meiningen approach that had been so successful in *Tsar Fyodor* was inoperative on such plays as *Twelfth Night* and *Hedda Gabler*. The day was saved when Nemirovich suggested a revival of Chekov's *The Seagull*; Stanislavsky was hesitant for he did not understand the play, but supplied a *mise-en-scène* rich in true-to-life details and evocative atmosphere. The novelty of producing a contemporary drama as if it were a Saxe-Meiningen historical play enthralled audiences, who also identified with the lyrical ethos of the intelligentsia portrayed on stage. Henceforth the Moscow Art Theatre adopted Chekhov as its house dramatist and the so-called Chekhovian "mood" with its pauses, subtle modulations, subdued longing and naturalistic trappings as the house style, adapted to all manner of plays. No matter whether the author was Gorky, Shakespeare, Ibsen, Turgenev or Hauptmann, the "mood" approach was preferred.

But as early as 1902, a rift could be seen to develop between the two directors. Nemirovich, essentially a man of letters with progressive political views, wanted the theatre to assume a more distinctly liberal profile, and preferred a repertory consisting of socially relevant plays staged in a suitably realistic manner. He pointed out that his own choices, *The Seagull* and *An Enemy of the People*, had been the two most popular productions in the repertory. Stanislavsky, however, a wholly apolitical being, always had a penchant for fantasy plays and interesting performance techniques, even though he equated the term "theatrical" with outworn clichés of the nineteenth century stock system. Work with actors was more appealing to him than work with a playwright. He was attracted by the experiments in improvisation held by Nemirovich's former pupil, a young actor in the company named Vsevolod Meyerhold, and in 1905 asked him to run a studio in which to develop a new acting style suitable for playing Maeterlinck.

Jealous of Stanislavsky's personal success as an actor even in calamitous productions, Nemirovich came to believe that his colleague was not so much interested in interpreting a play according to its author's intent as in controlling a group of actors, and that their aims as partners were too divergent to permit the Art Theatre to continue. Matters became so embroiled that by 1907 Nemirovich was considering a move to the state-supported Maly Theatre and Stanislavsky was planning to step down as a manager of the MAT. Things came to a head when Stanislavsky wanted to take on Leopold Sulerzhitsky as a personal assistant to foster experiments in avant-garde stagecraft and his embryonic "system" of acting; he had to pay his assistant out of his own pocket.

The upshot was that Stanislavsky, one of the few solvent shareholders in the MAT, sold out his shares in 1908, ostensibly so as not to ruin his family financially, and limited himself to directing two plays a season with an experimental play subject to veto by Nemirovich who had become Chairman of the Board. As it happened, the experimental production for 1908, Maeterlinck's *The Blue Bird*, was such a huge success that Stanislavsky was emboldened to consider an additional play for the following year. He was anxious to show that the Art Theatre was capable of producing tragedy, especially Shakespeare. It was at this juncture that Craig's name came to his attention.

1
OVERTURES

Although Stanislavsky had been exposed to and inspired by such European exponents of Shakespearean tragedy as Salvini and Rossi, it was the tour of the Duke of Saxe-Meiningen's troupe in 1890 that chiefly influenced his attitude to the production of Shakespeare. The playwright Ostrovsky had commented on an earlier appearance (1885) of the Meiningers in Russia, "These are not the dramas of Shakespeare and Schiller but a series of tableaux vivants made from those dramas";[1] the impressionable young Stanislavsky, however, was greatly taken with the disciplined crowd scenes, atmospheric sound-effects and pauses and, above all, the creation of a mood even before a word had been spoken. His own first major Shakespearean production for the semi-amateur Art and Musical Society, *Othello* (1895), was not so much a reading of a play as a variation on the theme of fifteenth century Venice. One member of the society, present when Stanislavsky related his concept to the company, recalled, "At his account of how the action was to develop in *Othello*, we simply were stunned. The splendid Shakespearean text remained somewhere in the background, there emerged only an account of the action itself."[2]

An excursion to the historical sites and museums of Venice had provided the raw material for the decor and costumes, for Stanislavsky was set on recreating the everyday life of the times. Real water flowed in the canals in which Iago paddled his hand; Brabantio, after his tantrum, was assuaged with a glass of water; Othello himself was based on a Moor Stanislavsky had met in a Paris café and although his own performance in the part exuded nobility, trust and up-to-date psychology, many found it to be lacking in tigerishness. Incapable of understanding the script from within, and personally unfamiliar with passionate jealousy, in the last act he fell back on operatic conventions. Audiences left, oohing and ahing about the splendid stage effects and admiring Stanislavsky as a sensitive actor, but with the comment, "He's no tragedian."[3]

In a frank letter, the French critic Lucien Bernard told Stanislavsky, "Even though you understood Othello's soul perfectly well, you did not play it in the Shakespearean tradition. . . . I have no doubt that if you were to work with Irving or Salvini, you would create a beautiful Othello."[4] Stanislavsky's reply was that, to his mind, tradition equalled lack of talent (*bezdarnost'*) and hollow formality, and he was seeking to rethink the classics along new lines. Unfortunately this rethinking invariably led to historical resurrection. His productions of *Much Ado about Nothing* and *Twelfth Night* in 1897 were partly conceived "to take advantage of excellent pictorial material" collected in Italy and the reviewers spoke more of the "historical truth" of the *mise-en-scène* than of its capturing Shakespeare's spirit.[5]

The same approach lingered on in the Moscow Art Theatre: It is significant that the success of the opening production of 1898, Aleksey Tolstoy's blank-verse chronicle play *Tsar Fyodor Ioannovich*, was founded on an "archaeological" interpretation, the careful use of museum artifacts to recreate the court life of sixteenth century Muscovy, rather than on the acting. Simultaneously, Stanislavsky had rehearsed *The Merchant of Venice* with the provincial tragedian Darsky as Shylock. The young actor Vsevolod Meyerhold recalled the preliminary discussions of the play as highly original and far from routine, when Stanislavsky insisted that the settings "clearly depict the contrast between two worlds — the filthy, sordid, craven and maliciously self-seeking Jewish quarter and the square in front of Portia's palace, heedlessly merry, exuberant and amorous."[6] This is certainly as modernist in its general "concept" as any of Harley Granville-Barker's notions. But to break Darsky of his old-fashioned mannerisms and penchant for emoting, Stanislavsky forced him to play Shylock with a Yiddish accent, which, to a Russian ear, was both comic and squalid. In the resultant production, once again the outward trappings were praised for their authenticity, but critics and audiences alike missed the tragic tone and the inner meaning of Shylock's scenes, and the play dropped out of the repertory almost at once.

The Moscow Art Theatre's most elaborate mounting of Shakespeare came in 1903 with a production of *Julius Caesar*, staged solely by Nemirovich-Danchenko whose directorial reputation was made by it. Stanislavsky had had no wish to be connected with the production but let himself be persuaded to play Brutus, even though he fought hard against giving up his splendid handle-bar moustache. The *mise-en-scène* suffered from acute Meiningenitis: Nemirovich-Danchenko and his assistants spent a year visiting Rome, sketching monuments and ransacking Mommsen's history for details of life in the later Republic.

The theatre was transformed into a veritable scientific institute. A special commission, headed by Nemirovich, went to Rome to collect the topographical and archaeological data. A special office was established: one section dealt with textual problems, stage traditions, cutting, publicity and literary criticism; another with everything concerning manners and mores of Caesar's era; a third with costumes, a fourth with weaponry, a fifth with scenery, a sixth with music, a seventh with crowd scenes, and so on. Not only the theatre set to work: all Moscow was eager to lend a hand. Museum curators and librarians, antiquarians, collectors and bibliophiles put their knowledge and their treasures at its disposal.[7]

To avoid the usual crowds of unpicturesque senators in togas, Nemirovich-Danchenko stressed the melting-pot element of Rome; he littered the stage with Egyptians, Syrians, Goths, Vandals, Nubian slaves and rude mechanicals of all sorts in crowd scenes of two hundred persons. Soviet commentators try to play down the Meiningen influence by asserting that the MAT production was ideologically the opposite: whereas the Court theatre had stressed the nobility of Caesar, that MAT made the People the protagonist. But on the face of it, the finished product owed more to academic painters like Alma-Tadema and Munkácsy than to a political idea, and the patent failure of *Julius Caesar* as staged by a leading modern theatre provoked a lively press debate in Russia on such questions as "Is Shakespeare obsolete?", and "Can the Art Theatre actors play Shakespeare?" The symbolist aestheticians seized upon it as a prime example of the bankruptcy of materialism: for Dmitry Merezhkovsky the production was sheer nonsense, and the poet and novelist Andrey Bely wrote, "I am convinced that at the present moment Chekhov means more to most of the members of the Art Theatre than does Shakespeare."[8]

Stanislavsky agreed. His Brutus had been thought noble enough but not very thrilling in the big moments, and he was unhappy about the experience. Shakespeare, or at any rate Nemirovich's approach to Shakespeare, seemed to him out of keeping with the theatre's goals; he wrote to Olga Knipper, "*Julius Caesar* won't take us as far as Chekhov will."[9]

After all, the Art Theatre's reputation had been consolidated by its productions of Chekhov, Gorky and Hauptmann, authors who lent themselves to the special blend of closely observed realistic detail, psychological subtlety and creation of mood that were the trademarks of the MAT. But the theatre had taken this direction somewhat at random, the success of *The Seagull* and Ibsen's *Enemy of the People* confirming it in its strengths. The original season had included, besides *Tsar Fyodor, The Merchant of Venice* and a revival of *Twelfth Night*, Sophocles' *Antigone* and Hauptmann's fairy-tales *The Sunken Bell* and *Hannele*. Problems with inexperienced actors, public disinterest and (in the case of *Hannele*) censorship curtailed the eclecticism of the theatre. Between 1899 and 1905 the only ventures into drama that required more than a naturalistic mode of presentation were a literal-minded rendering of Ostrovsky's *The Snow-Maiden* and the failed *Julius Caesar*. (An exception might be made for the 1900 staging of *When We the Dead Awake*, but the MAT approach to Ibsen was always staunchly veristic, with considerable research into the Norwegian ambience.) By 1905, Stanislavsky was beginning to feel, with Sorin in *The Seagull*, "as stale as an old cigarette-holder."

Stanislavsky's dissatisfactions were echoed by others. As early as 1902, the Art Theatre had been under attack for its adherence to naturalistic stage techniques. In an influential article "Unnecessary Truth," Valery Bryusov, a young symbolist poet and member of Merezhkovsky's cadre of mystics, had argued that the essence of theatre lay in the actor's performance, and that cluttered sets and verisimilitudinous stagecraft simply got in the way of his creativity. Moreover, he opined, there was something incongruous about a three-dimensional living body juxtaposed against two-dimensional elements professing an equivalent reality.[10] Bryusov had not read the works of Adolphe Appia, but he concurred with many of Appia's notions of a unit set, plastic elements of décor and a return to a more "Shakespearean" environment for the performer.

Yielding to such external pressures and to his own sense of failure, Stanislavsky turned to his former student Meyerhold to form a studio in which to carry out experiments in producing non-naturalistic drama; the studio's literary adviser was the same Valery Bryusov. After a year of conferences and rehearsals, the Studio prepared a production of Maeterlinck's *La Mort de Tintagiles*, which observers at the dress rehearsal pronounced to be brilliant. But the general public never saw it. Stanislavsky disbanded the Studio before it could open its doors. Financial difficulties and the uncertain political climate (the street riots of the 1905 Revolution were going on) were the reasons advanced to explain this censorious move; but another likely explanation is Stanislavsky's dissatisfaction with the acting, which failed to meet the demands of Meyerhold's stylization.[11] Stanislavsky was convinced that new acting techniques, not new methods of picturization, were the desiderata of theatrical innovation.

Meanwhile the Moscow Art Theatre strove to expand its repertory. Ibsen's *Brand* and allegorical dramas by Knut Hamsun and Leonid Andreev were performed with varying degrees of success; the choices were, for the Art Theatre, admirably daring if less adventurous than those of other theatres which (under the guidance of Meyerhold and his generation of directors) were staging the latest works of contemporary symbolists. Yet whenever the MAT tried to convey some meaning beyond the psychological it failed. In his "Report on the Past Decade's Artistic Growth" in 1908, Stanislavsky informed his Board of Directors that the theatre was incapable of interpreting poetic drama and Shakespeare in particular. "On the one hand," he stated, "the company seemed unprepared for sincerely and simply breathing life into the great feelings and lofty ideas of a universal genius. On the other, the theatre's essential objectives did not permit us to seek artistic inspiration in commonly used theatrical techniques. . . . "[12] Now it was time to strike out into that *terra incognita* and stake fresh boundaries. In the uncharted regions a guide would be helpful.

Neither Craig nor Stanislavsky knew anything of one another until the match was made by Isadora Duncan. The MAT was so ignored by the English theatre that the *Stage Year Book* for 1909 could run an article entitled "The Russian Stage" and not mention it.[13] The Russian theatrical avant-garde was on the alert for Western innovations, and so had some slight acquaintance with Craig's ideas, but Stanislavsky, in many ways a traditionalist, was not of their number. Only when Isadora presented him with the German translation of *On the Art of the Theatre* and the first issue of *The Mask* did he get some glimmer of Craig's principles.

That Stanislavsky would break with tradition and invite a little-known Englishman to work within the confines of the Art Theatre is a credit to Isadora's powers of persuasion. The relationship between the American dancer and the Russian director was unlikely. Stanislavsky, confronted by her untrammelled, loosely-draped exercises in movement, admired the "artistry" but was deeply shocked by the bohemianism. "You have to be Isadora Duncan to have the right to come on stage half-naked and not shock anyone," he warned his students.[14] Isadora herself was exempt from his ordinary moral strictures on account of what he deemed her genius. Even so, when she launched her usual seduction tactics against him, the tall, handsome director was terrified, for Stanislavsky was as prudish as Isadora was aggressive. When she invited him to her hotel suite to view some new dance movements, he rang up his wife to join them. A climax of sorts was reached, Stanislavsky told the young actor Mgebrov:

"You know," Stanislavsky began, "Duncan is a remarkable woman . . . God has endowed her with much . . . but she doesn't know herself . . . she doesn't know how to watch out for herself, she does herself harm . . . I forced her to realize this . . . look" he unfolded several pieces of paper. "This is a letter of hers . . . look . . . lots of pages . . . all tear-stained . . . And you know why? Because I forced her to understand herself . . . This letter is her profound repentance. . . ." S. stopped momentarily, to catch his breath, — so passionately and anxiously was he talking at that instant. Then he resumed: "A few days ago . . . when she was dancing, she asked me afterwards to go with her to a restaurant!" S. opened wide eyes filled with childlike wonder and terror, "Whew, you understand." Almost in a whisper, he continued, "I went, we got to the restaurant and Duncan insisted on a private room . . . then she ordered champagne . . . I didn't know what to think . . . suddenly she sat on the sofa, but she started to behave so oddly . . . Well, you understand, don't you . . . so wantonly . . . you understand?" Stanislavsky gazed into my eyes with the same fear. . . .

". . . Well anyway, when I saw that . . . for a long time I didn't know what to do . . . then she put her hand on my knee, — " at this point Stanislavsky's voice rang with the notes of an austere and stern pastor . . . "and I said to her: 'God dwells within you, and here you are jiggling knees.' At these words of mine Duncan suddenly burst into sobs . . . she sobbed . . . and I didn't know how to console her . . . Now, you see, I've had this letter from her. It breathes profound penitence . . . you see — it's all over tears . . . Duncan writes me that from that moment she understood everything . . . that now, she will live a new life, that I have shown her the artist's true path, that henceforth she will stop being frivolous and so on. . . ."[15]

However sincere Isadora's repentance at that moment, it was uncharacteristic of her resilient character to linger on it, although apparently she renounced any further attempts on Stanislavsky's virtue. His wife, the actress Mariya Lilina, a woman of great wit and understanding, had observed these manoeuvres from the sidelines untroubled, for she knew her husband's character. Stanislavsky, however, always felt that he had narrowly escaped a dreadful pitfall and was nervous that others, with less moral fortitude, might succumb. This attitude of mingled respect for the artist and alarm at the person was to color his relations with Craig as well; and would be shared by others in the Art Theatre.

Despite the rocky break-up of Isadora's affair with Craig, she was anxious to effect a collaboration between her favorite geniuses, sure that it would be productive of brilliance. Very early in 1908, she wrote to Craig:

Mr Stanislavsky, the regisseur of the Theatre, is a wonderful man — really Beautiful & Great — I talked with him many hours about you — He says he would love to have you come & be regisseur altogether, as he prefers to *act*. The plays for this year are all fixed, but he says if you came next August & prepared a piece Aug. & Sept. to be given in October, then if you liked & all went well you might stay with them — They are wonderful people all of them & he is Beautiful. So kind & unassuming — a *really great* man — I have never met anyone like him —

He asked if you would write to him. I told him he should write to you first — he seems shy — said he would write you a long letter but that it would take him a couple of weeks to compose it. He wants me to telegraph & ask you only to come & visit them & see if you like them — but I didn't think you'd care to come for anything not sure. He says he would give you a perfectly free hand in the Theatre — that the actors would all follow your directions as to movements, etc. & that you could do what you liked & take all the time you like to do it in —

All the people belonging to the Theatre are so simple & sweet & unassuming. There are 300 pupils in the School. I told him 6000 gulden for two months. He said he would put it before the directors. He said afterward you could take a troupe from their Theatre & go on tour —

He said "Tell Mr. Craig we are very simple people, that we care nothing at all for ourselves but very much for Art & that if he will come we will all be glad to follow his ideas."

I can only repeat that he is great & simple & Beautiful — such a man as one doesn't meet with once a century —

I showed him your book & he thought it very beautiful —

He is very anxious for you to come. He is a bit afraid of your prices — The Theatre is not very rich — [16]

If one reads between the lines of Isadora's effusions and her optimistic overstatements (the MAT had about a dozen pupils at the time, not 300), Stanislavsky's caution is evident. He was desirous of being gracious but not of committing the theatre to a promise that might prove expensive. In late March, no longer in Russia, Isadora reported to Stanislavsky: "I wrote Gordon Craig and told him both about your theatre and your own great art. But don't you want to write Craig yourself? If he can work with you, it would be *ideal* for him. I hope with all my heart that it comes to pass."[17] Stanislavsky's reply was cool: "At present I cannot promise Mr Craig anything definite, because the financial status of the theatre is so problematical."[18]

This reticence did not appear in Isadora's letter to Craig in early April: "He said he would be quite willing to give you entire control of what productions you wanted. I wonder how it would be if you came together."[19] This roseate prospect combined with Craig's usual ungrounded optimism led him to take her word for Stanislavsky's deed and he announced in *The Mask* that he had been invited "to Moscow to produce a play by Shakespeare which has not yet been decided upon ... If the production at Moscow is to be 'Hamlet' ... it will be a phenomenal sign of the trend of events."[20]

This is the first mention of *Hamlet* in relation to the Moscow Art Theatre and, significantly, it came from Craig. At this time, he was negotiating for the lease of the Arena Goldoni, a derelict open-air theatre outside Florence. He had begun to feel bitter about not having a theatre of his own and the Arena Goldoni would provide a private world in which to carry out experiments, hold classes and play lord of the manor. Almost simultaneously with these letters, he had received an offer from Max Reinhardt to come to Berlin and stage *King Lear*, with the proviso that the sketches be ready by the year's end. Another nibble was to come from Herbert Beerbohm Tree, for a *Macbeth* at His Majesty's in London. Nothing was to develop from these proposals but Craig was gratified to be wooed by three of Europe's leading managers and tried, in his amateur Machiavellianism, to play them off against one another.

With a *King Lear* for Reinhardt and a *Macbeth* for Tree, it was likely that he wanted to create a trilogy of Shakespearean masterpieces. More appositely, he had been using the screens that embodied his notion of kinetic theatre to stage a production of *Hamlet* on his model stage in the studio at Il Santuccio. Craig's fixation with Hamlet and his concept of the tragedy will be examined later, but at this point it appears that his announcement of *Hamlet* was a loud hint to Stanislavsky, a hopeful try at coercion.

He must have been surprised to receive a telegram from Isadora offering him two productions on behalf of the MAT, one of them to be *Peer Gynt*. The offer was tempered by a suggestion of low pay. Deciding to go to the top, Craig wrote directly to Stanislavsky on April 20. "Miss Isadora Duncan has sent me several telegrams and letters in which she conveys your desire that I should bring some work of mine into your theatre ... Am I right in supposing that Miss Duncan has made a mistake ..."[21] A week later, a telegram came from Stanislavsky: "Mademoiselle Duncan a raison je dois vous écrire quand un repertoire sera décidé excusez retard salutations."[22] Others would have taken this as a deferential postponement, but Craig, typically overconfident, read into it a positive commitment and began to barrage Stanislavsky with proposals, demands and shameless bluff. The first such letter, on May 2, expressed Craig's desire not to hurry the Russian director, *but* — commitments to other theatres in other countries compelled a rapid reply. Moreover, Craig's busy schedule made it imperative that plans should encompass a future year. *King Lear* is already spoken for, but

> It would give me *great pleasure* to produce *Hamlet* for you.
> In no case could I produce any play which I have not studied for a long period of time.
> — Do you understand — ?
> — Yes — Of course, you do.
> You say you have not yet decided on your repertoire.
> I hope the play for me to produce should be selected if possible after consulting me. It would give me great pleasure and some satisfaction to reieve [*sic*] a letter from you if it is not asking too much from so busy a man.[23]

The blend of solicitation and sarcasm was typically Craigian, and the Englishman was to use it in his correspondence with Stanislavsky throughout their association, usually with little effect. Without awaiting an answer, he drew up a list of plays he was willing to produce, including *Everyman*, *Agamemnon* and the dialogues of Plato, all of which he was to omit from his final roster as unsuitable for Russia.

When Stanislavsky finally wired to say that the repertory was to be settled in a few days, after which he would leave for Hamburg for a month's vacation, he proposed that Craig meet him there for discussions.[24] He obviously had no intention of committing himself to a man he had never met. Craig shot off a telegram regretting his own inability to leave Florence and assuming that Stanislavsky would visit him there.[25] This was followed by a brief letter to "Dear S" with the hope that "you will let me hear from you SOON." "I have to arrange my tournée to several cities, if possible within the next month and should not like any other date to clash with the date for Moscow."[26]

On July 10, Craig capped this barrage with a long letter that reads like a *cri de coeur* muted by a calculating mind:

> *5 Piazza Donatello. Studio 9, Firenze*
> Alas! I cannot come to Hamburg and I cannot come to Moscow in September. If I could *come* to either place I would do so.
> I cannot come because I am at work upon four very difficult plays to be produced in Berlin . . . Deutsche Theatre. One of these (King Lear) is to be ready September: as you know "King Lear" is not very easy.
> I wish I could come to see you. I wish I could come.
> As I cannot come I wish to write to you as though I had known you for a long time and as if I understood what you want. By doing so we may perhaps understand each other. I therefore drop the role of "Regisseur" or "Stage Reformer" and whatever mask you may think covers the real man and will attempt to show you myself and my wishes . . . . . hopes!
> > Is that right? Clear? Good; then let us proceed.
> > My wishes first.

Ist I want to work with you: I want to come to Moscow and produce with your help the best thing yet seen on the best stage in Europe. This must be a play which we *know* . . . n'est ce pas?

For my part I am familiar with Hamlet, Macbeth, The Tempest, Midsummer's Night Dream [*sic*], Ghosts (Ibsen), Vikings (Ibsen) and *fairly* familiar with Peer Gynt.

Could either of those plays be chosen by you?

2nd. I wish to do this work between October and January, for the plain and simple reason that I shall be free then and not free before . . .

3rd. I wish to make money.

So much for my wishes, and now about myself.

As I cannot visit in Hamburg or Moscow you will not be able to know what I look like that therefore what kind of a creature you are dealing with.

And even if I could come to see you you would probably not be able to judge . . . so now let me tell you.

I am poor . . . always was and always shall be. That is why I can refuse so many small offers to do *small* productions in a small way for a *small* sum.

I am really in love with my Art . . . and with the Theatre, vile and mad as it is I have no other interests in the world than to remain true to the Art, and I am not able to continue a work in a theatre where there is more than one master. I studied under Henry Irving who rules his theatre sternly and justly. I have not had the pleasure of meeting any such ruler since he died.

In the European theatre intrigue rules and the director is merely a figurehead. I understand this is not the case in your theatre. I should be glad of this assurance from you, and in this event glad to work under you.

I would rather remain in Italy than go to any land and produce what has been seen before . . . and so if I visit Moscow it must be understood that I come there with that purpose and the theatre must be prepared to make things possible.

All *Enthusiasm* has left the hearts of those who work in the theatres of Europe. They work without *playing*. They work without laughing or singing. To me the Art is a game. . . . a wonderful and exciting game. I hope your workmen would be prepared to play it with me.

And now my best greetings.

Write to me as you would to someone you were inviting to go on a shooting expedition . . . then I shall understand.

Gordon Craig[27]

This remarkable epistle contains the seeds of all the problems that were to bedevil the Craig-Stanislavsky relationship over the next few years and well into the future. At first glance, it looks straightforward and candid, with its asseverations of sincerity and masks off. But the posing continues throughout: Craig the idealist, Craig the reformer, Craig the art-lover trots out these personae as impressive credentials. Demands, rather than requests or inquiries, pulsate beneath every statement: the need for money, the insistence on a single autocratic leader, and the assumption that everyone in the theatre be prepared to sacrifice himself unquestioningly to Craig's wishes. Contrasted with these, the assurances of playfulness sound hollow. But somehow Stanislavsky was won over or, at any rate, worn down, and agreed that Craig might send an emissary to treat with him.

The envoy Craig elected to execute this delicate mission was his whilom business agent Maurice Magnus, an American journalist who swam in and out of the world of fashion and who had translated *The Art of the Theatre* into bad German. Like Craig, Magnus had delusions of adequacy about his prowess as a businessman, but his suave manners and dapper façade apparently reassured Stanislavsky who made proposals that Magnus conveyed to Craig on August 22. Craig was to come to Moscow on October 13 to see the Art Theatre, talk things over and, if agreeable, hire himself to the MAT by the year. By working with them during their seven-month season, Craig could thus more efficiently instill his ideas into the troupe and stage more than one production. Stanislavsky allowed Craig the right to come and go as he pleased, provided that his contracted work was completed. Two productions were suggested for the first season and, as an earnest of his intent, he sent along 1000 marks for travelling expenses. Magnus recommended that Craig agree to the offer: "It is the best proposition I have yet heard and certainly one which is more dignified than any other, for you deal with first class people."[28]

Pleased with the freedom to leave Russia at will, beguiled by the artistic respectability of the Art Theatre, and dazzled by the ready cash, Craig accepted.

The invitation to Moscow came at a propitious time for Craig, when he was feeling a fresh upsurge of creative impulse. His new enterprise, *The Mask*, had put him on a regular routine meeting deadlines, and the task had not yet become onerous. Editing a periodical enabled him to publicize his ideas, puff his prejudices and feel that he was communicating to the world. In the first issues, he had set forth the radical and somewhat overstated concept of replacing live actors with Uebermarionnettes, a concept so vivid that it defined him for many, to the exclusion of his other, less extreme positions. Even as he gave his assent to Stanislavsky, his attention was held by *Hamlet*. The seventh issue of *The Mask* which appeared the next month contained his article, "Shakespeare's Plays," in which he made a plea for uncut performance.

Cut the passage between Ophelia and Hamlet in Act III Scene 2 when he is lying at her feet and you rob the character of Hamlet of very much of its force. Ophelia instead of becoming a woman of intelligence, becomes an early Victorian debutante, and Hamlet instead of being a man of his time . . . becomes a kind of preaching curate.[29]

Over the next three years, these principles would be traduced in a production that was to cut a third of the play, in which Hamlet would barely approach Ophelia in Act III, and during whose preparation Craig would insist again and again that Ophelia was a nitwit. How and why word and deed were so disparate is the subject of the following pages.

2
FIRST IMPRESSIONS

Gordon Craig arrived in Moscow at 4 P.M. on October 26 and immediately checked into the Metropole, the most expensive hotel in the city, where he took a room with a bath. In one of the most memorable passages of *My Life in Art*, Stanislavsky recalled arriving to find his new colleague in "his Adamic costume" "splashing about in icy water."

> The discussion of art that began between us seemed to be the continuation of a discussion that we might have been having the very day before. In his bathrobe, with his long wet hair, he heatedly explained to me his beloved fundamental principles, his original researches in the quest of a new art of movement. He showed me sketches of this new art in which lines and clouds and stones and something that resembled tree trunks created an unceasing impetus upward, and one believed that out of this there would come some still-unknown and new art. He spoke of the indubitable truth that it is impossible to put the human body side by side with flatly painted canvas, that sculpture and architecture and objects of three dimensions are needed as the background for the body of the actor. He admitted painted canvas only at the further end of architectural passages on the stage . . . . What he needed was a simple background for the actor, out of which one would be able however to draw an endless number of moods with the help of lines and light spots.
>   Further, Craig said that every work of art must be made of dead material, stone, marble, bronze, canvas, paper, paint, and fixed forever in artistic form. According to these fundamentals, the living material of the actor's body, which endlessly changes and is never the same, was not useful for the purposes of creation, and Craig denied actors, especially those of them who had striking or beautiful individuality and who were not of themselves artistic creations . . . .[1]

Stanislavsky, who acceded in principle to Craig's scorn of painted scenery, was somewhat taken aback to find that actors, on whom he relied for theatrical truth, were thoroughly discounted; and he was further troubled to hear the personal animus behind the theories, when Craig continued, "Women . . . ruin the theatre. They take a bad advantage of the power and influence they exercise over men. They use these evilly and bring intrigues, favoritism and flirtation into the realms of art."[2]

But practical considerations took precedence over ideologies. Twenty-five degrees of frost prevailed outside and Craig had arrived in his ordinary Italian garb, his artist's uniform of wide-brimmed sombrero, trailing scarf and spring topcoat. These flamboyant garments were exchanged for an equally picturesque costume: an enormous Napoleonic fur pelisse and hat from the wardrobe of the MAT's production of *Woe from Wit*. Muffled in those shaggy trappings, Craig felt enveloped in a symbolic bear-hug.[3]

At seven o'clock he was taken to the theatre where he saw *The Blue Bird*, one of the MAT's more successful sorties into fantasy. The style of the décor was deliberately naïve, to reproduce a child's dream, and the transformations and magical effects were delicate variants of the tricks of Christmas pantomimes Craig knew so well. He thought the show "lovely" but too cluttered, and especially enjoyed Ilya Sats' music for it. During the mother's song he exclaimed "Very good" over and over again.[4]

After the performance at eleven o'clock, he was collected by some of the MAT's mad wags: Nikita Baliev, the moonfaced actor who played Bread in *The Blue Bird* and would later found and compère the revue *The Bat*; Ivan Moskvin, a charter member of the Art Theatre and its finest comic player; Leonid Leonidov, an actor of massive build and fiery temperament; Leopold Sulerzhitsky, Stanislavsky's assistant who will become a leading character in this narrative; and the millionaire share-holder Nikolay Tarasov who deposited them all in a scarlet and gold motor-car that impressed Craig far more than had Maeterlinck's fairy-tale. He was whisked away on an epic tour of Moscow night-life: the Hermitage for Russian food and caviar, the Yar for two ensembles of gypsy singers and dancers, "who shrieked and wept and leapt for me", the Mauretania, Jean's in Petrovsky Park for lobsters and champagne, and the Chinese Room at Egorov's for pancakes. Sulerzhitsky danced ("a God's dance — nothing short of it,"[5] Craig wrote) and Craig, warmed by the drink and the exuberant affection, like a proud papa, pulled out photographs of the Arena Goldoni. On the back on one snapshot, his hosts entered their regards in uncertain English. Tarasov: "You are a splendid man that I have ever seen in my life." Suler: "And I also." Baliev: "Mr Gordon Craig you are Alfe et omega." He finally crawled into bed at six in the morning.[6]

Stanislavsky had invited him to attend a Russian church service the same morning, but that was out of the question. Craig penned a note of apology:

Signor —
First, a thousand thanks for the beautiful play last night —
    unforgettable —
    quite wonderful —
    often beautiful —
    I could not come to church I was — dead —
    killed through kindliness showered on me by you and your associates.
    I am now risen again —
And because I do not wish a second death, and because I know I should give you trouble enough I think it best that I stay here in this hotel for the present. I wish you could take your 'Bluebird' to London this Winter — to Drury Lane. No one should do it there except you.[7]

Recovered from his hangover, that night at the MAT Craig beheld Leonid Andreev's allegorical drama *The Life of Man*, a pessimistic and somewhat hysterical play about Man's impotence in the face of his mortality. The designer Egorov had based his scheme on Aubrey Beardsley and carried it out entirely in black velvet. It had made Isadora ill and had the same effect on Craig, who took the opportunity of the intermission to leave the building and walk off the impression. In his Daybook he noted,

Black is not to be used as a basis of design unless much colour is also employed. The Russians used nothing but white to relieve the blackness — it was cleverness overreaching itself. This is typical of the Art Theatre which is admirable when it deals in Realism but which fails altogether when it indulges in attempts to avoid realism. Then it becomes only clever and never inspired.[8]

The next day Stanislavsky's wife, the actress Mariya Lilina, sent roses to Craig with a note "To make you forget the sinister black velvet. You can find flowers in Russia also.[9] She spoke excellent English and Craig ardently desired that she act as interpreter between him and her husband, for the two men of the theatre could converse only in halting German. "Edward Edwardovich," as she named him, would become a regular guest at the crowded teas in Stanislavsky's flat where she presided over the samovar, and was invited to dine there daily, with leeway to leave directly after dinner if need be.[10]

Among the guests Craig met at the Stanislavsky's was a twenty-year-old girl with black brows, short black hair, and widely-spaced almond eyes that gazed intently at him all the while he spoke. Alisa Georgievna Koonen was the daughter of a lawyer with no clients and of a pianist too ill to play; she had been accepted into the Art Theatre school when only sixteen years old and soon appeared in small parts in *Woe from Wit*, *The Drama of Life*, *The Life of Man* and *Brand* (singing Agnes' song offstage). Her first sizeable role had been Mytyl in *The Blue Bird*, when she was noted as the most promising young actress in the company, and in the next few years would be cast as Verochka in *A Month in the Country*, Masha in *The Living Corpse* and Anitra in *Peer Gynt*. Her tasteful oriental dancing as Anitra would owe much to her studies with Elli Knipper, one of Isadora Duncan's pupils, and Alisa Koonen met Isadora herself in Petersburg. Having joined the MAT at a time when it was in turmoil, experimenting with a varied repertory, Koonen was more interested in outward form than in inner nuances. Like the cultivated youth of the pre-war period, she was washed over by the fashionable wave of decadence: her intellectual nourishment was the poetry of Bryusov, Balmont and Jurgis Baltrushaitis (all of whom she knew personally), the plays of Maeterlinck and the fiction of Knut Hamsun. Musical speech and fluid movement were her prime objectives on stage.

Koonen and Craig hit it off immediately. He, mildly smitten with the beautiful girl, saw her as a disciple and a play-fellow; she, after the first flush of being impressed, discovered that he was not only a source of inspiration but great fun to be with. People even seemed to move faster with Craig around, she observed. In later life, when she had become Russia's greatest actress and the wife of director Aleksandr Tairov, she could compare Craig with "another Irishman" of her acquaintance, Bernard Shaw. There was the same eccentric carriage, the same malicious wit, the same skeptical attitude to things English.[11]

Craig's first claim on her mind was as an expert on Shakespeare. Shakespeare was not in fashion among the Russian youth of the time, and although she had had to prepare the scene between Laertes and Ophelia for a class, Koonen had been unfamiliar with the Bard's work until the director Mchedelov suggested she read *Measure for Measure*. This taste of tragedy so addicted her that she turned next to *Richard III* and *Anthony and Cleopatra*, this last overwhelming her with its power. When she asked Craig his advice on acting Portia in *The Merchant of Venice*, he replied:

I told her it would be a good thing if all the serious actors & actresses could take service in some small position at the Court of Petersburg. There only can the style of fine breeding with its outward show of good & grand manners be seen in Russia. Thus the beauty of Hamlet shows up against a golden pomp . . . his personal simplicity & beauty are only to be thoroughly perceived in such a setting. By splendour I mean all that is arrogant — tyrannical — contemptuous and ceremonious. For the presentation of Shakespeare's plays splendour is necessary & above all the inner splendour (fresh or degenerate both are in his plays).[12]

The ideas broached in these conversations with an awed and receptive young lady turned into important elements in the *Hamlet* to come.

Pole-axed by Russian hospitality and the theatre's earnestness, Craig confided his frenetic first impressions to a friend in London, the painter Will Rothenstein, with characteristic exaggerations in the telling.

Moscow, Metropole Hotel
Dear Will — I am in Russia — & the theatre here has asked me to be their regisseur or stagemanager & for life!

God. dear Will this kind of thing takes ones breath away — it's like a leap year proposal — heavenly because so innocently new, & who knows if I won't be ever at the disposal of this theatre which has prevented applause — by preventing its actors appearing to bow before the curtain — this vivid theatre which has dared to waste years in the production of one piece — this darling theatre which is so generous that it gives its audience a 3 1/2 hour's show — bless its innocence — if I loved anything but a Theatre which must obliterate the Theatre I would stay here for ever & do my dull best — but *I* must do my gambling *worst* — & must risk all & again all to drag the soul of the theatre out of its cursed body & free it of all tricks & trappings — then — then — others!!

Tree — the charming fellow — I could murder him with *great pleasure*.

Here they are all so good — so true — so wildly believing in it & its trappings as moths the candle — their faith wins me back for one moment — makes me *miserable* & them — terribly happy.

. . . I have lived 2 days here & lived a year in each . . .[13]

The heady blend of condescension and affection was typical of Craig and illustrates the germ of aloofness, of personal reserve, he injected into every collaboration and relationship. Of course, he had not been offered a life term as regisseur, and in fact was not even to meet Stanislavsky's co-director, Nemirovich-Danchenko, until the next day. Nemirovich-Danchenko rather resented being kept out of the limelight by his colleague's fame as an actor, but at the same time he was curious to explore Craig's ideas. Unfortunately someone told Craig that the two directors were not in agreement and since the Englishman already felt loyalty to Stanislavsky, he decided to treat Nemirovich as a figurehead for the Board of Directors. This decision was to sour their work together and decades later, Nemirovich the silent partner would tell Craig, "Stanislavsky wanted to pick me up and put me here, and he wanted to pick you up and put you there."[14]

What drew Craig even closer to Stanislavsky was that at last he saw him as an actor in some of his best roles, including Dr. Stockmann in *An Enemy of the People* and Astrov in *Uncle Vanya*.

Stanislavsky shows us how to act Dr. Stockman without being "theatrical" and without being comic or dull. The audience smile all the time that they are not being moved to tears, but never does a coarse roar go up as such as we are used to in the English theatre . . . this company is able to handle any play admirably.[15]

All in all, he got a strong sampling of the MAT's repertory, for before his departure Craig saw them perform Griboedov's *Woe from Wit* (he found the stage management of detail in the Act III soirée masterly), *The Cherry Orchard*, *The Lower Depths*, two acts of Ibsen's *Brand* with Vasily Kachalov in the lead, a rehearsal and a performance of *Three Sisters*.[16] The Chekhov and Gorky pieces showed the company at its best in atmospheric realism and the report Craig wrote for *The Mask* was glowing:

The Russian actors . . . give me the impression that they experience a keener intellectual enjoyment during their performance than any other actors in Europe . . . Nothing is slipshod. Everything is treated seriously . . . [Stanislavsky is] a master of psychology, his acting is most realistic . . . yet he avoids nearly all the brutalities . . . his performances are all remarkable for their grace. I can find no better word.[17]

But he was put off by the emphasis on realism, and his Daybook for the period is full of counterarguments to refute the idea that the soul can be revealed through emphasis on physicality.[18]

Whatever the doctrinal differences, Stanislavsky had been impressed by his eccentric English guest and on November 6 proposed to the Board that Craig, "to give our art a new impetus forward and pour more yeast into the dough," be commissioned to direct Hugo von Hofmannsthal's *Oedipus and the Sphinx* and design Ibsen's *Emperor and Galilean*.[19] There was no mention of *Hamlet*.

These were not random selections. From the start, when Craig had suggested *Peer Gynt* as a possibility, he had been linked with Ibsen, not least because of his designs for *The Vikings at Helgeland* in London in 1903. *Emperor and Galilean* was a project of epic scope, but, with Craig, there would be an avoidance of the sterile historicism that had undermined *Julius Caesar*.

As for Hofmannsthal, Craig had already designed his plays for Brahm and Duse. *Oedipus and the Sphinx*, a Freudian recasting of Sophocles' tragedy, had already been successfully produced by Reinhardt in 1906 with a setting by Alfred Roller. Roller, a member of the Viennese Secession group and a disciple of Appia, had brought Craigian staging to the professional European theatre while Craig himself was still trying to get managers to take him seriously. Interested in simplifying the design elements to a symbolic use of color and light and reducing set pieces to a minimum, Roller had used light in *Oedipus* not for naturalistic effect but to create a psychological mood. Some of his sets were extremely Craig-like in their blocky monumentality. Also in 1906, he had designed a *Don Giovanni* for Gustav Mahler at the Vienna Hofoper, which utilized the famous Roller-Tuerme. These towers were neutral forms which could be moved anywhere on stage and arranged in various positions against a cyclorama; although three-dimensional, they were, in principle, akin to Craig's screens and provided a kinetic stage setting.[20] The Russian theatrical cognoscenti knew Roller's experiments and it may have been Nemirovich-Danchenko who conceived of using Craig to compete with the Austrian designer on the same play. But Craig's mind continued to dwell on Shakespeare.

Novalis said of Spinoza that he was "a God-intoxicated man." Gordon Craig might as aptly be called "a Hamlet-intoxicated man." From the very dawning of his artistic consciousness, he seems to have bound up his own aspirations, disappointments and sensibility with those of Shakespeare's hero. Hamlet became for him a touchstone by which the world was to be judged and usually found wanting. The performance and production of *Hamlet* were the *ne plus ultra* of his theatrical ambitions because he saw the play not only as a dramatic masterpiece but as a mirror of his own creative preoccupations. His earliest published reference to it is a *jeu d'esprit* in his private magazine *The Page* (1898) in what purports to be "an extract from a letter written by a gentlewoman at the court of Elsinore." She comes across the melancholy Dane slouching in a chair "biting the nails of one hand whilst with the other he drew caricatures of his uncle on a copy of a play which is to be performed there to-night."[21] This Hamlet, who studies the expression of his grief in a mirror, seems less Elsinore than Thames Ditton, where the twenty-six-year-old artist was living at the time. The identification of Hamlet with idle and rebellious young men and thus with himself became Craig's *idée fixe*. Reading Hogg's life of Shelley in 1904, he jotted down on the fly leaf, "Shelley is young Hamlet," and the depiction of the poet's room at Oxford is also glossed as *"Hamlet."*[22] Later on, Craig was to write of this period, "Hamlet almost seemed to be myself . . . *Hamlet* was not only a play to me nor a role to be played — I somehow or other lived Hamlet day by day." His interest in the tragedy was obsessively proprietory and would prevent him from accepting not only modifications of his interpretation, but the intrusion of anyone else into his private Elsinore. His son has stated that "he saw in the Ghost his own father, Horatio was Martin [Shaw], Hamlet was himself, and the actors . . . were his familiars in the theatre, beautiful creatures from the land of his imagination. Ophelia was a mixture of all the foolish girls that he had known!"[23]

If the Ghost was his father, E. W. Godwin the scene-designer, Hamlet was also in part his surrogate father, Henry Irving, whose subtle and refined interpretation was the authoritative one on the late Victorian stage. And Craig had a chance to supplant this father figure by assuming the role himself. In 1897 he played it for six performances in place of Nutcombe Gould, with Ben Greet's company at the Olympic Theatre. Irving, as if acknowledging Craig as his heir apparent, lent him the dagger and costume from his own wardrobe.[24] But far more significant to Craig's monodramatic conception of the play was his earlier appearance with a minor touring company in 1894. In the industrial town of Salford, he had been puzzled during the performance by nut-cracking in the audience, and unable to discern what the noise was. He later wrote of his first entrance, "I, who am short-sighted and see very little without glasses, saw practically nothing at all when I looked out towards the spectators, because a grey fog of smoke seemed to fill the auditorium."[25] Short-sighted actors who play without their spectacles are not easily distracted on stage, because they are enrapt in their own concentration; other forms are dimly seen as colored blurs. If Craig was always muffled in this myopic solipsism when he played Hamlet, what could be more natural than his extrapolating that hazy atmosphere on to an imagined production, in which all the characters but the lead would at times be blurred by gauze curtains, at other times merged together as a solid golden mass, and at still other times clarified by an intense shaft of light? What more paranoid than a Hamlet who could not see the machinations around him without peering closely, who had to be jolted out of his self-involved purblindness? As those around him advanced or retreated, Hamlet would apprehend them as dream figures, fluctuating in clarity. The resultant image is the paradoxical one of a myopic visionary.

Craig returned to an intensive study of *Hamlet* some time in 1907, when penniless and homeless, he was given shelter in the villa Il Santuccio overlooking Florence and the Arno. There, working on model stages, he began to test his theories of stagecraft with figurines and the screens which he had devised to replace ordinary painted scenery. His first experiments were carried out with Greek drama, but he soon rejected that in favor of *Hamlet*, because of his close familiarity with the play, and recorded all the configurations he came up with in an exercise book.[26] With typical exuberance, he began to conceive of a published volume containing all of his annotations, and, in July 1908, *The Mask* carried an advertisement for an edition of *Hamlet*, based on the First Folio.

This Edition will contain the Text of the Play, Descriptions and Designs of each scene and full directions as to how to light the play. Every movement of the Actors will be noted at the side of the Text, and at times a design will help the student to the full significance of the movements.

. . .

This Edition will be the work of Mr Gordon Craig, the reason impelling him to such a task being the absense [sic] of any stage directions by Shakespeare, and the desire to give expression of what he considers to be the entire Art of the Stage Director.[27]

Had this *magnum opus* been carried out in the three volumes Craig projected, it would have been a major statement of the new stagecraft applied to Shakespearean production. But, with typical lack of follow-through, Craig remained content with a statement of purpose. Meanwhile, he had discovered a means of printing black figures by inking the cut-out wooden puppets for his model theatre: the annotated *Hamlet* was now conceived as an illustrated *Hamlet*. In any case, *Hamlet* was uppermost in Craig's mind when Stanislavsky confronted him with an offer, and it was natural, that, like a King Charles' head, the tragedy would keep bobbing up in conversation. The inducements to stage Ibsen or Hofmannsthal paled before the chance of realizing his private impressions of his favorite play in the flesh.

While Craig still propagandized for the Bard, a kindred suggestion came to Stanislavsky from another quarter. The writer Ivan Bunin wrote to him on November 18, proposing to translate a Shakespearean play for the MAT, for he had heard that Craig was to direct there. Stanislavsky turned down the offer on December 3, remarking, "It is true that Craig has been invited and will work in our theatre. An an Englishman, the best thing for him would be to stage Shakespeare. We are considering it, but, I repeat, nothing is yet decided."[28] He had earlier explained to the critic Lyubov Gurevich the reasons for taking on a foreign director.

Of course, we have returned to realism, enriched by experimentation and work, a more refined, more profound and psychological realism. Once we get a bit stronger at it, we will again be on the road to discovery. That is why Craig has been sent for.[29]

Stanislavsky therefore was envisaging a realism fortified by aesthetic control, and characterized any approach other than realism as "false and dead." Craig simultaneously was discussing with the actor Moskvin whom he considered "the best fellow & best actor of the Russian art theatre" his designs for Shakespeare, his etchings of motion, and ways of becoming a finer artist by discovering "a new land."[30] Stanislavsky and Craig both dreamed of discovery but even at the start of the voyage their sea charts were divergent.

On November 25 Craig left Moscow and arrived in Florence three days later. He had had his way. Before his departure, it was agreed that he was to stage a Shakespearean play, probably *Hamlet*. This concession on the part of the Board no doubt resulted from incessant canvassing on Craig's part. He was offered an annual salary of 6000 rubles, but he recommended instead that he be paid separately for each visit.[31] Craig's picture of himself as shrewd businessman lies behind this proposal: he must have thought he could up the ante each time he returned. The Board, composed of shrewd businessmen, was astounded by his lack of commercial acumen but acceded to his terms. What Craig wanted to be paid and what the Moscow Art Theatre was willing to pay him would prove a source of unending contention over the next three years.

On December 24, the Moscow *Evening News* made the first public announcement that an Englishman, Edward Gordon Craig, had been appointed to direct at the Moscow Art Theatre.[32] The revolutionary decision was now official.

3
MONODRAMATICS

A few days after Craig had returned to Florence from his first Russian jaunt, a paper was read at the Moscow Literary Artistic Club which he would have found remarkably appealing. A speech promulgating the concept of monodrama was delivered by Nikolay Evreinov, former law and music student, now a young director and playwright, who made his name by his reconstruction of medieval miracles and moralities at his own Theatre of Yore and by his theory of theatricality as a basic element of human life. The idea of monodrama was in the air, Evreinov was candid enough to admit, but he wanted credit as the first to formulate it.

According to Evreinov, an audience member can experience aesthetic pleasure in the theatre only when he co-experiences those things that happen to the characters, sympathizing with and sharing their emotions. But human perception is limited and easily distracted; hustled back and forth among the various feelings of many characters, it grows weary and surrenders. A more effectual means of promoting co-experience would be to reduce the angle of perception to a single protagonist, who would be the audience's *alter ego* in a monodrama.

Now what I mean by monodrama is the kind of dramatic presentation which, while attempting to communicate to the spectator as fully as it can the protagonist's state of mind, exhibits on the stage around him the world just as the protagonist perceives it at any given moment of his stage existence.[1]

Agreeing with Craig that words and mime are insufficient to embody a dramatic idea by themselves, Evreinov suggested that monodramatic moments can best convey a play's meaning. He used the apt example of a ghost: if the protagonist sees a ghost, why must the audience be distracted by the other characters on stage who do not see it or see it only reflected in the protagonist's fear, characters whom the protagonist himself, engrossed in his terrific vision, does not notice? Logic compels us to insist that the external spectacle be consistent with the internal experience of the one character with whom we are asked to identify.

Can it be that Hamlet, as he utters "To be or not to be" sees at that moment the rank luxuriousness of the court furnishings? And were not you, hard-bitten playgoers, angered at such a moment by the obtrusive splendor of the scene-shop luxury, all this superfluous precision of outline, so meaningless to Hamlet? . . .[2]

The protagonist's environment must bespeak his inner state and alter with his shifts of mood: lighting, scenery, even properties must change to express to the audience the protagonist's spectrum of emotions.

Evreinov's paper was an attempt to make practicable the symbolist aesthetic of a unified consciousness, the presentation of the world beyond as apprehended by a unique vision. Critics pointed out that his illustrations were those of a director and not a playwright, and that a stage monopolized by monodrama would soon become monotonous. In fact, few monodramas were written: Evreinov's own play *Backstage at the Soul* perhaps comes closest to the ideal. The Crooked Mirror dramatist B. F. Geyer made several interesting attempts; one of his plays depicted a wedding retrospected through the recollections of its various participants and, in another, the stage picture changed radically as the protagonist got progressively drunker. But these were more in the nature of revue sketches than serious drama.[3]

The concept of "monodrama" was only the latest in a series of innovations by which Russians aesthetes hoped to deal with the so-called "crisis in the theatre." When Craig, himself an unknown quantity, first came to Moscow late in 1908, he had no more inkling than did the rest of Europe that Russia was seething with debates about the nature of theatre and its future direction; and because he was co-opted by the Moscow Art Theatre and spent most of his time within its walls, he had scant opportunity to see and hear the alternatives. But even as the Art Theatre was attracting critical acclaim with a naturalism tempered by poetry and psychological nuance, others were finding naturalism of any sort a dead end.

Inspired by the millennial urges that develop whenever a century draws to a close, and actuated by a feeling of apocalypse as the political situation in Russia worsened, many writers and thinkers judged the theatre to be hopelessly unable to cope with the mind and aspirations of modern man. They came under the influence of Nietzsche and Maeterlinck: from the former they derived a notion of Dionysiac drama in which the spectator and the performer become one; from the latter, they derived a notion of "the tragedy of everyday life," transpiring within a man's soul without the need for external action.

The leading exponent of Dionysian drama in Russia was the poet, philosopher and classicist Vyacheslav Ivanov, who hoped the theatre would recover the religious function it once possessed. Through the dramatist, an artist-hierophant, the audience would be brought to awareness of the Platonic Ideals or the higher reality; the best means for this, Ivanov postulated, was a return to the ritual origins of the theatre and the choric involvement of the spectator. Unlike Nietzsche, Ivanov identified Dionysus with Christ and stressed the need for new mystery plays. The task of the artist was to remake the theatre into a combination of the ancient Greek *orchestra* and gnostic rites that would reintegrate the alienated audience into the ecstatic schesis.[4]

Ivanov's ideas were widely popularized, not least because the *fin-de-siècle* intellectuals in Russia, as elsewhere, looked forward to the new century as a harbinger of a brave new world, when such a communal transformation in the theatre might be possible. These hopes were dashed in 1905 when the failed revolution and defeat by the Japanese produced a mood among the intelligentsia of cynicism, bitter irony and disillusionment. Some indulged in predictions of the death of the theatre and its replacement by the cinema and puppet-show. There was a general turning-away from the view of theatre as divine salvation to a less portentous idea of theatre as play. There was a revival of earlier secular theatrical styles: the *commedia dell'arte*, the *sotie*, the fairground booth, and of conventionalized staging that, instead of merging actor and spectator, sharply divided the world of the footlights from that of the audience.

In 1908, the same year that Craig was invited by the Art Theatre, an important anthology of essays appeared in St. Petersburg: *Theatre, a Book about the New Theatre*. Its contributors, among them the symbolist poets Andrey Bely and Valery Bryusov, the designer Aleksandr Benois, the director Vsevolod Meyerhold, and the socialist ideologue Anatoly Lunacharsky, were for the most part members of Vyacheslav Ivanov's Wednesday salons. Hence his mystagogic concepts permeated the book, which, oddly enough, was dedicated to Stanislavsky, by no means an initiate or sympathizer. One of the more bizarre essays, and one especially pertinent to Craig, was "The Theatre of a Single Will" by the decadent poet, playwright and novelist Fyodor Sologub. Sologub was a rank pessimist, a believer in black magic and Satan's control of human life; he was deeply convinced that God and man were mutually self-denying entities and that we are all pawns of Aisa, the goddess of chance. His theatre appealed to man to return to the unself-conscious play-acting of childhood, so that the participant and the spectator might be mingled in the frantic ecstasy of a dervish dance. So far this was warmed-over Ivanov. But concomitant with this, Sologub prescribed a rather contrary theatre in which the poet's will would reign supreme. Sitting beside the stage, the poet would read his works, even to the stage directions, and the actors would be mannequins, illustrating his recital. "The drama," he wrote, "is the product of a single concept, just as the universe is the product of a single creative idea."[5] So the artist is equated with divinity, a romantic notion; but Sologub cherished no romantic notions about the divinity of most men. Since the human being is no more than a pawn in the hands of fate, there is nothing degrading about being a puppet on stage, manipulated by the superior being who alone is capable of creativity.

Strip away Sologub's arcane figures of speech and one had essentially Craig's idea of the stage-director as prime mover in the theatrical work, and his reduction of actor to Übermarionette — more *unter* than *über* in this case. Craig's first dialogue had been pirated and published in Russia in 1906, and a German translation was also available. Since none of his practical work, itself limited, was known outside of London, he was regarded by the Russians as yet another prophet of the theatre's imminent demise, although he at least proposed a new kind of theatre in its stead. "Craig is a sympathetic cutthroat, frank and, moreover, singing in a youthful basso, like Sparafucile in *Rigoletto*, 'I'm a bravo, of course . . .'" was one Russian critic's comment.[6] But prior to the Moscow *Hamlet*, no one had tested the Craigian or Sologubian ideals on stage, and it fell to the Moscow Art Theatre, uncharacteristically, to do so.

The on-stage experimentation that was going on in Russia at the time was never made known to Craig. Professional jealousy and doctrinal differences prevented Stanislavsky and Nemirovich-Danchenko from suggesting that their competitors were doing anything of value. As Craig later recalled, "if there was one thing that made Stanislavsky furious, it was the thought that anything in his theatre should be theatrical. It seems that what he meant by 'theatrical' was what they do in the Paris theatre."[7] Yet Craig would have found exciting Meyerhold's experiments with decorative stasis and rhythmic movement at Vera Kommissarzhevskaya's theatre in St. Petersburg; he would have been attracted by Evreinov's attempt to reproduce premodern methods of staging at his Theatre of Yore, and by his insistence on blatant theatricality as the central motive of human life; he would have sympathized with the producers of poetic drama in innumerable cabarets and "miniature" theatres. It was not until 1930, on reading a new book about the Russian theatre, that Craig "realized to how great an extent [Tairov] and others — Evreinov, for example — were in agreement with me."[8] It was an irony that symbolized what would become the basic fault running through the *Hamlet* production.

Craig's euphoria on his return from Russia took some time to dissipate. He immediately began a *Regiebuch* to contain his comments, ideas and sketches for the forthcoming production of *Hamlet*, and at the same time drew up a rough draft of an agreement with Stanislavsky delimiting the boundaries of their relationship:

I ask no definite position . . . merely at your disposal . . . as the family call in another doctor to consult on the illness of a patient. [This indiscreet line was crossed out.]

. . . enroll me as one of your company [at Moskvin's salary]. Will not produce a play proper but will give you ideas for that play which you can take or leave without offending me. I will not paint you scenes or . . .

For example you may decide to produce "Faust" or "Hamlet" & might then ask me for some designs and ideas for the representation of those plays — & you might accept or reject as many as you like — provided you did not *argue* with me about it I should be quite delighted.[9]

The rest of the page was covered with salary estimates. Luckily this letter was never sent, for its projection of Craig as an unanswerable "idea man" who scorns to descend to the nuts and bolts of actual production was not exactly what the Moscow Art Theatre had in mind.

The lease on the Arena Goldoni had been taken and Craig and his family installed there. In view of what he foresaw as a shuttle back and forth to Moscow, he put the management of *The Mask* in the hands of the urbane Magnus, even as he was discovering that his man of business was a good deal less trustworthy than he had suspected. He also had to deal with the imminent advent of a loving woman, which threatened to upset the equilibrium of his domestic life.

Not only Alisa Koonen, but Olga Knipper, widow of Anton Chekhov and a charter member of the Art Theatre troupe, had dallied with him in Moscow. The original Elena in *Uncle Vanya*, Masha in *Three Sisters* and Ranevskaya in *The Cherry Orchard*, she was a woman of considerable intellectual resource and charm, but, like so many others, she misread Craig's preliminary blandishments as something more than erotic etiquette. It was his customary technique in love to mount an elaborate and courtly assault and after continued rejection or satisfied vanity beat a swift retreat. The reserve he displayed in artistic collaborations also obtained in his sex life. When Olga, whom he had nicknamed "Temple" (for Temple of Art), wrote to him suggesting that she pay a visit to Florence that summer, he answered in a letter on January 11 that is a masterpiece of evasion and fanciful self-revelation:

Dear Temple. I like answering a letter like yours — it lends itself to me to excersise [*sic*] my cynicism and affection on it.

I too send you love . . . but I will not keep my cynicism to myself either. You are so charming — and so much more — something so mysterious that I can say at once

I love you very much —

I fear you very much —

You tell me "not to think that you have forgotten me" . . . of course I don't . . . I never do. I am so concieted [*sic*] that I know men and women never forget me —

You know that I am concieted — don't you? You ask what is the matter with me — that I am dying — must go to China Egypt — Temple darling, don't you know man, even now? don't you know he dies a death once a week if he lives a life once a week . . . I die, live, travel to India and back again . . . to Moscow and back — spend a year inspecting the secret caverns between Vesuvius and Hechla — dive into the deepest oceans and surprise unknown families of unthought of beings who dwell *deep deep down the* [*sic*]

This, and more (just as you are charming, and much, much more) I do in the space of an hour lying under a tree or sitting in my chair . . . a while passing from one to another.

And you wonder why I am dying. Darling Temple I am dying because I devour more time and expend more force in an hour than most people do in a year. That is to say I am 9570 years olds [*sic*] — for I was born in 1900 . . . having been asleep until that year! . .

All of which I am sure, does not interest you at all!!!

I wonder what does interest you — ?

What can I say which will interest you who have known such dear and great things that all other things can but be sense*less* —

Ah my dear Temple I see such wonders in your face — I see there the reflection of all the wonders you have looked at.

You ask where Isadora is? I am not quite sure whether she is in the island of St Helena or in Paris, but I have reason to suppose she is in Paris.

but why do you speak about Isadora? Do you think that she has anything to do with my "dying."

[Here Craig drew a huge *NO* as a sun emerging from clouds.]

If Isadora cared more for the Art which we are all dying to give birth to, if she cared less for money and power, and more for the old love of Love — and if she gave her whole being up to this dangerous desire, then I might have less weight on my eyes and on my hands — but a little extra weight will not be the cause of my death.

Heavens no! for I am devilish full of fight and am confident I shall win — but I shall only win dead if I fight alack —

Whoop!

But I cannot write clearly —

When I look at you, and see on your face "the eyes! the eyes!" the gravity of great beauty, then with my eyes I try to tell you all about this Love of Love for which I know we all care so little — But I must go and do some fighting somewhere to keep my hair nice and curly.

That, Temple, was always a great deep sorrow with me, that my hair never would curl . . . I could have been a success on the variety stage or in the pulpit with curls —

So you are playing Revisor —

How nice — I like to think of it.

[Here followed a sketchy impression of the set with a caption "You dear people."]

And you in your dressing-room — half Japaneese [*sic*] and awfully jolly — not at all horrible —

Do you know that the horrible should never be shown on the stage — *"Macbeth"* murdering should not be shown nor Hamlet bemoaning his fate —

Why then do we go on with the grotesque farce —

You in your dressing room *"pretending"* to be horrible are lovely.

You on the stage *being* horrible are utterly wrong.

Could you not one day keep these eyes and ears attentive you would do something no one has ever done.

You ask me where I will be in the summer

Ah, Temple, there's a saying in England that "one swallow does not make a summer" and the other evening one swallow nearly ended all my summers and winters. I was reading in bed — it was dark — I heard 12 o clock strike — then I heard *one*. Then I heard 2. t h e n . . . then I felt something which is utterly indescribable but which suggests the approach of a monster. My bed rocked . . . the windows shook . . . and I felt the whole house moving. It was like nothing I have felt before . . . and I was conscious of fear . . . fear is disgusting but in this case there was some excuse. The house swayed backwards and forwards for 8 seconds — but it seemed like ages, the mystery of the force which could act so, is what was so alarming. The approach of the unknown. They say that on January 25th it will come again . . . I shall try and understand it then, but the 1st experience is _____. Therefore, lovely, angelic, demonaic *dear very dear* Temple [Craig's underlining is intense here], when you ask me *where* I shall be in the summer I look up and down and grin at the walls and ceiling and think *"where."* All being well with my cieling [sic] and the top of my head I shall be in this room working like a good little boy. I may have one of my children here — a splendid boy — but I dare say I shall be all by MYSELF. Isadora will be sure to come here but Isadora will be full of little ambitious plans — and only HUGE impossible plans please me — — — And *you:*

[The rest of the letter concerns a poem written by his postman.][10]

Craig's epistolary fandango is a mating-dance: even as he allures Olga Knipper with compliments and asseverations of profound affection, he tries to prevent her intrusion into his family life by the report of an earthquake. Still, for all the double-talk, the connection between Knipper and Shakespeare had been made, and it may have occurred to him that she would be an excellent Gertrude.

While Craig was weaving "HUGE impossible" fancies, the Board of the Art Theatre, in its pragmatic way, set the wheels in motion. It sent him a check for 500 rubles, his salary from December 15, 1908, to January 15, 1909, and Stanislavsky followed this with a telegram, "We are rapidly setting about the production of *Hamlet*. We ask you to come at once. Impossible to start without you."[11] At the same time, the Board also appointed V. E. Egorov, who had designed the black velvet sets for *The Life of Man*, and the childlike fantasies for *The Blue Bird*, to travel through Denmark, Germany and England, to make sketches of medieval artifacts. Craig was still an unknown quantity, and the Board wanted the security of a second set of drawings to fall back on if he defaulted.[12]

Unused to such expedition, Craig responded to Stanislavsky that he requred another £300 before he could think of travelling and would be in Moscow in two months' time, when he had completed the sketches for *Hamlet*. Deferentially he asked information on Stanislavsky's plans for the staging. But in the same post he wrote to the Board, petulantly complaining that he had been summoned *"at a moment's notice"* when he had expected to receive two months' warning. For their benefit he put down his delays to troubles over *The Mask* and the opening of his school in September.

This shows you my position. I am also well aware that I have agreed to work for you and *I shall therefore start designs for Hamlet at once* — and I shall work at them with great delight.

My only sorrow is that I am not able to take train and join you *at once.*

But if you will read telegrams and letter carefully you will see why it is impossible. My suggestion that perhaps some one in Moscow might care to possess some of my pictures was made so that a way could be found to make it possible for me to leave *The Mask* at once.[13]

The note struck in these two letters was to remain dominant throughout Craig's correspondence with the MAT. Stanislavsky he would regard as a friend and colleague, albeit a wealthy amateur unacquainted with the vagaries of genius. The Board was to be characterized as a pack of pluto-cratic Philistines. His suggestion that they become agents to sell his render-ings was typically tactless.

> Meantime perhaps you will send me a few words HOW you intend to produce *Hamlet* so that I may bear them in mind while preparing my designs.
> Also names of the actors and their roles.
> I am grieved at not being able to come up to you tomorrow — perhaps if you could see and hear me you would understand how unhappy I am . . . .
> Will you let me hear which Edition of *"Hamlet"* you use.
> In how many scenes — do you omit any scenes — ?
> You might get an English copy and mark it for me — yes? If I can come (by some good luck) in a week or 2, I will write at once.[14]

The willingness to cut the script testifies to Craig's practical rejection of principles enunciated in *The Mask*. While waiting for a remittance, he went on annotating the text of the play and preparing drawings for the sets and costumes. As he fantasized about *Hamlet*, he confided some of his conceits to Mariya Lilina on February 1, using her both as an intercessor with her husband and a sounding board for his more extravagant notions.

Dear Mrs Stanislavsky,
Magnus, the gentleman who took over the Mask and raised its circulation to 10,000 has run away! leaving the Mask in a dangerous position.
It must not die: it ought not to die, so I am going to Paris to see Magnus who must be mad!
I thought at first that he was only ill, but now he writes madly that I think he must be off his little head!!
I go to Paris tomorrow . . . I think I shall also be able to see Miss Duncan who I shall tell of all your sweetness and goodness to me.
If I arrange as I want in Paris and if I have enough money in a week from now I shall try to come up to Moscow at once, . . . that is earlier than we hoped or expected.
I long to be there talking and sketching and skipping through Hamlet, . . . my little scrap of taste adding one touch more to the finely built building which your husband will construct out of the Shakespearean material.
I hope he will simplify everything, . . . the meaning of the simple old love story and the manner of it.

Once upon a time there was a man who loved all things except himself, and whatever was ugly he went far off from and looked at from far and found it beautiful; and that was Hamlet.

Hamlet who was made of searching eyes. I like to see nothing else in Hamlet. Father? Mother? Friends? Girl? even Uncle? are what he is asked to love . . . all so ugly . . . He steps back, shades his eyes with his hand and dies because he cannot succeed in finding beauty in them.

It is this desire to love and for love which breaks him. This desire, so beautiful because so pure has not been shown by Hamlet on a stage.

In appearance I see him as a large man with grand huge limbs and a heroic head of hair and large open eyes.

He is no ordinary man; his words and looks and actions are so extraordinary, so superfine, that men whisper (as they have always done) that he is mad. So was Dionysus mad, Christus mad: but they were Gods: here Hamlet is a man who is so full of the intoxication of love that no one can understand him, not his mother, nor the critics, to this day!

I talk too much say too little.

Tell some of what I say to your husband, if you think it worth while.

I hope he is going to play Hamlet: he was born for it, and I see him as Hamlet and I hear him too.

I see him standing motionless, standing secure, firm like a snow-capped mountain, at whose base many small figures of mean men and thin women creep or scramble.

Do write to me. I rely on you as my real good friend to translate only what is sensible in this letter and to leave out what is dull. Please.

    Love to you four.
                                  Gordon Craig.[15]

The identification of Dionysus and Christ with Hamlet would have pleased Vyacheslav Ivanov and his followers, but the portrait of Hamlet as a seeker after beauty, misunderstood both by his mother and the critics, had never been seen hitherto on a stage because it was a projection of Craig's own self-characterization. He naturally gravitated to strong authority figures in theatre, and so he selected Stanislavsky to embody this personal image. The image of the snow-capped mountain surrounded by ant-like nobodies could apply equally well to tall, grey-thatched Craig or tall, white-haired Stanislavsky with his entourage of sycophants and regisseurs; it barely fits a young prince fresh from university.

Stanislavsky did, in fact, dream of playing Hamlet — in the first years of the MAT he had wanted to play all the leads —, but he was going through a period of uncertainty about his acting and willingly yielded to the objections of Nemirovich-Danchenko who thought him unsuited to tragedy. Nemirovich had long considered that the only member of the company capable of taking on Hamlet was Vasily Kachalov and, ironically, the very day Craig penned his description of Hamlet for Lilina, the Board cast Kachalov in the role.[16]

Vasily Ivanovich Shverubovich had been born in 1875, the son of a priest, and began acting as an amateur while in high school. His success in a law-students' dramatic group in St. Petersburg determined him to take up the profession and, to avoid embarrassing his family, he had adopted the name Kachalov. (Since the Art Theatre, unlike most professional companies, was composed of many middle-class persons with higher education, *noms de théâtre* were common: Stanislavsky, Lilina, Leonidov, Luzhsky were all pseudonyms.) After playing major roles in various troupes, including the part of Horatio, Kachalov joined the Art Theatre in the spring of 1900, where he made a success with his first assignment, King Berendey in Ostrovsky's *Snow-Maiden*. Stanislavsky had been sceptical of Kachalov's promise and saw only his provincial mannerisms and stereotypical reactions; but even in 1900 Gorky had noted his voice of "rare beauty and flexibility."[17] Kachalov devoted himself to the Art Theatre techniques and soon replaced Stanislavsky as "leading man" (if one dares refer to an *emploi* in such a company). By the time he was cast as Hamlet, he had distinguished himself as Chatsky in *Woe from Wit*, Brand, Julius Caesar and the Baron in *The Lower Depths* as well as Chekhov's original Tusenbach and Trofimov. Tall, elegant and near-sighted, he exuded intellect and nobility. No vestiges of barnstorming survived in his measured and austere performances, quickened by flashes of mischievous comedy. He was the darling of the Moscow intelligentsia, the closest thing the MAT had to a matinee idol; young bluestockings quivered with delight at his resonant and mellifluous tones. They had long awaited his Hamlet.[18]

The rest of the principals were also cast at this time: V. V. Luzhsky and A. L. Vishnevsky, as Polonius and Claudius respectively, were the only members of the MAT's old guard to be enrolled. Claudius was also apportioned to Leonid Leonidov, to be rehearsed in tandem with Vishnevsky. Horatio was N. O. Massalitinov, Laertes the brilliant young actor A. F. Gorev, whom Stanislavsky had been grooming to play Don Carlos, and Gertrude, an all-purpose character woman, M. G. Savitskaya. The role of Ophelia was to be shared between Alisa Koonen and V. V. Baranovskaya. By the time *Hamlet* opened three years later only three of these actors would still be in the cast and only one of them in his original role.

Clearing the decks for action, both Stanislavsky and the Board sent telegrams to Craig approving his postponement of the journey, but requesting his recommendation of a text and its cuts, his over-all ideas and treatment of the works. Drawings could wait until his arrival. Then, on March 9, without waiting for a reply, Stanislavsky opened the first discussion of *Hamlet* with the actors and the directing staff. It is worth noting that rehearsals were well in hand, under his guidance, long before Craig took over the reins. The cast and crew were therefore indoctrinated with many concepts of Stanislavsky's that later had to be uprooted or accommodated to Craig's more radical taste.

Egorov had returned from his research trip to Denmark which he had toured Baedeker in hand, and he laid his portfolio open to them at this meeting. The sketches were chiefly of medieval castles, details of Teutonic costume and weaponry, and copies of paintings by Cranach and Holbein. His approach was stolidly archaeological. He and Stanislavsky agreed that the ambience should be that of a provincial court with its everyday routine and shabby ceremony; pomp and "theatricality" were to be avoided. Egorov suggested Kronberg Castle as a model, but it was not sufficiently prison-like for Stanislavsky's taste, so barred windows showing glimpses of cannon on the ramparts were worked into it.[19] Stanislavsky then discussed the characteristics of Hamlet, Ophelia and Laertes, indicating which critics were to be consulted, and appointed the youngest cast members to make extracts from them.

On March 13, Stanislavsky went over his ideas with the directorial staff.

Winter. A cold sea. Elsinore is a cold stone prison. Two hours away from Norway. The Norwegians have invaded Elsinore many times. The cannons in Elsinore are always primed. A rough militarism prevails. The castle is a barracks.[20]

The architecture had to suggest the barbaric might of the Middle Ages, but the costumes and interior decoration were to bring in elements of the Renaissance. Three days later experiments were carried out on the Ghost's appearance. Stanislavsky viewed the Ghost as

A soul in torment — this is his essence. A tortured, noble soul; find the incarnation of a tortured, suffering soul — throw out everything else. The rest is unnecessary and unimportant: who he is — a warrior, a state councilor or anyone else is what clothes him. Rags hang from him. We probably won't actually use rags, but something slightly silvered.[21]

The lighting was therefore planned so that the Ghost's shadow would rise gradually to the very top of the stage, like the wings of the Angel of Death in Hauptmann's *Hannele*, waxing and waning to create an effect of phantasmagoria and mystery.

Three days later Act I, Scene I, was rehearsed. Stanislavsky saw it taking place during a blizzard, the guards swaddled in furs to protect them from the icy, penetrating cold up on the crenellated fortress wall. The Ghost was to appear fleetingly behind falling snowflakes.

Some coarse soldiers are changing the guard, and suddenly mysticism breaks in; everything begins to tremble, the tragedy begins at once. I should like it if, when the Ghost intrudes, mysticism so take over the stage that the castle itself begins to rock, and everything is changed.[22]

As for Scene 2 and Claudius' council,

Entrances and exits are destructive — they are no good at all, involve a lot of movement and drag things out. On a golden throne sit the King and Queen and at left,

1. Vladimir Egorov's preliminary design for Act I, Scene 2, the Court assembled. The Cranach influence is very evident. A blond Hamlet is seated to the right of the Queen. (N.N. Chushkin, *Gamlet-Kachalov* [Moscow: Iskusstvo, 1966].)

2. Craig's conception of Act I, Scene 2, with the Court a mass of gold. Hamlet is seated in profile down left. (N.N. Chushkin, *Gamlet-Kachalov* [Moscow: Iskusstvo, 1966].)

beside them, sits the pensive Hamlet . . . It must be calm. The characters must be King, Queen and Hamlet. The rest is only a background of vileness, richness, density. An enormous throne behind a magnificent baldachin, where the King and Queen sit, and on a step below or perhaps right beside them, Hamlet. On benches along the wall sit the courtiers, and down front in a trap, back to the audience, stand warriors with spears. The problem is to show the throne, the three characters, and the retinue, the courtiers, merge into one generalized background of gold. Their mantles flow together, and they cannot be perceived to have individuated faces. They are rough brushstrokes, saturated with majesty, a background.[23]

These comments remarkably prefigured Craig's own views of the scene, even to the words used, and would partially be incorporated into the finished production.

But if the décor was to take on an emblematic character, the acting was to be very much in the MAT tradition of nuanced psychology. When the actors erupted with questions about how to relate to a Ghost, Stanislavsky referred them to the general line of "inner experience." As to playing the Ghost itself, he laid stress on the basic tools of an actor's skill.

You need not recite the words, but you do need to understand the author's idea — those feelings for whose sake the words were written . . . These feelings, those ideas must be understood and to understand them reach them accurately through physiology . . . Every feeling is apprehended through sight or sound or realization. If you ask someone something, you look in his eyes, you await his answer. If you start asking without looking at your respondent, if your eyes don't verify that he is the respondent, you put yourself in a false physiological condition. If, on the other hand, you start by linking eyes with your partner, even though the feeling that causes you to look in his eyes is known to you only in your subconscious, thanks to the accurate physiological set-up, you can convey it to the realm of feeling. Which is bound to happen. But if you get into a conventional physical state of nerves to stand for inner experience in advance and listen to your voice to find the intonation you think corresponds to a given word, you will certainly come up with nothing but the theatrical stereotype which always accompanies such words on stage.[24]

Egorov devised a design of narrow windows that revealed the various levels of a winding staircase, and Stanislavsky seized on the pictorial tableau of silhouettes moving up and down it. It would be the perfect setting for "To be or not to be": as Hamlet moves ever lower and lower, Ophelia ascends to the top; during the scene they would occasionally stop, look back at one another and then go their separate ways in a gliding motion. As one actor recalled, "Stanislavsky got very carried away and fantasized a lot at these pre-Craig rehearsals."[25] If this smacked of symbolism, the conception of Fortinbras and his soldiers did not. Stanislavsky wanted them to appear as Vikings, animal-like in iron and pelts, an ultranaturalistic depiction. In his flat, he examined material for costumes and when it was approved, tested it on the main stage. On the "New" or studio stage, whole acts would be read with the actors.

Despite this intensive work, Stanislavsky held true to his commitment to Craig. On April 1 he wired him that the MAT was about to leave for its annual month's tour to St. Petersburg, and asked him to meet them there by April 15. Two months' salary was sent to cover expenses. As we shall see, Craig's presence obliterated all this advance work and, in particular, Egorov's designs. When Stanislavsky was shown them again in 1935, he confessed that they were "Very interesting but I remember absolutely nothing of it. The impression Craig's concept made was so strong that it totally forced out of my recollection everything I seem to have done with Egorov."[26] Egorov, for his part, was very bitter at being bypassed and resentment rankled for decades. As a consolation prize, Nemirovich-Danchenko offered him his choice of Ibsen's *Lady from the Sea*, Strindberg's *Ghost Sonata* or Hauptmann's *Helga* for the next season, but none of them was eventually staged. Instead, Egorov's last project for the MAT was a set for Yushkevich's Zolaesque *Miserere*, a dismal failure.[27]

4
GRAND ILLUSIONS

Craig arrived in St. Petersburg, bearing his sketches which Stanislavsky found to be "very talented." On this second trip, the Englishman had time to confirm his first impressions and consolidate the friendships he had made earlier. Isadora was then in Petersburg and a stormy dinner party with the Stanislavskys deepened the rift between her and her former lover.[1] On the other hand, Craig grew more fascinated with Alisa Koonen with whom he had long soulful talks. "She has been loved before, but more than this she has *loved* before and lost her lover — he left her. It would be unworthy of Love therefore if she did not torture me, rend me & break me if she can."[2] Even as Craig jotted these warnings in his Daybook, he envisaged her as the ideal Ophelia, not least because of her checkered past.

"What would you say if I took Miss Koonen to Italy and built a small theatre for her, where she would play all by herself? I think it would be an interesting experiment,"[3] Craig remarked, half in jest, to Stanislavsky. The director took the proposition seriously and drew the young actress aside, warning her not to let herself be taken in by such wild schemes. The next day she got a letter from Isadora cautioning her to be wary of trusting Craig, for he was a seductive fellow and yet indifferent to young girls.

Fascinated by such a character-sketch which failed to correspond to Craig, I at once guessed that the letter had been written not without Stanislavsky's participation, and I dropped by the Hotel Europa to see Duncan. Very spontaneously and sincerely, she confirmed my guess, and we both laughed at Stanislavsky's charming and naïve officiousness, his constant attempt to protect me from nonexistent perils.[4]

However, the individual to whom Craig felt closest was Stanislavsky's assistant Sulerzhitsky. Leopold Antonovich Sulerzhitsky was one of those men whose talents are so diverse and whose personality so malleable that their lives are dissipated in a search for direction and in service to single-minded but dominant individuals. He had been born in 1872, the son of a bookbinder, and soon showed a penchant for painting; after aiding the painter Vasnetsov in cataloguing the frescoes in Kiev Cathedral, he matriculated at the Moscow School of Painting, Sculpture and Architecture. But he became a convert to Tolstoyanism, that hazy cult of passive resistance to authority so popular among intellectuals at the time, and was expelled from school for an antigovernment speech made on examination day. For two years as a pilot he sailed before the mast. In 1896, at his refusal to take the oath of loyalty to the Tsar when he was called up for military service, Sulerzhitsky was tried and put in solitary confinement. After a psychiatric examination, he was sent to a fortress in Kushka, a pesthole in Central Asia where death by fever was intended to be his fate.

After a fortuitous release by General Kuropatkin and an adventure-filled return to civilization, Sulerzhitsky finally met his master Tolstoy who wrote of him to Chekhov, "he possesses a really valuable possibility for disinterested love of people. He is brilliant at this"[5] — just the man, Tolstoy thought, to aid in resettling the Dukhobors ("Wrestlers with the Spirit"), a pacifistic religious sect persecuted by the authorities. So Sulerzhitsky spent two years in bringing them via decrepit steamer to Canada and establishing a farm community there in the most primitive conditions. Another settlement mission to Cyprus culminated in a serious bout with yellow fever. On his return to Russia in 1900, Sulerzhitsky then worked an underground printing-press for which he was arrested two years later and exiled, a pardon being issued to him after a year.

Like so many Russian liberals, Sulerzhitsky was severely shaken by the failed revolution of 1905. His pacifism had always been at odds with his revolutionary radicalism, and the rift in his opinions kept widening. As a result of this spiritual crisis, he turned to the theatre, hoping to find in it an artistic sodality that would "sustain his faith in mankind in our terribly cruel world."[6] It was not so much an escape from reality as an attempt to harness art to his aims. For despite his psychic crises and poor health, Sulerzhitsky was the life of any party, a practical joker, a singer who intoned folk ballads with Shalyapin, a dancer who impressed Isadora Duncan — "all three musketeers rolled up in one,"[7] Tolstoy had said, for he exuded a great zest for life. Gorky and Chekhov had introduced him to the Art Theatre in 1900, and in 1905 he began directorial work there as special assistant to Stanislavsky, who was struck by Sulerzhitsky's idealism and fealty. "Suler brought with him into the theatre an enormous baggage of fresh, lively spiritual matter, straight from the soil . . . He brought a virginally pure attitude to art, totally ignorant of its old, outworn and hackneyed professional gimmicks."[8] He was among the first adherents of the "system," Stanislavsky's newly evolved method of acting, and was later to organize the famous Moscow First Studio as well as an actors' commune in Evpatoriya.

"This wise child," as Gorky called him, was a special favorite of the youngsters in the Art Theatre troupe, for he represented a background of "real life." It was one thing for a wealthy industrialist like Stanislavsky and an aristocratic litterateur like Nemirovich-Danchenko to preach devotion to one's art; it was another to see this ex-sailor, ex-political prisoner, ex-colonist and ex-farmer spending long hours perfecting a stage effect and dedicating his energies unstintingly to achieving someone else's concept. Forbidden by the authorities to live in Moscow, Suler dwelt in a railway guard's shack outside the city limits or spent the night on the floors and sofas of the actors' apartments. Much of the technical success of *The Blue Bird* had been due to his ingenuity and effort.[9] A man who wore his heart on his sleeve, Suler was fiercely loyal. Still devoted to Stanislavsky, he immediately transferred some of that devotion to Craig, and his attempts to reconcile his two idols artistically and personally over the next three years was to destroy his peace of mind. The production of *Hamlet* was to be Suler's purgatory.

At this stage, however, they were inseparable, a Bohemian Mutt and Jeff: the tall, long-haired Craig in his costume-shop furs, and short, bearded Sulerzhitsky in his navy pea-jacket and middy blouse. Later, when a work-shop in the theatre had been set up for Craig, the two men would sing English folksongs together, and Suler's critical commentary would often make Craig abandon his model without a murmur. Stanislavsky recalled, "Craig spoke an Anglo-German jargon, Sulerzhitsky an Anglo-Ukrainian patois, and this gave rise to a mass of *quid pro quo* anecdotes, wordplay and laughter."[10] Craig himself characterized Suler in his Daybook as

A dear man, this Suler, a rough diamond, full of intelligence and with natural talent for almost everything. He couldn't draw or paint — wrote a little, I believe — was not a composer of music and had never acted, but he seemed, by instinct, to under-stand all the essential things about the stage. He had also been a farmer, and he spoke very good English. A rare creature! Yes — and we all loved him. He talked of the actors to me — and probably to them — as a pack of stupids. *"They know nothing and they won't try and learn,"* he said.[11]

With his prejudice that some persons are "born" histrionic and that actors cannot be made, Craig was bound to take to this instinctual man of the theatre. Even after they had quarrelled irreparably, he still called him "a most loveable character."[12]

In late April, Craig and Stanislavsky began detailed discussions of *Hamlet*, progressing through the play scene by scene. Craig would begin with general statements about characters or an episode and Stanislavsky would interject questions and comments, chiefly to elicit a more precise elu-cidation of given points. Suler was invariably present, trying to clarify the Anglo-German *lingua franca* in which the two directors sought to com-municate; he reassured Craig that Stanislavsky's questions did not neces-sarily represent his opinions. These discussions were recorded, *verbatim* in some cases, paraphrased in others, by Ursula Cox in English and in Russian by Mikhail Lykiardopoulo, the secretary of the MAT Board, who were bilingual, and occasionally by Suler himself. This transcription was stan-dard operating procedure, for the MAT, with its pervasive sense of history, kept copious records of every production, realized or not. But Craig found the taking down of his every word unsettling; he was used to indulging in extravagant flights of fancy on café terraces without being called to account for them afterwards. And so he began to "feed" the stenographers, weaving elaborate and impractical *mises-en-scène*, or adopting outrageously perverse stands, all of which Stanislavsky took seriously and felt obliged to consider or contravene.

They write down *everything* and find each idea so important to register so that later it may all be brought to bear with full force and nothing lacking . . . The whole aim of S[tanislavsky] is that his company may *all* be filled with the same knowledge of the piece. But one must not forget that his company is composed of university men and women — they understand something beyond payday.[13]

After the general discussion, they would proceed to a line-by-line analysis, Craig correcting the inaccuracies of the Russian translation of the play and laying out blocking and lighting patterns as well as interpreting motivation. Stanislavsky and Suler would take their own personal notes, from which the *Regiebuch* was to be composed. Significantly, no actors were present at this stage of the proceedings.[14]

The original scheme had been to use Craig as an adviser on the physical aspects of the production, hence the need for Egorov as an alternative designer if the Englishman failed to work out. But as the talks wore on, Stanislavsky found himself seduced by Craig's novel approach, and although he had misgivings about the feasibility of many of these new ideas, he was willing to try them out. Craig wasted no time in declaring that Shakespeare had no interest in everyday life or historical reconstruction. *Hamlet* was a mystery play, a monodrama about the conflict between spirit and matter. Thus, the setting, by its architectural and pictorial nature, had to present an abstract realm of shapes and lines with no relation to external or material existence. The tragedy took place within Hamlet's soul, and the other characters were to be psychic emanations of his loves and hates. Means other than straightforward characterization had to be found to convey this interpretation.

Typical of the progress of these discussions as well as the format for recording them are Stanislavsky's notes for Act I, Scene 1, and the character of Ghost. Craig family legend has it that when the two directors had first met, Stanislavsky had dumbfounded Craig with the earnest query, "How do you imagine the character of Hamlet's father?" The answer when it came was provocative.

INTRODUCTION

I. Craig did not know a better beginning to a play than the first three scenes of "Hamlet." They speak for themselves.

Ordinarily, actors who play Hamlet take special pains in the first two acts, hoping at once to arrest the spectator's attention and sympathy, which is why these first two acts tend to wear them out.

To no avail, for wouldn't it be better to trust Shakespeare?

II. Craig sees three tones for the performance of the play.

1. Tone I — Abstraction. This is the inner experience [*perezhivanie*] of Hamlet himself.

2. Tone II — Semirealism, *i.e.*, wherever the tragedy begins and develops. For instance, in the first scenes of the play.

3. Tone III — Realism, *i.e.*, where the wedge of comedy cleaves through, at which points Craig permits the realism of Chekhov's plays. For instance, in the scene with the gravediggers or Polonius' scene with Hamlet.

The curtain is open.

The stage is barely lit.

Servants in special costumes enter and set the screens in place.

Bell to let in audience.

The audience is seated.

All at once all the lights are turned out — both those in the auditorium and those on stage (see Figure 1).

Resultant blackout.

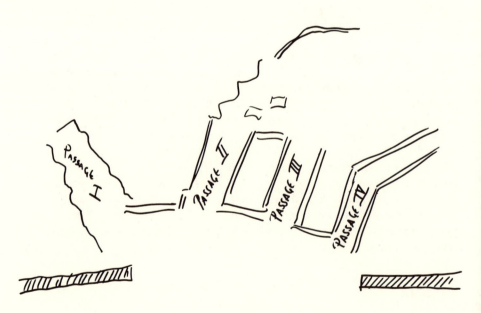

Figure 1

At Point A a mysterious glow appears — barely visible.

That is where the Ghost will appear, *i.e.*, the place where the play begins.

The glow is accompanied by some sort of shade of Hamlet's father. It moves from left to right and in its wake light pours in and fills the stage. As to the constitution of this shade, Craig came up with contradictory and ambiguous statements. This is what he said about it at various times under various circumstances.

THE GHOST OF HAMLET is an important role.

The apparition must not be theatrical. God help us if this apparition gives off a smell of gimmickry or heavyhanded stunts. Let the apparition be real, *i.e.*, in other words, let the spectator's relationship to it be real, with total faith in its actuality. "Can this be done?" Craig asked fearfully, like a child, as if afraid he had said something silly, impractical and fit only for dreams.

At other times, as if entranced by the possibility of such a real apparition and recalling the everlasting nuisance of stage effects, which involve the creation of an apparition from gross matter — Craig urgently insisted that the Ghost be a real tragic figure, who arouses pity and fear simultaneously. It is a shame that there's no way of turning it into the kind of tragic figure one sees in ancient plays. This impossibility results from the father's Ghost's talking too much about petty earthly matters and his life beyond the grave.

He remembers only too well all the realistic details connecting him to earth, and at the same time talks about his torments beyond the grave. He is a tragic, semirealistic figure out of the Middle Ages, not the ancient world of Greece.

Through such fancies Craig arrived at another notion. He would like to give an impression of the dead man's tragedy by means of realistic effects and therefore, as I see it, descends to ultrarealism and with its aid tries to achieve abstraction. At such moments Craig begins dreaming about a figure and outward semblance of the dead king in this way: He is bolt upright, because of rigor mortis. He is a skeleton gnawed away by worms. Only fragments of flesh hang from the bones in places, as in certain illustrations of Death (a skeleton with shreds of flesh) pursuing living creatures in pictures by medieval painters. No armor on him at all. That is only an hallucination of the frightened soldiers, who are used to envisaging the late king in full kit at marches and tourneys. The bones of his skeleton glow and glimmer with a mysterious, unearthly light, which the fantasies of the terrified take to be shining armor. The Ghost is swathed in some kind of material (as Lazarus is depicted emerging from the tomb in paintings). This material winds round its legs, droops and hinders it from walking; nevertheless, no one can stop the impeded Ghost from leaving and, shadow-like, moving through the light. It would like to tear these impediments asunder. This material is a tattered shroud, putrescent or ripped to shreds — fabric decaying on the rotting, once comely body, winding-sheets which bandage the dead when they are entombed. This skeleton with bits of flesh, these shredded garments will give the apparition the appearance of some emaciated, starving beggar in tattered rags — with scraps of hair, apparel, flesh and bone. "Sic transit gloria mundi" speaks from the entire figure of this best of men, wherein only his beautiful and suffering soul now resides with the rent, mouldering, ephemeral remnants of a fabric which once was gorgeous and really splendrous. The figure ought to make a picture. Remnants or vestiges of this regal exterior should be descried throughout his skeleton. He is, without question, tall and well-built. "I repeat," Craig exclaimed more than once, yanking on his long hair and casting a despondent look backwards, "this is a very important and difficult role, because it must portray a human figure and yet be inhuman in this realistic guise."

There was one other aspect which refused to fit Craig's ideas concerning the shade of Hamlet's father and the relationship of the living to it.

Why did Shakespeare despatch this fine, best of men — a deceased king — to hell and doom him to such cruel tortures beyond the grave?

Because he hadn't time to be shriven before death?

This hidebound, ritualistic and unthinking belief does truly exist among a majority of Christians. Perhaps such a view was strong in the Middle Ages, but it is the view of narrow-minded, dull-witted persons. Let Marcellus, Bernardo, probably even Horatio believe it, but Shakespeare could not hold such a narrow creed, and consequently, Hamlet himself could not believe such a thing — not Hamlet, in whom Shakespeare placed the best, sublimest of his own feelings and ideas.

Shakespeare's genius cannot brook such petty, Philistine views. Both in ancient times and the Middle Ages, great minds have known how to extract from the great teachings and dogmas whatever is of importance, whatever constitutes their eternal value, and to discard the trivialities that, like a membrane, dull and disfigure the great idea.

In any case, Shakespeare, as a genius, must have been an unbeliever from the orthodox viewpoint.

Shakespeare's, and consequently Hamlet's, adherence to this narrow, hidebound dogma would not hold up in the eyes of Craig the critic.

The fact that in Scene V, at the Ghost's exit, Hamlet appeals to earth and hell is no explanation. Such exclamations have been uttered in all ages and therefore are typical not only of the Middle Ages. And besides, the covert meaning of these exclamations should sooner lead us to suppose a denial of hell (the anathematizer's hell) than a belief in it.

To support this notion, Craig told us an anecdote.

One of the English museums preserves a book of the famous English actor Macready.

It lies under glass, open to that very page where Hamlet, at the Ghost's exit, appeals to earth and hell. Against each of these exclamations Macready wrote in the margins: "murder," "murder," "murder." These glosses express the actor's feelings relating to Hamlet's exclamations.

Perhaps these outbursts break forth from hatred of his uncle's crime and nothing else . . .

How does the Ghost speak? Usually an actor declaims the part, crooning it stagily. This is very bad, but one cannot speak words from another world realistically. And here Craig goes off on a tangent, proposing all sorts of possibilities and recalling the great impression made on him once by a Gospel reading in a cathedral or the pronouncement of an anathema which he heard in Moscow in a Kremlin cathedral. From memory he portrayed the deacon's manner of uttering the phrases, raising and lowering his voice a semi-tone.

This would be unhackneyed and majestic as well, *i.e.*, it's what the actor needs who plays Hamlet's father's Ghost. But even then, overjoyed with his discovery, he rapidly grew disappointed, remembering that for the accustomed Russian ear the deacon's reading style has a different meaning than for him, a foreigner, who was

hearing a Russian church service in an unusual and alien setting for the first time.
    After such general remarks, Craig returns to the following directions.

HAMLET

Act I
Scene 1
    Elsinore. A platform before the castle. Francisco on guard. Enter Bernardo.

BERNARDO
Who's there?

FRANCISCO
Nay, answer me. Stand and unfold yourself.

BERNARDO
Long live the King! [*No. 1*]

FRANCISCO
Bernardo?

BERNARDO
            He.

FRANCISCO
You come most carefully upon your hour. [*No. 2*]

BERNARDO
'Tis now struck twelve. Get thee to bed, Francisco.

FRANCISCO
For this relief, much thanks. 'Tis bitter cold,
And I am sick at heart.

BERNARDO
Have you had quiet guard? [*No. 3*]

FRANCISCO
Not a mouse stirring. [*No. 4*]

    No. 1. If an actor plays the ghost in this scene, he must slink along cautiously, seeking Hamlet.
    From behind, in back of a sort of low wall, only Francisco's head must be visible, as he stands guard.
    Bernard enters to relieve him.
    The first three lines are spoken. (See Figure 2.)
    No. 2. From Bernardo's line "You come most carefully upon your hour" to the line "Have you had quiet guard?", Bernardo and Francisco speak, walking along Passageway III.
    While they are walking towards the *audience* along this passageway, the Ghost moves upstage, away from the audience, along Passageway II to point "a."

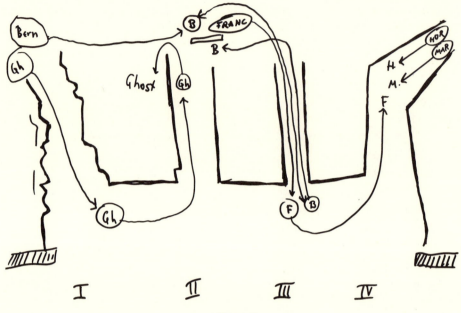

Figure 2

No. 3. The Ghost disappears around the corner.

No. 4. At the line, "Not **a** mouse stirring," the Ghost, mouse-like, creeps around the corner and is concealed in the wings.

BERNARDO
Well, good night.
If you do meet Horatio and Marcellus,
The rivals of my watch, bid them make haste. [*No. 5*]

FRANCISCO
I think I hear them. Stand ho! Who is there? [*No. 6*]

HORATIO
Friends to this ground. [*No. 7*]

MARCELLUS
                    And liegemen to the Dane.

FRANCISCO
Give you good night.

MARCELLUS
                    O, farewell, honest soldier. [*No. 8*]
Who hath relieved you?

FRANCISCO
                    Bernardo hath my place.
Give you good night. (Exits.) [*No. 9*]

MARCELLUS

Holla, Bernardo! [*No. 10*]

BERNARDO

Say —

What, is Horatio there?

HORATIO

A piece of him.

BERNARDO

Welcome, Horatio! Welcome, good Marcellus!

No. 5. At the line "If you do meet Horatio and Marcellus, the rivals of my watch, bid them make haste," Francisco goes along Passageway IV upstage, while Bernardo returns along Passageway III upstage back to his post.

No. 6. Francisco's line, "Stand ho! Who is there?" — Horatio and Marcellus come from the depths of Passageway IV to meet with the departing Francisco.

No. 7. From Horatio's line "Friends to this ground" to Marcellus' line "O farewell," the conversation takes place at the back of the corridor. The speakers are barely visible.

No. 8. After this last line of Marcellus', "Farewell," they split up; *i.e.*, Horatio and Marcellus walk downstage along Passageway IV, while Francisco moves upstage along Passageway IV.

No. 9. The line "Give you good night," — Francisco shouts on his way out, turning towards the audience, *i.e.*, in the direction in which Bernardo might hear the voice of the departing Francisco. (See Figure 3.)

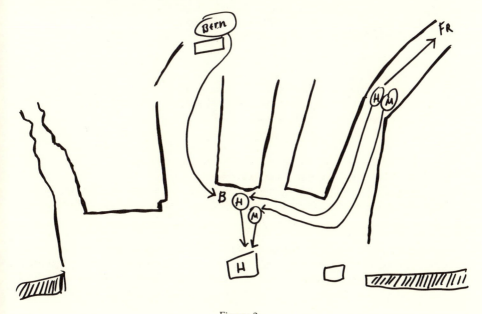

Figure 3

No. 10. On Marcellus' line, "Holla, Bernardo," Bernardo walks along Passageway II from his post to meet Horatio and Marcellus. They meet downstage, between Passageways II and III.

MARCELLUS

What, has this thing appeared again tonight? [*No. 11*]

BERNARDO

I have seen nothing.

MARCELLUS

Horatio says 'tis but our fantasy,
And will not let belief take hold of him
Touching this dreaded sight twice seen of us;
Therefore I have entreated him along
With us to watch the minutes of this night,
That, if again this apparition come,
He may approve our eyes and speak of it.

HORATIO

Tush, tush, 'twill not appear.

BERNARDO

                    Sit down awhile,
And let us once again assail your ears,
That are so fortified against out story,
What we have two nights seen.

HORATIO

                    Well, sit we down.
And let us hear Bernardo speak of this.

BERNARDO

Last night of all,
When yond same star that's westward from the pole
Has made his course t'illume that part of heaven
Where now it burns, Marcellus and myself,
The bell then beating one — [*No. 12*]

No. 11. Horatio's line, "What, has this thing appeared tonight" — from that moment what is truly important to the play begins.

Everything up to that point is unimportant to the tragedy and therefore ought to be spoken and performed lightly by the actors. Do not let the actors move far downstage in the early part of their roles, otherwise it will spoil what is important to the tragedy, that the red thread, *i.e.*, the thing for which the play was written, run through the play. Up to that moment Horatio and Marcellus have been sitting on a stone, their backs to the audience, while Bernardo stands facing them, leaning against the wall between Passageways II and III. Marcellus sits further left of the audience and therefore Passageway II is not visible to him. Horatio, who sits further right, cannot see the passageway either, because his view faces the wall on which Bernardo is leaning.

No. 12. Backstage a bell tolls the hour.

MARCELLUS

Peace, break thee off. Look where it comes again . . .
[*No. 13.*] (The Ghost enters.)

BERNARDO
                    In the same figure
Like the King that's dead. [*No. 14*]

MARCELLUS

Thou art a scholar; speak to it, Horatio. [*No. 15.*]

BERNARDO

Looks 'a not like the King? Mark it, Horatio.

HORATIO

Most like: it harrows me with fear and wonder.

BERNARDO

It would be spoke to.

MARCELLUS
                    Speak to it, Horatio.

HORATIO

What art thou [*No. 16.*] that usurp'st this time of night,
Together with that fair and warlike form
In which the majesty of buried Denmark
Did sometimes march? By heaven, I charge thee, speak.
[*No. 17.*] (The Ghost exits, *i.e.*, disappears.)

MARCELLUS

It is offended. [*No. 18.*]

BERNARDO
                    See, it stalks away. [*No. 19.*]

HORATIO

Stay! Speak, speak, I charge thee, speak! [*No. 20.*] (The apparition exits.)

MARCELLUS

'Tis gone and will not answer.

No. 13. The Ghost appears in Passageway II. Naturally, Marcellus, who sits facing this passageway, sees it.

No. 14. Bernardo hastens to peer round the corner at the entering Ghost (see Figure 4).

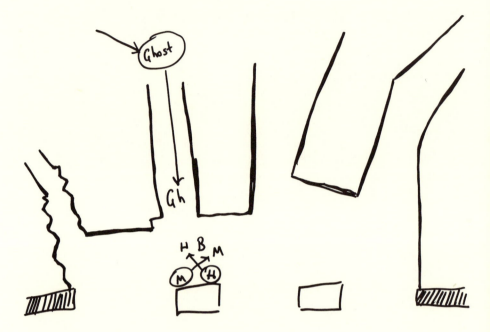

Figure 4

No. 15. Marcellus quickly walks over to Bernardo. Horatio is behind them. As the Ghost comes closer, not seeing the soldiers, they seem to cling to one another in wonderment and fear, pressed up against the wall.

By the way, Craig imagines all the soldiers as tall. As was said earlier, the Ghost is also tall. These tall, well-built figures, terrifying one another, create a tableau like a bas-relief . . .

The Ghost stops at the corner.

The soldiers hide behind the corner and freeze. The Ghost and the soldiers do not see one another. (The line: "What art thou that usurp'st this time of night.")

No. 16. The Ghost searches, crosses into the niche of Passageway II. Moves about. Horatio is frozen in place with fear, the rest draw back. All of them are tense with terror. Meeting the Ghost seems to make them taller or forces them to stand more upright. At this encounter the soldiers instinctively and out of habit stand at attention, as they did during the King's lifetime, being military men. (See Figure 5.)

No. 17. The line "By heaven, I charge thee, speak." The Ghost is offended and quickly vanishes, quivering with fright. His folds of clothing quaver rapidly and tremble.

This disappearance must be done deftly to conceal the actor in the wall. After the actor-Ghost has disappeared, there remains in the spot where he disappeared the Ghost's shade (done by lighting), which gradually fades away.

No. 18. Horatio, Bernardo and Francisco look about from behind the corner into Passageway II, seeking the Ghost. They have all moved (audience) left.

No. 19. The Ghost has barely disappeared when he has reappeared from behind Passageway II (do this with a stand-in so that the Ghost's appearance and disappear-

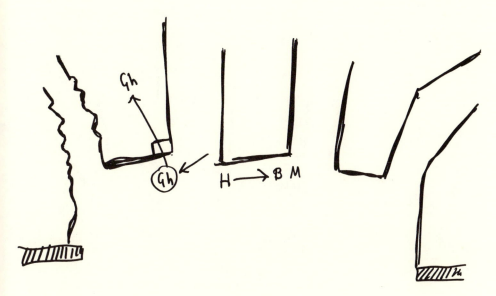

Figure 5

ance are produced almost simultaneously). Bernardo sees him in Passageway II. Wishing to follow the Ghost, they all make a rush audience right, *i.e.*, to the corner of Passageway III.

No. 20. The Ghost (perhaps another stand-in) almost simultaneously with the disappearance behind the second passageway appears in Passageway III and is concealed (see Figure 6).

BERNARDO

How now, Horatio? You tremble and look pale.
Is this not something more than fantasy?
What think you on't? [*No. 21.*]

HORATIO [*No. 22.*]

Before my God, I might not this believe
Without the sensible and true avouch
Of mine own eyes.

MARCELLUS

                Is it not like the King? [*No. 23.*]

HORATIO

As thou art to thyself.
Such was the very armor he had on
When he the ambitious Norway combated:
So frowned he once, when in an angry parle,
He smote the sledded Polacks on the ice.
'Tis strange.

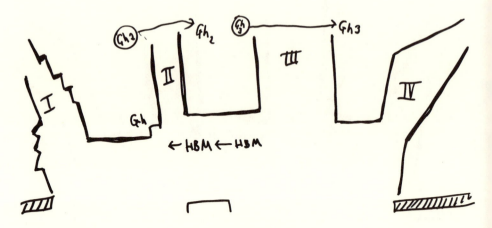

Figure 6

MARCELLUS

Thus twice before, and jump at this dead hour,
With martial stalk hath he gone by our watch.

HORATIO

In what particular thought to work I know not;
But, in this gross and scope of my opinion,
This bodes some strange eruption to our state. [*No. 24.*]

MARCELLUS [*No. 25*]

Good now, sit down, and tell me he that knows

Later on Craig said that at this disappearance of the Ghost everyone except
Horatio runs after it. Horatio is aware that it is no good chasing a Ghost.

No. 21. After a pause of perplexity, looking at one another, striving to explain
what has happened.

No. 22. Horatio, panic-stricken, goes and sits on the stone, *i.e.*, in his original
place.

No. 23. Marcellus draws near Horatio to ask his question. Stares fixedly in his face
and also sits in his original place.

Bernardo stands by the wall on guard, as before.

What has happened does not lend itself to acceptance and analysis by the materialistic human brain. Therefore intuition strives to comprehend the superhuman.
Hence there arises a mood of mysticism, expressed by great, intense concentration,
nervous tension and resonance (mysteriousness, concentration, seriousness, ner-
vousness).

One might think that the Ghost has some particle of reasoning power; has it not decided to inveigle Horatio into its search for Hamlet?

One must not forget, however, that the everyday, professional conditioning of a soldier's life manifests its influence even at such a ghastly moment.

Soldiers explain everything supernatural through their own individual, banal superstition, which finds food for terror in the soldier's workaday life. Naturally for them, war and enemy invasion are the most important and dreadful question of life. Thanks to their rudimentary development, their suppositions are materialistic and their mysticism of a commonplace nature.

Of course, Craig jokes, if his ghost appeared to actors after his death, they would start supposing that even there, in the other world, the director was struggling in quest of new "screens" and linear combinations on stage.

These remarks about war and Denmark, in Craig's opinion, are not interesting in themselves and unimportant to the basic framework of the tragedy, they merely abet whatever interest there is in actors conveying a feeling of the impression made on people by an apparition from beyond the grave.

No. 24. Horatio in his agonized surmises rises and speaks mysteriously, inclining towards Passageway I, where the Ghost appeared.

No. 25. A short pause. Horatio, and behind him the risen Marcellus, mysteriously cross beyond the place where the Ghost appeared, *i.e.*, to the next stone, further right, and there they sit at Marcellus' behest. Bernardo, glancing round, walks over at once and stands by the stone abandoned by Horatio and Marcellus, and then, growing interested in the discussion, sits down on it. They all whisper — fearfully, pointedly and mysteriously (see Figure 7).

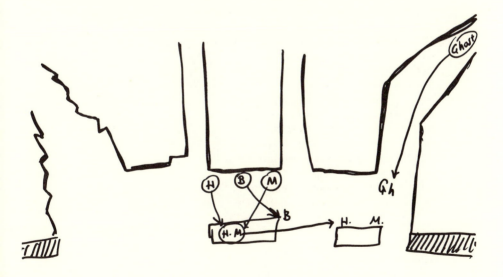

Figure 7

[MARCELLUS — continued]

Why this same strict and most observant watch
So nightly toils the subject of the land,
And why such daily cast of brazen cannon
And foreign mart for implements of war,
Why such impress of shipwrights, whose sore tasks
Does not divide the Sunday from the week,
What might be toward that this sweaty haste
Doth make the night joint-laborer with the day?
Who is't that can inform me?

HORATIO

That can I.
At least the whisper goes so: our last king,
Whose image even but now appeared to us,
Was, as you know, by Fortinbras of Norway,
Thereto pricked on by a most emulate pride,
Dared to the combat; in which our valiant Hamlet
(For so this side of our known world esteemed him)
Did slay this Fortinbras, who, by a sealed compact
Well ratified by law and heraldry,
Did forfeit, with his life, all those his lands
Which he stood seized of, to the conqueror;
Against the which a moiety competent
Was gaged by our King, which had returned,
To the inheritance of Fortinbras,
Had he been vanquisher, as, by the same comart
And carriage of the article designed,
His fell to Hamlet. Now, sir, young Fortinbras,
Of unimproved mettle hot and full,
Hath in the skirts of Norway here and there
Sharked up a list of lawless resolutes,
For food and diet, to some enterprise
That hath a stomach in't; which is no other,
As it doth well appear unto our state,
But to recover of us by strong hand
And terms compulsatory, those foresaid lands
So by his father lost; and this, I take it,
Is the main motive of our preparations,
The source of this our watch, and the chief head
Of this posthaste and romage in the land.

BERNARDO

I think it be no other but e'en so;
Well may it sort that this portentous figure
Comes armed through out watch so like the King
That was and is the question of these wars.

HORATIO

A mote it is to trouble the mind's eye:
In the most high and palmy state of Rome,
A little ere the mightiest Julius fell,
The graves stood tenantless, and the sheeted dead
Did squeak and gibber in the Roman streets;
As stars with trains of fire and dews of blood,
Disasters in the sun, and the moist star,
Upon whose influences Neptune's empire stands,
Was sick almost to doomsday with eclipse.
And even the like precurse of feared events,
As harbingers preceding still the fates
And prologue to the omen coming on,
Have heaven and earth together demonstrated
Unto our climatures and countrymen.
(The shade appears again.) [*No. 26.*]
But soft, behold, lo where it comes again!
I'll cross it, though it blast me. [*No.27.*] Stay, illusion
Speak to me.
If there be any good thing to be done
That may to thee do ease and grace to me,
Speak to me.
If thou art privy to thy country's fate,
Which happily foreknowing may avoid, [*No. 28.*]
O speak!
Or if thou hast uphoarded in thy life
Extorted treasure in the womb of earth,
For which, they say, you spirits oft walk in death,
Speak of it! [*No. 29.*] Stay and speak. Stop it, Marcellus.

MARCELLUS

Shall I strike at it with my partisan? [*No. 30.*]

HORATIO

Do, if it will not stand. [*No. 31.*]

BERNARDO [*No. 32.*]
                                    'Tis here. [*No. 33.*]

HORATIO [*No. 34.*]
                                    Tis here.
(The shade vanishes.) [*No. 35.*]

MARCELLUS

'Tis gone.
We do it wrong, being so majestical

No. 26. The Ghost seems to sail out from behind the corner of Passageway IV.
The soldiers take fright and run left. Bernardo hides in the niche of Passageway II.

Marcellus runs to Passageway I, and Horatio to the forestage between Passageway I and II (see Figure 8).

No. 27. Best to take some definite action, if only to terminate this painful scene.

No. 28. During this time, the Ghost draws nigh, as if wishing to say something (see Figure 9).

No. 29. Long pause. It moved once, stopped. Moved twice, stopped, opened its mouth to speak.

A cock crows.

It moves as if to vanish.

No. 30. While the Ghost is gliding towards the wall in order to disappear, the guard, cowering in fright, clears a path for it.

No. 31. The Ghost has made haste and arrived at the wall (a) and immediately the second one (a supernumerary double) passes by, simultaneously with the disappearing one, — from behind (see 6).

No. 32. Bernardo does not rush at the Ghost as is always done, but on the contrary, hides in numb fear.

No. 33. The Ghost emerges from within the wall and returns home — to hell by way of Passageway I (see b) and disappears.

No. 34. Horatio doesn't run after it either, but cowers in numb terror.

No. 35. The Ghost was vanished. Bernardo and Marcellus would have rushed after it, but suddenly realize the futility and stop short. Long pause. All three seem a bit fuddled in their wits.

At the first moment after the disappearance of the apparition, they had almost lost consciousness.

At the second, they scratch their heads. They think they've suffered a stroke.

The third moment — all three draw close together in a troubled awakening. They cling to one another.

Fourth moment — Horatio moves away from them and goes to Passageway III.

His first notion is to run to Hamlet and acquaint him of their rushing at his father's shade and offending it (see Figure 10).

[MARCELLUS — continued]
To offer it the show of violence,
For it is as the air, invulnerable,
And our vain blows malicious mockery.

BERNARDO
It was about to speak when the cock crew.

HORATIO
And then it started, like a guilty thing
Upon a fearful summons. I have heard
The cock, that is the trumpet to the morn,
Doth with his lofty and shrill-sounding throat
Awake the god of day, and at his warning,
Whether in sun or fire, in earth or air,
Th'extravagant and erring spirits hies
To his confines; and of the truth herein
This present object made probation.

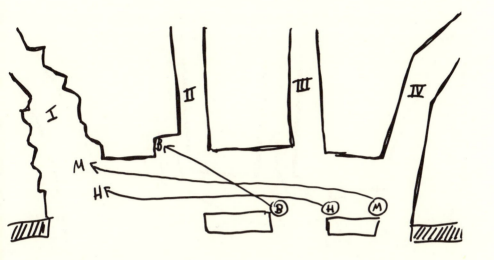

Figure 8

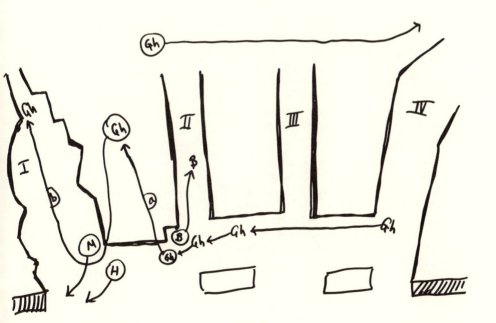

Figure 9

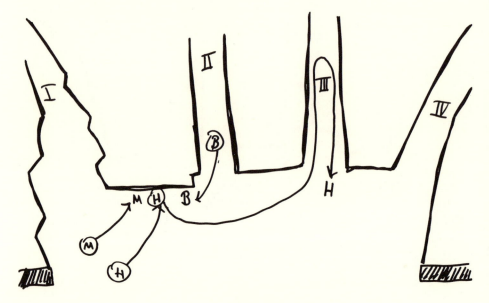

Figure 10

MARCELLUS

It faded on the crowing of the cock.
Some say that ever 'gainst that season come
Wherein our Savior's birth is celebrated,
This bird of dawning singeth all night long,
And then, they say, no spirit dare stir abroad,
The nights are wholesome, then no planets strike,
No fairy takes, nor witch hath power to charm;
So hallowed and so gracious is that time.

HORATIO

So have I heard and do in part believe it.
But look, the morn in russet mantle clad
Walks o'er the dew of yon high eastward hill.
Break we our watch up, and by my advice
Let us impart what we have seen tonight
Unto young Hamlet, for upon my life
This spirit, dumb to us, will speak to him.
Do you consent we shall acquaint him with it,
As needful in our loves, fitting our duty?

MARCELLUS

Let's do't, I pray, and I this morning know
Where we shall find him most convenient.
(Exeunt.) [*No. 36.*]
No. 36. Horatio, Bernardo and Marcellus, having spoken all these lines, depart

upstage, where Bernardo had been at the beginning of the scene. There they all three whisper. Only their heads are visible. The light fades out.

Only the glimmer of a glow remains as at the beginning of the scene, *i.e.*, in the same place where the Ghost had appeared.

When the glow dies out, a bell is heard.

The chime changes to a rumble — the pealing of wedding bells. The rumble increases, and the notes of a cracked bell grow prominent. They are mingled with the sounds of a funeral march, growing ever more distant.

Craig says that Shakespeare has no flourish of trumpets in the original.

During this rumble the set is quickly changed.[15]

With the discussion of the first court scene, where a more naturalistic psychology might be considered apt, Craig's interpretation jarred with traditional versions of the play. For him, the whole Polonius family was a vulgar personification of courtly etiquette, with Laertes an embryonic Rosencrantz who would grow up to be another Polonius. Craig wanted to cut all of the character's noble speeches. Ophelia was negative until purified by sorrow and madness, and the Queen "a fat woman who flops on sofas all day and night." In the throne-room everyone was to whisper inaudibly and tiptoe about, incessantly soliciting the king and queen, to give an effect of animal life.

But his most radical notion was the personification of Hamlet's death-wish, yet another manifestation of the monodramatic protagonist. In itself, a thanatotropic Hamlet was not out of keeping with the play. Kachalov was especially taken with Hamlet's contempt for the meaninglessness of life, for it enabled him to interpret what looked like weakness as an intellectual's sensitivity. The Prince was aware both of life's imperfection and any man's ability to improve it, an awareness that leads to inertia, and finally, the acceptance of death.[16] But Craig's attempt to turn the consummation devoutly to be wished into a discrete character seemed like upstaging to Kachalov. And however redolent of Maeterlinck the result, Stanislavsky regarded it as wholly un-Shakespearean.

On April 29, Stanislavsky, Craig and Sulerzhitsky discussed Act I, Scene 2. Here is that conversation as it was transcribed by Ursula Cox. Owing to necessities of retranslating the Craig-Stanislavsky patois back into standard English, she occasionally came up with unidiomatic phrases which require glosses. But her versions, taken down on the spot, are much more vital and interesting that those translated many years later from a Russian redaction.

29 APRIL 1909   DISCUSSION OF ACT 1, SCENE 2

CRAIG. I should like when I speak of that calmness desired by me in the performance of the play, for you to understand that in this calmness there should not be that tension which usually accompanies calmness on the stage.

*   *   *   *

In this play (*Hamlet*) I have found many parts which are not in the least important to the action, and I do not want the important to be lost on account of the unimportant. For example, in Hamlet's monologue in the second scene, Act I, beginning: "Not seems, madam; nay, it is; I know not 'seems.'" — In this monologue only the first two lines and, at the end of the monologue, the last two lines are important. These four lines express an important thought and must be spoken accordingly. All the rest of the monologue must be pronounced more as music, so that the thought becomes so much lost in the sounds that the audience simply *does not follow* the thought except in the above-mentioned four lines. How this music is done will depend on the individuality of the actor.

*   *   *   *

I want all this (*points to the scene*) to be in no way realistic. In the staging of this we must speak not so much of what *to do* as what *not to do*. I think it is possible for the actors, without getting into stiff and unnatural poses, and without speaking with unnatural pauses and emphases, quietly to convey the thought and feeling.

*   *   *   *

More than anything in this work I am afraid of misunderstandings. We must have many discussions as to what Shakespeare wants in this play — not what he *wants to say*, not by any means, but what he wants as an artist.

*   *   *   *

All the tragedy of Hamlet is his isolation. And the background of this isolation is the court, a world of pretence. The only person to whom some ties still join him is his mother, who would like to answer him only something does not let her. And in this golden court, this world of show there must not be various different individualities as there would be in a realistic play. No, here everything melts into a single mass. Separate faces as in the old masters of painting must be colored with one brush, with one paint.

*   *   *   *

In the king's monologue there must be felt vulgarity, falseness, insincerity. Here Shakespeare paints with a large brush. There must be especially a certain roughness. All this is necessary to show up the main drama. If you do this as you do Chekhov there may be too many details which cannot be used.

STANISLAVSKY. I understand what you say about monodrama. Let us try by every means to make the public understand that it is looking at the play with the eyes of Hamlet; that the king, the queen and the court are not shown on the stage such as they really are, but such as they appear to Hamlet to be. And I think that in the scenes where Hamlet is on stage we can do this. But what are we to do with the characters when Hamlet is not on the stage?

CRAIG. I should like Hamlet to be on the stage always, in every scene, all through the play; he can be in the distance, lying, sitting, in front of the people acting, at the side, behind, but the spectator ought never to lose sight of him. I want the public to feel the connection between what is going forward on the stage and Hamlet. So that the public should feel as keenly as possible all the horror of Hamlet's position.

STANISLAVSKY. I should suggest that in the scenes in which Hamlet does not take part, we should show the characters not as with the eyes of Hamlet, but realistically, such as they really are.

CRAIG. I am afraid that in following out the idea of seeing everything through the eyes of Hamlet, we may be pedantically consistent in the execution of this idea. But, on the other hand, to make the characters realistic is also dangerous. They can at once lose all their symbolism, and then the play may lose very much. The voices, gestures, etc. will appear too realistic.

STANISLAVSKY. If the queen, for example, appears without Hamlet, the audience will have to think too much, and will ask itself: "With whose eyes are we now looking at the stage, with Hamlet's or with our own?" The public may get into a muddle.

CRAIG. I should like something beautiful always to be on the stage side by side with the criminality of the characters taking part; Ophelia, for instance, who by her presence during the speech of Polonius would be symbolic of truth and so would show the falseness of Polonius.

STANISLAVSKY. Well that can be done by the tone of the actor who acts Polonius, the king, etc. and on the appearance of Hamlet this tone of falseness can be exaggerated into a slight caricature. So, in fact, can all the scenes.

CRAIG. And perhaps one might put on the stage instead of Ophelia — in the scene between Laertes and Polonius, for instance — some very realistic workman, working at something, in order that by his presence, and his honest, genuine labor he might show the falsity of the world in which Polonius and Laertes live.

STANISLAVSKY. We have tried this, but nothing ever came of it. Perhaps we did not know how to set about it, and you will succeed, but we never succeeded. All the theory of Meyerhold rests on this. The audience lost all the beauty of the play because all the evening they were wondering and asking: — "What is the meaning of this workman?"

CRAIG. I think that as a matter of fact one could act Hamlet without the text, but I don't suppose anyone would like it.

STANISLAVSKY. If you treat your ideas all at once, you will repulse the public and so hinder the carrying out of your theories in life. Things can only be done very gradually. Christ made the same mistake — he demanded *all* at once, for which reason people to this day do not understand him.

CRAIG. I don't believe at all in doing things gradually. You can *think* if you like for 2,000 years, but you must show what you have thought out *all* at once, and quite clearly and definitely.

STANISLAVSKY. I beg your pardon. We have gone off on to general principles. Let us return to the second scene.

CRAIG. Cannot one bring a musician with some sort of instrument in order to give a definite tone for the sound of the voice? In order not to leave this in the hands of every actor on the stage?

STANISLAVSKY. If the actor catches the tone of all the mise-en-scène, this music in the execution will come to him of itself.

CRAIG. Are you convinced that it comes to the actor by itself, or do you think that he must be taught by the help of music?

STANISLAVSKY. We can try of course; but my experience is that if the actor gets the music in his interpretation from his emotions, then it is good but if he does not feel any music in the emotions and tries to get the music in intonation, by ear, then he loses everything like Kommissarzhevskaya who in one year lost not only the power of living on stage, but lost even diction. It is difficult to understand what she says.

CRAIG. I should even like everything to be conveyed without words, by the movements of the actors illustrated by music.

STANISLAVSKY. Yes, but that would not be Shakespeare's Hamlet. It would be a new art founded on the theme of Shakespeare's Hamlet.

CRAIG. Not even on the theme of Shakespeare's Hamlet, but on the theme of the original legend which served Shakespeare as the basis for the work.

STANISLAVSKY. I should be glad to try something of this sort with you some time. Something without words, as I myself hate words.

CRAIG. We should hate not words, but ourselves who make use of words, of this kind of art.

STANISLAVSKY. Yes, but for such an experiment I should not be able to find you many artists, even among our own troupe. I think we find only very few — four or five people who could try this to a certain extent. Knipper, Lilina, Moskvin, I . . . but I think it is advisable to divide the work. At present we are working at Hamlet and parallel with this, we might look for new forms of art.

CRAIG. Yes, but we stopped at the question of how these people are going to speak.

STANISLAVSKY. We must try that in twenty different ways.

CRAIG. Of course I don't want to be theatrical, I don't think you want that either. At the beginning of the scene I want the voice of the king to sound like metal, like falling chains, something like the heaviness of a battleship. I want him to blaze up in the fire of hate, whilst round him is something festival. Then it seems to me one must feel bells, the ringing of marriage bells, and at the same time, as if in answer, an underground murmur.

STANISLAVSKY. That can be done by music.

CRAIG. No, I do not think it can be done by music. The actors must do it, and everything else must help in as far as it is possible.

STANISLAVSKY. The music must not be symphonic, must not give a definite melody, but must consist of dull, somewhat incomprehensible, subterranean sounds. At a distance bells ring in sound-deadening chests, and, like a continuation of this sound a choir of male voices hums some motive through closed lips . . .

CRAIG. All this is not the *most important thing* in this scene. The most important thing is the king. If he is a bad actor, then we can go no farther.

STANISLAVSKY. We will try these sounds at the rehearsals.

CRAIG. Yes, but I am not speaking of these bells as of something sounding in the theatre. I only hear them in my imagination. And the most important thing is the king. On him *everything* must rest. I am not looking for a definite sound. What I want is a definite impression.

STANISLAVSKY. We must explain to the actor that he is acting the king such as he appears to Hamlet — energetic, blunt, etc.

CRAIG. First of all, he must give the idea of an unearthly strength in the king.

STANISLAVSKY. At first he will perhaps try to give it realistically, and then he will try to make it more abstract. Because while he does not feel it in himself he can do nothing.

CRAIG. Oh, certainly, certainly. Can we not make the actors realize that Hamlet himself *is* the spirit, buried in matter, that is to say, not Hamlet himself is buried in material, but that Hamlet is spirit, and all that surrounds him is material.

STANISLAVSKY. Oh, our actors understand this perfectly.

CRAIG. I am not sure of that. One, is accustomed to show Hamlet weak for some reason or other. I am sure that if you asked your company one by one what sort of a character is Hamlet, strong or weak, they would all answer weak.

STANISLAVSKY (*laughing*). For our purpose it would be better not to speak to the actors of the intention of the stage-manager to make a strong Hamlet. Going through the whole play psychologically, you can arrange these points in such harmony and proportion that a strong Hamlet must necessarily be produced. Otherwise if you simply tell the actor of your intention he will at once come on the stage with expanded chest, and strong theatrical voice.

CRAIG. Oh! that is awful! You have an even worse opinion of actors than I have.

STANISLAVSKY. I have not at all a bad opinion of actors. These are simply stage habits from which it is not easy to free oneself.

*   *   *   *

STANISLAVSKY. Let us begin to go through the text with remarks. Do you want the sound of trumpets?

CRAIG. I think not. Do *you* want to have it? In Shakespeare there are no stage directions whatever — absolutely none. The only thing that he has done in some of the historical plays is to show the places. All the stage directions have been put in afterwards. In Hamlet he had not a single stage direction.

*   *   *   *

I should like the play to begin without a curtain — in fact to have no curtain at all so the public on coming into the auditorium should have time before the beginning of the play to take in these screens and new lines, and this, for them, new appearance of the stage. It would be good also if each scene began by people in special costumes coming on to the stage, arranging the scenery, seeing to the light and so on, in this way making the audience feel that this is to be a performance.

*   *   *   *

It is necessary that in acting the second scene, the court, the voices of the courtiers should not sound too definite or sharp. They must be blended as much as possible into one general effect so that the spectator does not want to trouble himself about who says this or that.

*   *   *   *

It seems to me, in fact I have even dreamed about it several times, that during Hamlet's monologue a figure comes up to him, a bright, golden figure. And at one time it even began to seem to me that this figure is *always* with Hamlet. Of course it is not on the stage, not in the theatre, but in my mind I feel the presence of this figure. All the idea of this play is the struggle between spirit and material — the impossibility of their union, the isolation of spirit in material. And I think that this figure which appears to me near Hamlet is Death. But not dark and gloomy as she generally appears to people, but such as she appeared to Hamlet — bright, joyful, one who will free him from his tragic position. I am not sure if it is possible to put her on the stage, but if she *were* able to appear her first appearance must be during the monologue "To be or not to be." She must be beautiful, glowing, and during his reverie she leans towards him and leans her head on his shoulder thus:

but he seems slightly to draw away from her.

STANISLAVSKY (*aside*). This is another play.

CRAIG. Let us go on with the staging. Cornelius and Voltimand go out with some noise. A short pause. Laertes remains on the left, listens to what is said to him, and after the king's speech to him goes out with Polonius. On the stage in the passages remain only servants. There must be many of them. The servants must be dressed in dusty costumes and the style of those costumes must recall the clothes worn by the inquisition. In proportion as the dialogue between the king and Hamlet develops, the servants move cautiously nearer and nearer to Hamlet; that is to walls dividing Hamlet from them, and endeavour by eye and ear to pierce these walls. Of course by this they portray only what Hamlet is feeling — he feels these slaves gathering round him, listening and spying. Then follows Hamlet's monologue. And then that wonderful, extraordinarily brilliantly written monologue of the king. His stupidity, his woodenness of feeling are marvellously expressed in it . . . Do you think the queen took part in the murder?

STANISLAVSKY. I think not.

CRAIG. How is one to show that even the mother whom Hamlet greatly loves, that she also, together with all the world, is his enemy.

STANISLAVSKY. By the one fact that she does not understand him.

CRAIG. Yes, that is so. Then she must be coarser and fatter.

STANISLAVSKY. Why?

CRAIG. To show the public that she is foreign to him.

STANISLAVSKY. You make a mistake in having so little confidence in the public. It understands a hint much better than something broadly and obviously thrust before its eyes.

CRAIG. Yes, but though I have seen many performances of Hamlet I have never seen a good rendering of the queen. Both the women in Hamlet, both the queen and Ophelia, are as a matter of fact very bad women, very worthless. I want this to make itself felt. I want that between Hamlet and all the rest of the world there should not be one single point of agreement, not the smallest hope as to the possibility of a reconciliation. I could see in Hamlet the history of the theatre. In Hamlet all that is living in the theatre is struggling with those dead customs that want to crush the theatre.

STANISLAVSKY. All the same you trust very little to the actors.

CRAIG. No! Everything is to be got through the actor.

STANISLAVSKY. In the words of the queen: — ["Good Hamlet, cast thy nighted colour off," etc.] the chilling influence of the artificial court life is felt, is it not?

CRAIG. No, I think not. The queen says these words not at all because she was brought up in the court circle, under the influence of the cold court life. She is capable of being much warmer. And only the presence of the king sitting beside her makes her speak to Hamlet with insincere coldness.

STANISLAVSKY. Then when she is in the bedroom why is she just as cold with Hamlet, although they are alone?

CRAIG. No, there she is not the same! There she is quite different! And there even Hamlet himself loses some of his spiritual beauty, because the feeling of relationship, the filial feeling draws him nearer to the man, to the animal, the creature loving its mother. In this scene his mother's voice sounds for him with much more strength and power . . . How are we to make as gentle as possible the transition from the dialogue to the monologue of Hamlet?

STANISLAVSKY. We might do that as in the third scene of the Blue Bird.

CRAIG. No, what interests me is not the mechanical part but the impression of softness. At the transition to Hamlet's monologue all behind the columns gradually darkens, the whole court fades away and becomes lost in a sort of warm darkness, and again one can hear the ringing of bells, beautiful and sad, though perhaps broken. This monologue does not consist of reflections. The man is on the verge of fainting, everything is dancing before his eyes. During the first four lines his thoughts are escaping him.

STANISLAVSKY. Then Horatio and Marcellus come in. Is this a realistic scene? When Hamlet hears the news of his father, surely such news cannot be received without a change of pose?

CRAIG. No, of course not. But this is such a mysterious moment that one should not be too realistic here.

STANISLAVSKY. At Hamlet's words: — ["methinks I see my father"] you won't bring in any appearance, shade of his father, will you?

CRAIG. Oh no. He sees his father all the time. Hamlet pronounces these words most calmly, but his listeners, on the contrary, receive them with great agitation. And when Horatio says that yesterday he saw Hamlet's father, Hamlet is frightfully offended and hurt. While this conversation is taking place they must all sit very close to one another and speak in low voices . . . Well, you know how to do this better than I. But I am very fond of this scene. When they tell Hamlet how they saw his father, he doubts if they are speaking the truth, and even thinks they are trying to laugh at him. And the presence of these people round him may arouse in him suspicions of them. I do not understand a few curious things: — why does Hamlet think that the vision of his father was a vision of hell and not of heaven? He almost seems to smell a smell of sulphur. I do not understand Shakespeare; surely he did not send the father to hell only because he did not take the communion before his death?

STANISLAVSKY. It is just in that that the tragedy consists; that he sees his father on the other side of the grave suffering and begging his son to free him from his sufferings. A man who has had even one glimpse of the life on the other side of the grave can hardly be normal in this life.

CRAIG. I do not agree with that at all. I cannot understand why Shakespeare sent such a good man to hell, I do not believe that Hamlet is suffering from the inability to take revenge. The tragedy of Hamlet consists in how he, being alive, shall avoid losing what is beautiful in himself. How he shall revenge justly and for the good of Denmark, his personal [sic], hence his tragedy.

      *   *   *   *

I should like the play to begin in great darkness. Then it becomes lighter and lighter, in the middle the brightness is greatest and towards the end it again becomes gradually dark.[17]

Even this early in the rehearsal period, certain irreconcilable differences are apparent. Stanislavsky's ruling concern was the effect on the audience and the pragmatic means by which this effect might be produced. Craig, on the contrary, was willing to spin idle skeins of surmise and supposition. The contrast is ironic, in view of Stanislavsky's claims of a fourth wall in his theatre, negligent of the audience. His readiness to adopt Craig's monodramatic concept was sincere, since it was in accord with the fashionable ideas of the time and would keep the MAT abreast of theatrical fashion. What is perhaps a more startling point of agreement between the two men is their contempt for language: Craig often stated in print his disdain for the words in a play, but Stanislavsky's published remarks on dialogue are more respectful. Still, his elaborate scenarios for productions, inventing novelistic situations under, around and outside the dialogue, suggest a basic disinterest in the literary or linguistic aspect of a dramatic work. Had they not both been irredeemably stage-struck, they might have been happiest working in silent film.

Stanislavsky's distrust of Meyerhold, his former student, is also intriguing. The only attempt that had been made in Russia to impose a single directorial vision by conventionalizing an acting style had been Meyerhold's experiment with formal grouping and hieratic stylization in productions of Sologub, Ibsen and Maeterlinck at Vera Kommissarzhevskaya's theatre in Petersburg. Kommissarzhevskaya, the Eleanora Duse of Tsarist Russia, had given him *carte blanche*, lending herself wholeheartedly to his manipulations, but Meyerhold's approach had been primarily pictorial and musical, with the actor reduced indeed to a kind of Übermarionette. Kommissarzhevskaya's fans were displeased, she herself felt her talents diminished, and Meyerhold had been acrimoniously fired the year Craig arrived in Petersburg. Stanislavsky's remarks on the disintegration of Kommissarzhevskaya's abilities relate to the static, formal stage picture and crooning delivery Meyerhold had imposed on her and her troupe. But Craig astutely jotted the director's name in his copy of *Hamlet*.[18]

Ironically, Craig and Meyerhold seemed fated to miss one another by inches throughout their careers. When the Russian director visited the Arena Goldoni in 1910, Craig was away; and they were not destined to meet until 1935 when Craig saw some of Meyerhold's work and averred in an article for *The London Mercury* that, given the opportunity, he would haunt Meyerhold's rehearsals exclusively, to gain an understanding of such an exceptional theatrical genius.[19] And yet when Craig first began work at the MAT, his most fervent champion in Russia was Meyerhold, who regarded him as both a precursor and a fellow adversary of naturalism. "It is remarkable that in the very first year of this new century," he wrote in 1909, "E. G. Craig flung a challenge to the naturalistic theatre . . . therefore, this young Englishman is the first to erect initial guideposts on the new road of the Theatre."[20] Meyerhold's own ideas were independently developed, for he had not read *The Art of the Theatre* when first experimenting at the MAT's Studio on Pozharsky Street, but he avidly followed notices of Craig's activity in the German press and even translated, from a German text, two of the Englishman's essays. What Meyerhold found so attractive in Craig's writings and sketches was support for the idea of the conventionalized essence of stage art, the need to create an enriched and monumentally poetic theatre, a theatre of symbols related to the traditional forms of the premodern theatre which had engendered the new techniques of stage expression. Craig's desire to begin *Hamlet* without a curtain and with actors setting the stage corresponded exactly with Meyerhold's contemporaneous projects for staging.

On the philosophical level, Meyerhold was impressed by Craig's directorial extremism, his striving to become the one and only "author of the spectacle," who subjugated everything on stage to the "almighty law of rhythm." He also shared Craig's distrust of the everyday, his fondness for abstraction, and his concept of the theatre as a *mysterium*, in which man the marionette is governed by the power of occult "unseen forces." Had Craig and Meyerhold cooperated in a production, they would have spoken a common language and avoided the conflicts in which Craig and Stanislavsky invariably landed. Meyerhold who required from the actor "tragedy with a smile on his lips" would have understood Craig's insistence that one must be playful to achieve tragedy, a notion which confused Stanislavsky. And Craig's desire to use grotesque masks and a statuesque plasticity cooperated with Meyerhold's attempts to leach psychology out of the performer's technique. Naturally, when Craig mooted these points in his colloquies with Stanislavsky, the latter dismissed them as the kind of thing that distressed and bewildered Meyerhold's audiences.

But to assume that Craig would have achieved fuller artistic understanding with Meyerhold is also to assume that he was capable of sharing his artistic prerogatives with anyone, particularly when the play involved was *Hamlet*. The extremity of his views became more manifest on May 7, when the discussion concerned Act I, Scene 3, Laertes' farewell. There he and Stanislavsky were entirely at cross-purposes, the Russian distressed that too much novelty might alienate the audience, the Englishman dismissive of any attempt to crib, cabin and confine his personal view of the characters.

7 MAY 1909   DISCUSSION OF ACT I, SCENE 3

CRAIG. The scene takes place in the family of Polonius. I want this family to seem distinct from all those who have been seen before. Laertes is in the essence nothing but a little Polonius.

STANISLAVSKY. In what way should this family be different? It must be unsympathetic?

CRAIG. Yes; the family is incapable — stupid.

STANISLAVSKY. And Ophelia?

CRAIG. I'm afraid so. She must be stupid and beautiful at the same time. There's the difficulty.

STANISLAVSKY. She must a negative type, or a decided [i.e., positive] one?

CRAIG. I should rather say negative.

STANISLAVSKY. Are you not afraid that the public which is accustomed to see Ophelia as a sympathetic character, when it sees her stupid and unpleasant, will say that the theatre has disfigured Ophelia? Must we not be a little careful?

CRAIG. Yes, I know.

STANISLAVSKY. Perhaps on the stage it would be more tactful to make her on the whole sympathetic and nice, but in some places to show her stupid. Would *that* do?

CRAIG. Ye-es. But I think that she, and the whole family, especially in this scene, are awfully worthless. And only when she begins to go mad does she become more definite [i.e., positive]. All the advice which Laertes and her father give Ophelia shows their extraordinary lowness of character.

STANISLAVSKY. How are the public to look at these characters — with their own eyes or with the eyes of Hamlet? Hamlet is not on the stage in this scene.

CRAIG. It does not matter — there is nothing of any good in this scene that ought to be pondered on.

STANISLAVSKY. But won't the public get muddled?

CRAIG. I don't think so — what do you think?

STANISLAVSKY. The Moscow public likes to hunt out the deficiencies of the stage-manager and might jump at this opportunity.

CRAIG. That's not important.

STANISLAVSKY. No, but in former performances we have seen that, thanks to such opportunities, the public has overlooked all the good that was in the play and has courted the chance of showing its acquaintance with literature.

CRAIG. Yes. — But you don't want to present Ophelia beautiful, pure, noble, as is generally done. Otherwise, it seems to me, there would be no tragedy.

STANISLAVSKY. I have not thought much about the subject. But as I am accustomed to think of Ophelia, and as our critic Belinsky explains her, Ophelia is a somewhat middle-class creature, but gentle, capable even of dying, but incapable of any sort of protest or active measure. Belinsky however conceives her to be poetical.

CRAIG. Well, all right. But how can this critic (Belinsky) consider Ophelia or Desdemona poetical, if he knows Cordelia? And Imogen —

STANISLAVSKY. Yes, but Belinsky, comparing Ophelia with Desdemona, thinks that Desdemona might . . .

CRAIG (*interrupting*). I think they are both rather stupid.

STANISLAVSKY. Then there is no tragedy.

CRAIG. She altogether has very little to do with the tragedy. I feel no sympathy at all towards Ophelia. The only female characters in Shakespeare's tragedies towards whom I feel great sympathy are Cordelia and Imogen.

STANISLAVSKY. But how does Shakespeare look at Ophelia?

CRAIG. I think, as I do.

STANISLAVSKY. I don't agree. If Ophelia were simply a fool, she would have lowered Hamlet.

CRAIG. She is necessary in the play in order to make the whole play rather more pathetic, that's all. The English critic, Jameson, thinks that from the very start, from her childhood, she is rather stupid. She tells a story of how some ploughboy frightened her by making grimaces sitting on a fence.

STANISLAVSKY. If Hamlet throws over a fool, it is not interesting, but if he has so gone off into the clouds that he throws up a beautiful, pure girl — then there is a tragedy.

CRAIG. I don't see it. She's a miserable little creature.

STANISLAVSKY. But why did he love her?

CRAIG. He loved only the imaginary Ophelia of his imagination. An imaginary woman.

STANISLAVSKY. One must explain that in the entr'actes.

CRAIG. Hamlet is a man of imagination. He imagined also that Rosencrantz and Guildenstern are his friends — well then??

STANISLAVSKY. But Hamlet never felt them to be his friends. People try to show them so on the stage, but it is quite untrue. He only loved Horatio.

CRAIG. Hamlet's mistake is that he thinks everyone is as simple as he himself, and therefore wants them to be his friends.

STANISLAVSKY. Shakespeare doesn't show this. He meets Horatio with affection, and the other two on the contrary — coldly.

CRAIG. No. One of the keenest moments in the play is the entrance of Rosencrantz and Guildenstern. Hamlet wants them to be with him. At school they had been good friends and he is therefore glad to have the possibility of renewing friendly relations.

STANISLAVSKY. But it was not Hamlet who sent for them. But the king.

CRAIG. Yes . . . But they were educated together.

STANISLAVSKY. It doesn't matter with whom a man is educated. That they were educated together is a long way from meaning that they are friends.

CRAIG. Quite true. When they found out that Hamlet did not succeed to the throne, they went over to the king.

STANISLAVSKY. These details are, of course, very important, but the chief, ruling idea must be the collision of two antagonistic objects — spirit against material. And our problem on the stage in all the play is to find the tone first of the material, then of the spirit. What manner for the one, what for the other. In addition to which the manner must be understood not by explanations but by imagery.

CRAIG. I see there only one free man. And these three, Ophelia, Laertes and Polonius are under the influence of the king. And Ophelia is also under the influence of Laertes.

STANISLAVSKY. Yes, these are quite everyday characters, quite realistic, and the actors must look for this in their characteristics. The actress (Ophelia) in this must look for middleclassism. Polonius is a capable, but low and abominable courtier, and all his manner, tone, must show the low-minded courtier in him. And he must be acted quite realistically, even to commonplaceness.

CRAIG. You think so?

STANISLAVSKY. And these same characters, in the presence of Hamlet must pass into caricatures, but not comic — tragic caricatures. Then the public will understand your idea.

CRAIG. I should like not to leave out anything in Shakespeare, but in this scene there is very little that is worth underlining or emphasizing in that way or any other. I like the Italians because they can speak so lightly in places where there is nothing of importance. They do this as lightly and nicely as if they were playing at ball. This relieves the public, does not weary it unnecessarily, and therefore the public can grasp the important places all the more strongly when their turn comes.

STANISLAVSKY. This is your personal opinion. I should not say so. This manner of acting is only the carelessness of the travelling player.

CRAIG. Not altogether. I have seen this in little companies where it was done quite consciously. This is a very subtle manner of acting.

STANISLAVSKY. An Italian stage-manager who organized these travelling companies told me how he did it. This is done because the player who takes the part of Hamlet has seldom any great talent and in order to emphasize him they resort to this plan, they only give an outline of all the places where Hamlet is not on stage.

CRAIG. This is not any special company. I mean that knowing how to emphasize the essential by two or three strokes, and how to pass over lightly what is of small significance is, in general, the particular quality of Italian art; not only theatrical, but also in painting they have the same power.

STANISLAVSKY. That is the general Italian system.

CRAIG. But I think it can be easily attained.

STANISLAVSKY. In order that this scene should pass lightly and not arrest the attention there must be as little movement as possible. To get this it would be good if they all sat.

CRAIG. But in the scene before they were already sitting! [*In a note pencilled in the margin of David Magarshack's biography of Stanislavsky, Craig claimed that of the last two speeches, the first was his, the second Stanislavsky's.*]

STANISLAVSKY. Don't forget, the most difficult thing for the actor is to stand still in the middle of an empty stage.

CRAIG. Yes, yes I know . . . Do you not see Ophelia here, with various affectations, crying without any special internal emotion — but standing in one place without any unnecessary movement, not moving.

STANISLAVSKY. Do you know of a single actress who could accomplish this? Duse, for example, do you think she could do it?

CRAIG (*laughing*). Oh! Duse here would fly about all over the stage.

STANISLAVSKY. Then who can do it?

CRAIG. I think you have not one but several who would be able to do it?

STANISLAVSKY. I know of only one, but she does not like to speak.

CRAIG. Who is that?

STANISLAVSKY. Duncan.

CRAIG. Oh no! She cannot.

STANISLAVSKY. I've seen . . . What you want from the actress is very interesting, but only a genius can do it.

CRAIG. Which of your actresses has the most *sense of humor?* I think Mrs. Lilina; it seems so to me. I think she could solve this problem. All the same I should like very much for this to be done almost without movement. Here there is no action; there is only conversation.

STANISLAVSKY. And where is Laertes to go to when he has to go off?

CRAIG. I think that all his scene takes place on the side of the stage to the right of the audience. I should think that, in proportion as the conversation draws towards an end, they all, imperceptibly and smoothly, move towards the exit by which they came on to the stage.
In Shakespeare there are no feelings or mood whatever, which one must read between the lines. He is too clear. In the modern plays the mood generally makes itself felt not so much by the words themselves, as by what there is between the lines, but in Shakespeare it makes itself felt before all and entirely by the actual words.

STANISLAVSKY. Yes, but one must know how to make the words heard.

CRAIG. It is to that end that I give such simple scenery. Against this simple and austere background, every mood, every tiny gesture can be heard, seen and felt. The *words* are *all of* value. The gestures must be no less valuable — but *all* very *slight*. And I should like the movements also to be simple and few in number.

STANISLAVSKY. And why do you think we make so many movements in Chekhov?

CRAIG. Because they flow out of the play.

STANISLAVSKY. Yes, but the thing is that in Chekhov there is no movement. We make the actors move simply in order to make the audience follow and listen.

CRAIG. Yes, yes.

STANISLAVSKY. And the most difficult thing of all is to put two actors on the stage and make them carry on a dialogue without moving. It immediately becomes theatrical. Not theatrical in a good sense, but commonly theatrical. What are we to do in order to obtain, not commonplace, but artistic theatricalness? In one of our plays, "A Drama of Life," we found a means . . .

CRAIG. But here in Hamlet words are beautiful in themselves and the idea lies in the words themselves.

STANISLAVSKY. Do not forget, in the first place, the words are translated and therefore not so fine as in the original, and secondly, and above all, that in order to get people to listen to beautiful words, they must be beautifully spoken. Let us move on farther: so you want the characters taking part in this scene to stand the whole time. I should like to say that a sitting posture is richer in poses. Standing, there are very few possibilities. If the actors sit, they can vary their pose far more.

CRAIG. Yes, but I should like to have as little movement as possible throughout the play. I should like them (the actors), without falling into the habit of speaking into space, to understand that the performing of Shakespeare does not demand a great variation of pose or movement. Shakespeare's ideas are in the words. To translate them into movement, into acting, is only possible on one condition, that there should be as little as possible of this acting and movement.[21]

Another reason why Craig and Stanislavsky had difficulty seeing eye-to-eye on an interpretation of Hamlet was because they had grown up with widely divergent traditions. The Russian Hamlet, performed in translations of variable accuracy and distinction, followed the manner of Pavel Mochalov "the Russian Kean" who had played the Prince as an impassioned temperament, given to soul-searing outbursts and flamboyant gestures. Such a rendering played hob with Hamlet's procrastination but it electrified audiences. This melodramatic approach became the standard among barnstormers and urban stars alike: in Stanislavsky's younger days the leading actors of Hamlet were the flashy Georgian prince Sumbatov-Yuzhin and the somewhat less sophisticated Ivanov-Kozyolsky. Reviewing Ivanov-Kozyolsky's performance in the early 1880s, Anton Chekhov had deplored the lack of thought in it but admired the profusion of feeling, and concluded that on the whole mediocre Shakespeare was better than no Shakespeare at all.[22] The last important Russian Hamlet prior to Craig's advent had been played by the Grand Duke Konstantin Nikolaevich, cousin to the Tsar and president of the Imperial Academy of Science. A poet of considerable skill, the Grand Duke had translated the play himself and his rendering is thought to be the best in Russian prior to Boris Pasternak's. There were no doubts as to the nobility and intellectuality of the interpretation he gave at the Hermitage Theatre in 1902 with officers of the Izmailov Regiment filling out the cast, but audiences were exclusive and it had little influence on the public stage.[23]

Stanislavsky had inherited these stage traditions, and those of the equally activist Hamlets of Rossi and Salvini, along with the literary interpretation of the role by Vissarion Belinsky. Belinsky's critique of Mochalov's performance in 1837 had become a *locus classicus* of Hegelian aesthetics. According to Belinsky, the central idea in *Hamlet* is that "of disintegration as a result of doubt, which in turn results from departing from the realm of natural consciousness."[24] For Belinsky, Shakespeare took the world as the prototype of his creations, and therefore his dramas are microcosms, which may differentiate between individual entities, but are raised to universals when they express an idea. The poetic idea or "pathos," the passion struggling towards the purely spiritual or divine, is revealed in *Hamlet* through the protagonist's soliloquies and "that eccentric inner force manifested which made the poet take up his pen in order to unbosom his soul of the burden weighing heavily upon it."[25] The character Hamlet is at once the author's spokesman and the instrument of the most supernal qualities of literature.

How Stanislavsky could reconcile in his own mind the dynamic cavalier of the footlights with the cerebral imago of Belinsky's analysis is not easy to fathom. There is no question that Kachalov was more comfortable with the latter. But Craig also entertained two disparate ideas of Hamlet. He had grown up with the interpretation of Henry Irving, whom he loved and revered. Although he had been too young to witness the iconoclastic opening night in 1874 when Irving revealed to a surprised but receptive audience his gentlemanly intellectual Prince, Craig had had occasion to view it innumerable times in revival. Irving's Hamlet dwelt in the domain of the mind, carefully nursing his schemes and weighing circumstances; on occasion, this pensiveness would be lit by the white light of inspiration, the cold flash of sardonic wit or the magnesium flare of anger, but over all the tone was *grisaille*. Irving's introversion was miles away from Mochalov's emotionalism, and perhaps they differed most over Ophelia: the Russian Hamlet was a lover, turbulent, no doubt, but still closely akin to Romeo. Irving had neither the physique nor the temperament of a stage lover, and tended to understate Hamlet's infatuation.[26] This may explain why in preliminary discussions Craig and Stanislavsky were so much at cross-purposes on this issue: the Russian director was used to a beautiful eidolon of the Eternal Feminine, while the Englishman insisted on an Ophelia who was a silly goose, unworthy of Hamlet's affection. Here, however, Craig's predilection for reading the girls in his own life into Ophelia is as potent an influence as Irving's interpretation.

But Irving, at the same time he instigated intelligent alterations in Hamlet, was a performer with an eye to stage-effect and audience-pleasing. Despite the refinement and sensitivity, he was capable of highjinks with the players, grandstand histrionics in the churchyard, a duel worthy of *The Corsican Brothers* and what one critic called "his expert murder of the King."[27] The student and the actor co-existed in Irving and consequently resurfaced in his

Hamlet. And Craig, for all his desire to spiritualize Hamlet and create an inner drama, was, as a born man of the theatre, drawn to colorful gesture, rapid diction and startling effects whenever the acting became too pallid for his taste.

In essence, Craig subscribed to the notion of the Romantics that Shakespeare's characters were not dramatic activists, but highly self-conscious solipsists: what they do, the dramatic element, is less important than what they think, the lyric element. The resurgence of this attitude among the Decadents led Arthur Symons in the 1890s to equate Shakespeare and Beethoven, and to call *Hamlet* a symphony. Consequently it is amusing to find Craig citing, as an English critic to confute Belinsky, Anna Jameson whose *Characteristics of Women* (1832) explored Shakespeare's heroines as excellent case-studies of the feminine sensibility, as if Ophelia, Portia and the rest had been historical characters and not fictions. Stanislavsky's own technique was invariably to "novelize" dramas by providing the characters with lives outside the dramatic framework; his famous "subtext" is the psychologizing of a Romantic impulse. But where Stanislavsky was eager to create a world peopled by all the characters in a play, even down to the lowliest walk-on, Craig's imagination was dominated by the protagonist whose "subtext" alone was of interest.

The secrecy of these discussions and the points of conflict in interpretation fed the theatrical rumor-mill. Nemirovich-Danchenko felt called upon, when interviewed by S. Spiro for the St. Petersburg *Living Word (Zhivoe Slovo)* to deny rumors of dissension in the company over Craig's appointment.

I must confess that I am greatly surprised at various articles which appear every now and again in newspapers, which speak of certain disagreements between us and Gordon Craig. . . . There are no disagreements whatever. . . . Stanislavsky is quite under the fascination of what he calls "Craig's genius." . . . Those few sittings at which I assisted have evoked in me such confidence in Craig; he illuminates so profoundly, so gracefully, with such taste and nobility the meaning and sense of "Hamlet" that I had nothing to do. . . . . He himself works very hard; he feels bored when sometimes half a day passes without work. . . . Craig does not leave anything out and assures us that the performance will not take long. . . .[28]

Craig was so pleased with this testimony of support that he reprinted a translation of the interview in *The Mask*, but matters were not as rosy as Nemirovich suggested. The co-partner himself was tentatively intrigued, if cautious: "The more I think about everything I have seen in Craig, the more I am attracted to the beauty, nobility and simplicity of that form. And particularly for Shakespeare. And many ideas have sprung up in me for their realization. But it must be talked over thoroughly before giving orders . . ." he wrote to Stanislavsky.[29]

Personally, Stanislavsky found in the Englishman an unprejudiced audience for the system of acting he had schematized on paper. On May 4, he explained his "circles" and "arrows" to Craig and Isadora. "I thought she would laugh at this theory, but it seems that it is interesting and useful to her and Craig, more than to any of our own artists. This cheered me up."[30] Later that night Craig got into an argument with some of the actors and Suler "supported me in my argument and he grew furious that the actors are so stupid. They do not know anything & wont try & learn' says Suler to me. 'They muddle everything up — are muddleheaded — & rely on instinct to lead them along.' I fear this is true — but they must be taught to learn to know by being taught to search."[31] Craig always found it ironic that he, the feared proponent of the Super-marionette, should be more indulgent to actors than their mentor Stanislavsky.

On May 8 and 9, the two directors discussed Act I, Scenes 4 and 5, and Craig in a note jotted down in his copy of the play testified to his growing dissatisfaction with realizing practically a private vision.

It is wrong to act these plays — in the worst of taste.

Let the actor go about trying to conceive the voice of a *spirit* conscious that he must in an hour go back to hell fire — and of course it is *unconceivable!* The best way is the little or simple way —

Poor old ghost — he surely doesn't want to frighten his son to death so would not assume a sepulchral voice.

The vision of the Ghost — the fierce impression made on Hamlet's brain is reflected during the next 4 acts — on the screens — light — what you will.

I find this Ghost who is in ½ hour to return to unspeakable agonies curiously given to human hates and personal details — he is not yet thoroughly "purged."

. . . Lines like no other writer — But I begin to believe it is a bad play.[32]

Stanislavsky, unaware of Craig's doubts, was excited by such ideas as the Ghost's injunction to swear rising "like steam from the earth." His wife wrote to their daughter, "Craig is working in a talented and heartfelt way. Papa is very pleased with him. But he is quite torturing poor Suler with his ill temper."[33] Stanislavsky himself evinced his pleasure to the composer Ilya Sats, who was charged with writing "plenty of music" for *Hamlet*.

If you take into account that Craig . . . and I spend from 12 to 7 every day talking about the nuances of Hamlet's soul in Anglo-German, you will understand the kind of head I'm going about with all week . . . Craig has turned out to be so talented and unexpected in his fantasies that I am amazed, for as soon as he turns something in me topsy-turvy, it opens new horizons . . . .[34]

5
PROJECTIONS

The Moscow Art Theatre returned to its home ground on May 20, and on the train, Craig inquired into Stanislavsky's methods:

"How do you deal with your actors" — I asked. He grimaced — then he smiled: his whole face puckers up at all points — the lips always closed.

He puts up his hands.

We take the actor like this (his left hand took him) we take his part like this (his right hand took it up and closed to a fist) and we bang it into him thus and one two three went his right fist into his left palm with slow thuds —

I thought — "how humane."[1]

The next day, these manhandled actors were called to a general company meeting, where Stanislavsky announced for the first time that Craig was to direct *Hamlet*. The company had thought that he had been engaged only as a designer and an "idea man"; their reaction was anxiety and discontent, even alarm, that a foreigner might upset the established work routines and atmosphere of the Art Theatre. Stanislavsky argued, "We need Craig — he is a rousing start, he forces us to think, argue, get excited. He will bring "the water of life" to our art, which, without these external jolts, might grow stale and antiquated."[2] He referred to the company's complacency and the need to inject new blood in it, and paraphrasing the passage in the old Nestorian chronicle about the summoning of the Varangers to rule Russia, he explained that the Viking Craig had been summoned not to be ruler and Tsar but merely to revitalize the theatre's formal technique. But these appeals to novelty left the actors no less uneasy. Craig himself recognized his false position: "Here is Moscow where they try to do as I want, there is too long a pause between my thought and the act of the subordinates — they are not used to me I suppose — but the thing grows cold."[3]

Cold or not, Craig was convinced that *Hamlet* was the ideal testing-ground for his screens, especially since the Moscow Art stage-frame was rectangular. Fifty years before John Bury popularized sets composed of organic materials at the Royal Shakespeare Company, Craig was arguing that only natural surfaces would do for the screens. Treated contact paper, scene-painting and factory goods were all to be avoided. *Hamlet* would commence with a symphony of screens in motion and come to rest only when the play ended. So Stanislavsky selected studio space and ordered large rehearsal screens to be prepared for Act I, one of iron and one of wood, and on May 22 began experiments for arranging the screens for Act III. Both men hoped that the production might be staged without the use of a scene curtain, Craig suggesting ten grey-clad masked stagehands shifting the set-pieces in full view of the audience, "thereby insisting on the unactuality of the whole piece a *show*."[4] Craig proposed a ground cloth of squares, powdered by the attendants in different colors for each scene; four arches flown in would meet the tops of the screens; and doors, windows and landscapes to be painted directly onto the screens or on shot-silk strips of backcloth in blue and rose attached to them at three points.

In operation, however, the iron and wooden screens proved to be too cumbersome. To shift metal required an electrically-driven system which the theatre could not afford, while the wooden panels were so heavy as to be dangerous. New transparent screens of grey gauze were next ordered, and on May 23 costumes came under discussion.

Mr Craig said that it was desirable that all costumes should be made as nearly as possible of the same tone and of the same material. He wanted a rough knitted material, heavy not flimsy, that would fall in good folds.

Mr St[anislavsky] produced such knitted material that had been used in Julius Caesar, and could be coloured with vegetable colouring matters. Mr Craig approved of them.

Mr Craig insisted on the importance of deciding whether the performance is to please the public or to realize the ideal of the artists, in order to know what to aim at, so that he might be in entire harmony with St[anislavsky] and his artists and vice-versa.

Mr St[anislavsky] said that the ideal would be aimed at and then modified to suit the capacities of the actors.

Mr Craig said that St[anislavsky] can do whatever he likes with his actors.

Mr St[anislavsky] replied that his actors fall infinitely short of what he wants and concessions must be made for them.[5]

Act II was submitted to analysis on May 27. Craig thought the uninteresting commencement of the act "had to be filled up with something," probably court ceremonial as rich and decorative as possible. The "Words, words, words" scene between Hamlet and Polonius was to be staged separately with a new setting, "Hamlet's room," to which Rosencrantz, Guildenstern and actors would later come. A new tableau, "Hamlet's soliloquy" was also called for.[6]

In the afternoon, although Craig still insisted on aged wood 28 feet high, Stanislavsky ordered new screens made of reed, cork and bamboo. They, as well as plywood, were to prove too pliable and prone to buckle. Craig then agreed to imitation bronze on condition that it so fool him that he think it the genuine article.[7] As to the shifting of the screens in full view of the audience, Craig began to conceive of a track hung with gauzes that would move in front of the screens during changes: a more diaphanous version of the standard "scene in 1" of the Victorian theatre. In the event, gauze was used only for the disappearance of the court in Act I, Scene 2.[8]

REHEARSAL DIARY

MAY 28

Craig received another installment of his salary, amounting to 4500 rubles since 25 October 1908.[9]

He and Stanislavsky discussed Act II. Vocally, Laertes was to have a barely audible lisp and Polonius a quiet but powerful voice. "Polonius like a great *Frog*. Green dress, spotted. Papa Polonius deeply hates Hamlet for excelling Laertes. His plot is to bring Laertes to the throne after death of Claudius."[10]

Craig visualized the scene with Polonius as talking place in a room with a narrow corridor leading upstage centre, with concertina-like walls. The King and Queen, in gold but without their mantles, perceive Hamlet entering at the top of the corridor and rapidly exeunt right with Polonius, who returns in a few moments. In the distance, at the back of the lighted corridor, a moving marionette of Hamlet is to appear slowly and zigzag its way to the forestage, gradually growing to the largest size and then halting. As Polonius hurries to Hamlet, the downstage area blacks out and only the corridor is lit. A powerful spotlight next floods the forestage, blinding us to what goes on upstage. Thus, Craig intended to swap the marionette for the actor Hamlet, who must slowly appear from below the steps, reading a book. Then the lighting alters, illuminating the upstage area, darkening the downstage where modernistic silhouettes, back to the audience, stand in for Hamlet book in hand and Polonius approaching him from the depths of the funnel — that is, the same blocking as before but with the characters reversed (the light change enables the screens that compose the concertina-corridor to move forward with the actor Hamlet, narrowing the shallow expanse of forestage into a funnel-shape). At the end of their dialogue, Hamlet goes back upstage to the light. Polonius follows him but is cut off by three nets of gold, bronze and steel, on the line, "My lord, I will take my leave of you." "This is not a symbol," insisted Craig, "but is to give a sense that Polonius is stuck in it like a frog, while Hamlet goes further and further and further."[11]

(In practice, these plans proved impossible to carry out.)

The scene then shifts to "Hamlet's room," a three-walled cube, with large round windows in each wall. Hamlet would be sitting reading in the embrasure of the central window, and the tiny marionette figures of Rosencrantz and Guildenstern would appear in the distance, sneering and pointing

3. One, very cluttered, version of Hamlet's room, before Craig scrapped the concept. The bull's-eye window was used to frame a number of various perspectives. (Humanities Research Center, University of Texas at Austin, Austin, Texas.)

at the unheeding Prince. Craig wanted either Rosencrantz or Guildenstern to be like the actor Baliev, "clever brains behind a stupid face."[12] The entrance of the players was one of Craig's favorite moments, for "Hamlet loves actors." In their scene, he hoped to fly them in through a window like "dream people" and cast their blue shadows on blue screens. Another tempting notion was that the players carried their scenery on rollers and unfurled a panorama of a ruin behind the First Actor and donned masks for his speech on Pyrrhus. This scene exhilarated Craig: he viewed the players as proud of their profession and a chorus to the Prince, while Polonius was the essence of a critic: "he sees only realistic external." "Hamlet has lost his life, is breathing heavily through is lost in the *acting*, the art."[13]

MAY 31

Stanislavsky and Craig worked on Act III. In discussing "To be or not to be," Craig expanded the idea of the figure of Death, mooted earlier. Now he considered it indispensable, the figure entering to music to bring Hamlet to a pitch of ecstasy. Suler noted:

Hamlet enters in exaltation, not pensive and depressed as he is always played. Before the soliloquy begins, Hamlet laughs, he is drunk with the music . . . He laughs in ecstasy in time to the music. It is a duet. A duet between Hamlet and the music, i.e. Death. Hamlet never sees the figure of Death, but always feels it drawing him on . . .

At the end of the soliloquy Hamlet stands behind the tulle with an enormous shadow in back of him. On the screens, side shadows are continually moving around him and with him, flickering like black fumes.

The figure of Death must be depicted as a girl or young man. If the figure is to appear or disappear, it will seem restless, but if it stands still it will seem wooden. Let it be lightly agitated. The actor or actress playing this figure must relate to this role as if to a real, living character.[14]

Kachalov, who was the only actor allowed into the discussion at this point, took early exception to the duet idea. In later rehearsals, when lanterns were used to cast the flickering shadows, he found himself constantly distracted.[15]

Stanislavsky proposed to work out the Ghost by various means: as a black silhouette cast on transparent blue glass as if by moonlight; a flying phantom as in *The Blue Bird*; a dark shadow on white tulle made by a magic lantern; or a colored reflection cast from the wings on to the darkened stage.[16]

JUNE 1

About this time, Craig wrote to his friend Edward Martin:

I have been here three weeks — Rehearsals have begun — in a most *orderly* fashion, and nice through and through owing to the really sweet nature of the manager . . . The entire company taking their lead from the manager, do *everything* I say. It may be a dream, dear old chap, but by God it's like Heaven, after years of Hell. First and foremost, they take time, and nerves are not allowed . . . consideration of every second — every move — every idea —

Again (for it must fade, it can't be real), it may all be a dream. It is nearer those divine Purcell days than anything I have experienced, though I am a *guest* in this case, and receive a nice salary into the bargain.[17]

He and Stanislavsky made notes on the Hamlet-Ophelia scene in Act III. Ophelia, Craig asserted,

is like a poor piglet, set out as bait in the crocodile hunt. . . . The King comes down stage all in gold and with shining eyes observes everything, ready any minute, like a tiger, to pounce on his victim. . . . Here the King must be horrible. A large head, blazing eyes, enormous hands like an eagle's talons. He must wear a clear mask so that his beastliness isn't lost on the audience.[18]

I hear music in the air and see the olden figure of death. The music is the voice of Death figure — it bubbles up like a fountain between the sentences. He hears the music and *he laughs* and laughs with it *a duet*. The figure who is sunlike calling him away and out of it all — Death.

When the golden figure of Death draws him and he repulses her she goes away with some show of regret.

The smile of Hamlet. The smile of the others. They always leer at him. This response is a true and sweet smile. Smiles at *all.*

The shadow of the fates behind and above him now begin to close in on him and
bend over him.

Hamlet is for extremes. Once it was *"Mother,"* now it is *"Harlot,"* once *"Angels"*
now, alas! *Devils.*

His face looks like an opening tomb. When he becomes aware that there are listeners he does not draw his sword and attack the arras — 1st he feels for his swords,
finds none — then searches in scene and finds nothing — strangle

This scene is love love love over and over again — no fury, no anger — nothing
but love in agony.

Oh, if Ophelia had been Imogen!!! What a place Denmark had been in 10 years.

You cannot *teach* an actor how to play such scenes. I can play them "indifferent
honestly" myself alone in my room — pray God, my actor, that you be inspired.

[When Hamlet realizes that he is being spied upon] I would like the actor to grow
quieter and quieter so the suffering becomes so unbearable that he moves more and
more calmly to the end . . . Hamlet pronounces those three farewells in particular as
if he were planning to depart. No, standing in the same place, quieter and quieter
each time, as *if dying of grief*, he softly sends her these breaths of farewell.[19]

Craig also wanted to cut Ophelia's speech beginning "Oh what a noble mind
is here o'erthrown," but Stanislavsky definitely objected.[20]

Alisa Koonen recalled that the plans also made impossible physical demands on the actors in this scene. Hamlet was to be propelled in, as if wind-
swept, rush to a screen, bend forward, stretching his hands to the ground,
twisting his torso in sharp, impulsive, yet musical and plastic turns, and
then stretching upwards with his back to the spectator. She, as Ophelia,
was to dash headlong from the top of a huge staircase in a frantic swoon. "It
was unrealizable," she complained. "No actress could do it."[21]

JUNE 3

Craig himself was coming to the conclusion that some of his cherished
notions would have to be changed. In a chat with Suler, he relinquished the
idea of performing the play uncut.

EGC. Quite impossible this long play of Hamlet — quite impossible to produce it as
to give most people pleasure.

SULER. — Yes — too long — too many things in it.

EGC. Yes & the people forced into separate & fixed places — Mr Jones must go & sit
in Row 5 No. 9 seat & stay there & cannot go round later or share a glance of the
play from Row 8.[22]

He suggested an extra-wide stage, providing identical views to all the
seats.

4. Cut-out figures for the model stage. The Play scene, 1909–1910. Note the resemblance of Hamlet to the figure in Plate 2. (Humanities Research Center, University of Texas at Austin, Austin, Texas.)

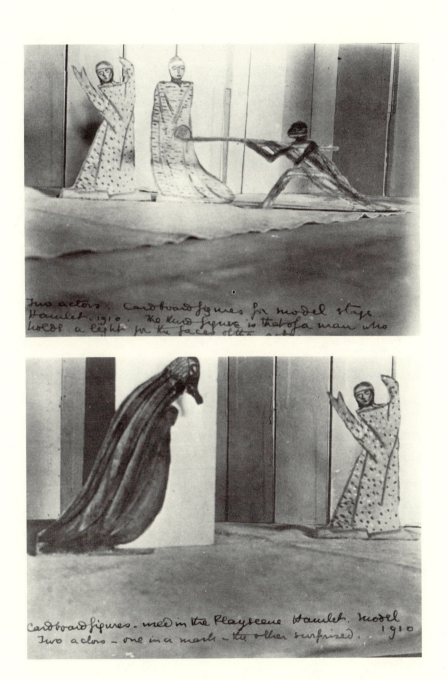

Two actors . Cardboard figures for model stage
Hamlet. 1910 . The third figure is that of a man who
holds a light for the faces of the ...

Cardboard figures - used in the Playscene Hamlet. model
Two actors - one in a mask - the other surprised. 1910

5. Cut-out figures for the model stage. The Actors performing the
Mousetrap, 1910. (Humanities Research Center, University of Texas at
Austin, Austin, Texas.)

JUNE 6

A lighting rehearsal was held on stage with plain wooden-frame screens, covered in ordinary grey canvas.[23] Eventually, they settled for twelve of these canvas flats, the staple of every theatre in the Western hemisphere.

JUNE 7

Stanislavsky and Craig discussed Act III, Scene 2. The actors preparing for the play within the play must be seen in their room through transparent screens. None of the dialogue before the play is significant and should be hustled through. "We in the audience only hear stray phrases but let it all be spoken and acted. This is for Stanislavsky to develop and such a thing he can do to perfection."[24] The dumbshow throws huge shadows on the back wall and ought to be "the most perfect work of art imaginable," accompanied by emphatic oboe music. The speeches in the Mousetrap should ripple along quickly, and the court audience must display great interest.

STANISLAVSKY. You think the play should make an impression on us?

CRAIG. Don't you think the impression on us is the reflection of the impression made on *that* audience?

STANISLAVSKY. No I think not.

CRAIG. It will make a great impression later on when the murderer comes in, but I don't see how it can make much impression now. I think Hamlet wrote not the dramatic lines to sting the conscience of the king, he wrote the very contemplative lines, the long speech of the Player King. When murderer comes on, there is a roll of music, then a drum begins to beat.[25]

JUNE 9

Craig spoke a long while with Stanislavsky of his conception of a "Platonic theatre," that is, an open-air amphitheatre, but found him unexcited by it. He visited Suler, ill with nephritis, but far more receptive. Suler wondered why so great an artist as Stanislavsky, a man of such feeling, should have no affinity for the open-air theatre and should think it sentimental. Craig's uspoken explanation was that Stanislavsky is a businessman first, a theatrical amateur second and "to the businessman of course, open air theatre is sentimental."[26]

For his enthusiasm, Suler was deemed by Craig "a remarkable man for his enormous fund of affection," but he began to grow increasingly critical of Stanislavsky.

I find Stanislavsky a man of curious nature — not original in the least degree — but very receptive & very eager to reflect truthfully the thoughts of others . . . a little inclined to think when he is *reflecting* an image that he is creating it. . . . In manner he is clumsy yet delicate & even graceful: in face a winning smile — often a very sharp cunning look, which is not sly — [27]

JUNE 8-15

Closing discussions of *Hamlet*. As Kachalov wrote to a friend,

. . . myself, Kostya [Stanislavsky], Craig and Suler conscientiously sat in the theatre all the way up to June 2, driving Suler to nephritis, and the poor fellow collapsed, while Kostya continued working with Craig until he began to talk to everyone in a kind of Volapük of Russian and German, beginning every sentence with "und" — for instance: "und where Guildencrantz is standing, I already hab vergessen." Or, "that means the last time the voice (Ghost) is heard aus dort — from the upstage passage." Well, anyway, Craig and I came off unscathed, probably because Craig has been highly flattered, fed dinners, told compliments, and this has sustained his strength, while I was allowed to sit quietly, smoking and listening, by which means I also preserved my strength to the last.[28]

Among Craig's ideas for the last two acts were these:
In *the closet scene*, Hamlet is too virtuous a prig, and so the audience sympathizes more with his mother; thus, his virtue must be played down, and he ought to look like a boy of twelve when in the presence of his parents. "It is remarkable that the Ghost after having been in the other world is not improved at all. Probably it is the influence of the room."
Ophelia's mad scene. The courtier who announces Ophelia's arrival should be a woman so that the whole scene is played by women. (Stanislavsky insisted that it be Horatio.)

I should like them to act the whole thing in masks. This comes into my head when there are such moments of changing expression as here.
When you work with Ophelia, tell her not to act anything wonderful in this scene — let her stand simply, sing simply and nothing more. She feels the song very much. She is in a state of great excitement, but she is calm externally.
It is desirable that Ophelia should have a deep low voice, like wind, that she should not chirp and should not try to act a madwoman.

He found her songs untranslatable because of their obscenity, but thought they proved that Hamlet had slept with Ophelia.
The King's plot with Laertes. Because this is such an uninteresting scene, it ought to be accompanied with music, which sometimes sounds like a wind.
The Graveyard. Hamlet on his return is calmer, more severe and serious, somewhat grey, though his senses are much sharpened, and his voice during the funeral should sound like Dante's voice in Hell. "Mr Craig apologizes for understanding Hamlet as an ideal man."
The final scene. The leitmotif of the scene is the line, "I shall win at the odds, but thou wouldst not think how ill's all here about my heart." Osric, hung with looking-glasses, is a grotesque figure of Death; his protruding eyes are reminiscent of a chameleon but his head is a death's head. Since he is strongly perfumed, there should be a smell of scent in the theatre.[29]

The ingenuity of these ideas could be realized only if the actors could find the proper means, and here the gap between Craigian fantasy and MAT practice could not be breached. Weary of "table rehearsals," Craig impatiently noted in his copy of the play that the writing of the *mise-en-scène* for Act V, Scene 1, from line 1 to line 70 took three hours. He escaped from the "gloom and earnestness" of textual analysis by deliberately expatiating on color and movement impossible to recreate. Kachalov had written on the first page of his script "Find the living man,"[30] and when Stanislavsky inquired of Craig the best means for acting Hamlet, the Englishman concurred "the answer is to live it — but we must not forget we *cannot* live it — and must perforce in the end be merely playing it. Therefore as we can neither live nor play it we must in future leave it alone."[31]

Craig, nursing these doubts, left Moscow, dowered with gifts by the company, including a carved wooden town with city gates and a small troupe of street musicians. It reminded him of his birthdays as a child. (Craig's own children, the ultimate recipients of these presents and of stories of Russia, would play their games by choosing the outlandish names: "I'll be Mr. Stanislavsky." "Then I want to be Mr. Nemirovich-Danchenko!")[32] But this festive departure marked the beginning of a rift which was to grow between Craig and the MAT until it expanded into an unbridgeable gulf. At a distance he began to regard the Art Theatre as a financial milchcow and the production of *Hamlet* as a thing of the past which had already been superseded. Having emptied himself of his fantasies about *Hamlet* while in Moscow, he bridled at having to engage in the tedium of making them practicable. Stanislavsky, once released from the spell of Craig's charm, looked upon this task of realization as inconceivably difficult, not least because he had to carry out another man's ideas. In addition to his usual managerial and repertorial responsibilities, he was preparing an important new production of Turgenev's *A Month in the Country*, which would be a test of his system of inner life for the actor.

As usual, trouble began over money. In June, when Stanislavsky was in Vichy on holiday, Craig telegraphed from England for funds, and when a draft on the bank in Florence was not honored, he requested a draft on Stanislavsky's Moscow account. "Banks are more timid than girls it seems — and less human — for I begged the Bank, I whispered to the Bank — I pressed the hand of the Bank, — I kissed its fingers — I threatened the Bank — I almost broke the Bank — but it remained placid and unmoved and it would give me nothing."[33] Stanislavsky replied in pidgin German that his checks were in Moscow and that the best he could do was to recommend that Craig write to the MAT business manager Rumyantsev.[34] In the midst of this, Nemirovich-Danchenko, who was still dubious about Craig's schemes and inwardly favored a Gothic Hamlet, suggested that the Craigian interpretation was unrealizable and Kachalov would never manage it. The whole enterprise, he hinted, was in peril.[35]

Stanislavsky replied to his partner on July 15, from the resort of Saint-Lunaire:

Apparently *Hamlet* is worrying you. Suddenly there isn't enough time?! Two things worry me — Kachalov and Craig. Not so much when he's in Moscow under our wing but when he's far away. In Vichy I got a desperate telegram. The bank hasn't given him the money. "Send 2000 francs." I made a formal reply. He pleaded. I risked sending him 1000 francs. Again he didn't wait for them in London and went off to Florence. Now I'm carrying on a correspondence to retrieve the money. When he's under supervision, he is businesslike, but who knows — on the loose is he drawing the designs? Am I not making a mistake helping him to support English workmen in Florence?[36]

These fears were not allayed when Craig's next letters ignored *Hamlet* entirely to discuss plans for his pet project, the school at the Arena Goldoni.[37]

On August 9, Craig officially applied to Rumyantsev for a salary advance of 2000 rubles, and shortly thereafter received a message from Lilina, written in English, French and German, telling him that if he wanted armor, shields, gloves and any other metallic items made in time for the production, he must send designs of the objects to scale.[38] Finally awake to his responsibilities, Craig wrote to Stanislavsky on September 5 to smooth things over with egregious flattery. Substituting wishful thinking for plain dealing, he claimed

The "Hamlet" work begins tomorrow and all being well everything shall be ready by the beginning of November. In the course of the week I hope to write to you again about the costumes.

I hope that your carpenters and mechanics will find some means of being able to make the screens turn easily, so that a single leaf at a time can move with least pressure.

I think that they ought to be making some experiments now with that, for my object in designing this scene, is that it shall be able to pass from one shape to another with great ease, and that is where your mechanics can greatly assist me.

I believe that I have for the last scene of all found something that is beautiful bringing a feeling of the immensity of the creation, when compared to the life and death of a single man.

The more I read "Hamlet" over the more I see your figure. *I cannot believe for one moment that anything more than the simplest rendering of his character can ever reach those heights which Shakespeare seems to touch* and the nearest to those heights that I have seen in the acting in your theatre is your performance in *Uncle Vanya*, and it was this fact which I could not quite express to you in Moscow.

How can there be anything higher and grander than the simplicity with which you treat your roles in modern plays? I mean *your* personal acting.

Does not the thought in *Hamlet* develop itself and find its words through precisely the same process as the thought in Chekhov's plays. If there are passages in *Hamlet* in which the words are less colloquial are they less sincere? It would be horrible if it were so. It would mean that Shakespeare was not a great artist.

How much I would like to see you as Hamlet I cannot possibly tell you. I can conceive no more ideal thing on the stage and each time that I think of the play being

6. Gordon Craig, *left,* and Sam Hume, *right,* working with the model stage at the Arena Goldoni. A photograph pasted into Craig's Daybook. (Humanities Research Center, University of Texas at Austin, Austin, Texas.)

performed in Moscow I am grieved to think of what the stage will lose without your presence. I am sure Kachalov will be very good indeed and that everyone in Moscow will think so. But I have a deepdown conviction that I cannot change that the whole of Europe would be moved and set thinking if they could witness your performance of this part. Is there anything that you want for the immediate plays that you are doing? Whatever it may be do not fail to send to me if it would help you.[39]

Yet a week later Craig's next letter to Stanislavsky merely demanded his honorarium, for "as I explained to you in Moscow I am one of those people that spend my money unevenly." To sugar-coat this pill, he also asked permission to use Stanislavsky's teachings to make up one-third of *The Art of the Theatre*, in which he hoped to prove conclusively that the only possible reform of the modern stage must be founded on Stanislavsky's principles.[40]

In October, Sam Hume, a young Californian, turned up in Florence, asking to become a pupil of the maestro. Craig was gratified and, as in all his relationships, set about to exploit the new disciple by putting him to work. The *Hamlet* experiments would be carried out with screens on a large model stage, and Hume was to cast the successful results in plaster. These finished models would then be sent to Moscow. Essentially Craig regarded Hume as a useful peon: "He was a good fellow," he noted condescendingly the following year, " – rough – & without a glimmering of taste, without a spark of the true enthusiasm. As the head of a cattle ranch he would have been admirable if he could first get rid of a bad temper."[41]

Hume, who was later to become an influential scene designer and a power in academic theatre on the West Coast, would have been chagrined to learn the Master's opinion, for he expected the exploitation to work both ways. Although he was sincere in his admiration of Craig's scenography, Hume hoped to advance his own career by association with an established celebrity. Later, when he had enrolled at Harvard to take a degree, his letters to Craig fulsomely expressed his desire to become "Ascanio to your Benvenuto."[42] In them, this pushing young particle boasted of his attempts to ingratiate himself with George Pierce Baker, even as he sought to protect his staked claim in Craig from other prospectors. When Sheldon Cheney hoped to elicit material from Craig for an article, Hume parried, "I don't think he is competent to write anything so I just want to forewarn you that you may hear from him."[43] Craig never did supply Hume with all the patronage he expected, content to view him as a migrant worker who dropped in on cue.

While Hume toiled away at the plaster models, an increasingly nasty correspondence began to grow between Craig and Stanislavsky on money matters. Craig kept demanding increments, and on October 10 he drafted a very long and acrimonious missive, complaining that his demand for 5000 francs had been met with only 2000. Consequently he had had to dismiss workmen without pay, he claimed, yet "I find that the work for your theatre has, with the exception of a three weeks' holiday, occupied my WHOLE time since the beginning of the year." This blatant falsehood was joined by another, that he was supporting six workmen (though in fact Sam Hume was the only paid assistant), and Craig requested that the Art Theatre set up exhibits of his work and publication of his writings to supplement his income. Then the attack became personal:

If I had a *Fabrik* by means of which I would make money for art all would be quite different. That is another story.
You have such a place, and I have always felt how admirable an idea it was, for with the money which it produces you are enabled to keep up a splendid little theatre and a fine house. . . . I have the merest necessities and some discomfort.

He demanded travelling expenses, studio rental and freight for the models, and concluded, "Hamlet goes very well. I am well."[44] In fact, a French translation of this letter was not sent until October 30 and, discreetly, the passage about Stanislavsky's textile mill was omitted.

Stanislavsky did not choose to reply. Instead, he left that onerous task to Nemirovich-Danchenko, who had recently been reassured about Kachalov's potential as Hamlet by the playwright Leonid Andreev, whose allegorical drama *Anathema* was running at the MAT.

If . . . Kachalov does the same thing as Hamlet as he does as Anathema, you will easily bring off "Hamlet," even if all the theatres in Petersburg were playing it daily . . . Whether he has yet become a great tragedian or not is still too soon to tell, but the entire theatre-going world has admitted it, the whole theatre-going world buzzes about Kachalov, is avid for Kachalov as it is avid for Shalyapin. . . .[45]

With this encouragement in mind, Nemirovich did not want to break off relations with Craig, even as he meant to bring him to book for his irresponsibility. In a grimly formal letter of November 19, which he rewrote before sending, Nemirovich pointed out that the Russian public's ignorance of Craig's name would vitiate the success of any exhibition. He declined to raise his salary, pointed out that Craig had fixed his own payment schedule, and stipulated that Craig had no contractual right to break matters off until the completed production plan for *Hamlet* was delivered. Then he drew up new terms: the production plan with all the costume designs had to be finished by April 15-28, 1910; Craig had to be in Moscow from February 15-28 to the April date and again for two months in August and September prior to the opening of the new production, at a salary of 1500 rubles a month.[46]

Craig, surprisingly, acquiesced to the MAT Board with an odd mixture of sarcasm and ingenuousness.

Dear Sirs. I will spare you another long letter. For I see that my last one has been misunderstood. Alas the language of the adroit business man is a language which must remain ever an ideal for me. I must give up all hope of ever acquiring it. But in plain oldfashioned English I can tell you that your proposal as expressed in the contract you have sent me is delightful and I accept it with all the enthusiasm which remains to me after a life experience of things theatrical.[47]

When the January 1910 issue of *The Mask* appeared, there was no hint that anything was affecting the successful completion of *Hamlet*. Craig's report to his alter ego "John Semar" painted a rosy picture of his work at the MAT.

We are all doing as we think best. The carpenters, dress makers, actors and stage managers are all working not merely in harmony . . . but with an enthusiastic and harmonious activity which it seems impossible to break . . . One reason why it is so nice entering the Russian theatre to commence work is that one goes there with the thorough confidence that there is going to be no ill-feeling anywhere about, no stiffness which will prevent exchange of thought, no conceit which will baulk progress and lead to "scenes."[48]

He praised them for their open-mindedness and declared that he would never again work in London unless he was given the same conditions as in Moscow,

that is to say, when I can come in to the theatre, change the production if I wish, cut or leave uncut the play if I wish, use a curtain or discard the curtain if I wish, take a year over the production of a play, or two years if necessary; select a first-class staff to work under me who have no other work except the one play which I am producing; experiment and have experiments made to the extent which I think necessary in the matters of scene, costume, acting and lighting upon a full-sized model stage made in the theatre and kept in special quarters entirely for my own use, and when I meet with a manager who will bring his troupe and me into such close union and such perfect harmony as I have experienced at the Art Theatre in Moscow whose leader is Konstantin Stanislavsky.[49]

The same issue contained the earlier interview with Nemirovich-Danchenko, as well as an article on the ghosts in Shakespeare's tragedies, in which Craig dogmatized that the Ghost in *Hamlet* cannot be an actor in gauze or armor, but "a momentary visualization of the unseen forces which dominate the action and is a clear command from Shakespeare that the men of the theatre shall rouse their imagination and let their reasonable logic slumber."[50]

In other words, no dirty linen was exhibited in *The Mask* for public delectation, nor was any mention made that Craig had not yet worked with the actors or the crews. The truth that progress was not guaranteed at the MAT was confirmed in a letter from "your old truly friend Suler" in Moscow, which told Craig,

I did nothing for a Hamlet.

No room in all theater. But during two or three week I will prepare your room, and will try a little work for to build small stage and model screens, and will look how to do that on a large stage.

His letter also expressed the hope of seeing "dear, young Craig" very soon.[51] In preparation for that hoped-for arrival in Moscow, Craig told Lilina on January 24 that the models were "very handsome and completely finished; they will save work and time for everyone, and the scene painters can work from them with ease. They are ten times better than those I made in Moscow."[52] They were sent off on February 11, with instructions that no one

7. Cardboard figures of the actors making up, 1909–1910. (Humanities Research Center, University of Texas at Austin, Austin, Texas.)

was to touch them until his arrival "for I think I can explain better how they are to be set up on the stage." Shortly thereafter, Rumyantsev sent the new contracts to Craig, stipulating 500 rubles a month, and requesting a receipt for the money already dispatched.[53] Once again Craig set out for Moscow.

The honeymoon was definitely over. Craig's impatience with human imperfection, his rankling discontentment over money and the rebukes of the Board, his contempt for those who could not immediately appreciate and carry out his ideas soured the project of *Hamlet* for him. His irresponsibility had shocked and disquieted the Board and Nemirovich-Danchenko, who were now anxious not to lose their financial and creative investment and desired to implement the production as soon as possible. Stanislavsky, who still believed in Craig's genius despite his disillusionment in the man himself, tactfully hoped to salvage the ideals and principles of the project in rehearsal, but he too realized the need for expediency. Only Suler, uninformed of the bickering in high places, kept faith, as he eagerly looked forward to the consummation of Craig's masterpiece.

6
REVERSALS

Returning to Moscow, via Berlin, on February 28, 1910, Craig was met at the station by Suler, and moved back into the Metropole. Because this trip was supposed to be his last, two rooms at the theatre next to the tea-room were set aside for him, as a combination workshop and óffice. One room, with three windows, contained an exact model of the theatre and its proscenium on a scale of one inch to the foot, on which Craig could arrange Sam Hume's handiwork and the miniature folding screens, as well as the colored wooden figures that stood in for the actors. The model theatre was equipped with eight banks of lights, which duplicated the electrical system used on the MAT stage. Next to the model-room was a study sparsely furnished with a large desk, a deep armchair and a thick carpet, the shelves on the walls laden with the Shakespearean library Craig had brought with him.

Students from the directing program were assigned to carry out the work in the model-room, and one of them, Nikolay Petrov, who was to become a leading Soviet director, left a vivid picture of the routine.

In the model-room the "directing" students were engaged in gluing together an endless number of models after sketches made by Craig. We would usually show up ahead of Craig, and be met by Vasily, who worked in the model-room and acted as commandant *cum* cleaner and handyman. He was not overly fond of Craig. After hearing about his aesthetics, Vasily would rejoin, "Well, maybe that's how it is, but all the same it ain't right."

Craig would enter unexpectedly.

"Look, here he is, gotta get his breakfast."[1]

Breakfast was invariably two boiled eggs, a French roll and a bottle of pasteurized milk. Craig's Russian was almost non-existent and he relied on pantomime and sounds to communicate; when he thanked Vasily with a wrongly stressed "SPAH-siboy," he would get in return and in Russian "And drat you too."

After breakfast, Craig would go into the workroom, place a drawing-board on the work-table, and with mat-knives of various shapes start cutting out wood engravings, humming loudly as he did so. When the cut was ready, he would press it against a cloth pad steeped in colored ink, then lay it on a lightly moistened sheet of Whatman paper, pile a stack of books on it and, as surplus weight, sit on top, humming all the more loudly. When the woodcut was finished, he would disappear into his study with an English-accented "poyzhaluistoy" ("Eef you plizz"). The students watched

8. Craig's workshop at the Moscow Art Theatre, 1910. The workman Vasily is standing at the back of the model stage. The young man seated at the left is probably Evgeny Vakhtangov. (Humanities Research Center, University of Texas at Austin, Austin, Texas.)

his exit with dismay for it was up to them to transfer the complicated scheme of light and dark masses into a feasible stage setting that utilized the screens, and into a lighting plot that used ordinary sources of stage illumination to achieve the illusion of chiaroscuro.

After the maquettes had been glued together, Craig would inspect them and make comments; if he approved the miniature versions of his fancies, the design was translated into large scale on the "velvet stage" (so-called because Stanislavsky has used it for his experiments with black velvet scenery in *The Blue Bird*) and the finished product exhibited to Craig, Stanislavsky and Suler. With a captive and unpaid staff to carry out his ideas, Craig's fancy burgeoned. Petrov remembers having single-handedly glued together one hundred and forty-four maquettes.[2]

The work-room and the study were located in a side-wing of the velvet stage, off the beaten track of the theatre, and in addition to the surly work-man Vasily and the handful of directing students, the only persons granted entry by Craig were Stanislavsky, Suler (who had the task of seeing that the technical adaptation went smoothly), and Lykiardopoulo to translate. One more member was added to the team at this point, Konstantin Aleksandrovich Mardzhanov. Mardzhanov was no green student. A Georgian whose real name was Koté Mardzhanishvili, he was thirty-eight years old when he joined the Art Theatre, and had been on the stage since 1893 as an actor and director throughout the Russian provinces as well as in Moscow. His own staging methods owed a great deal to the World of Art movement, its symbolism and scenographic principles, and he may have felt out of place amid the realistic modes of the MAT. The chance of working with Craig greatly excited him, and when he defected from the Art Theatre in 1913 to form his own Svobodny Teatr (Free or Independent Theatre), he first consulted with Craig and Reinhardt. The Svobodny Teatr (which had Aleksandr Tairov on its directing staff) was to enrage Stanislavsky for it not only was eclectic in approach, using elements of Chinese theatre, ultrarealism and futurism indiscriminately, but it wooed Alisa Koonen away to be its leading lady.

This however was three years in the future. In 1910, Mardzhanov was still an obedient assistant, keen-eyed and assiduous but not unaware of his masters' shortcomings. In his memoirs, he reconstructed the chain of command:

[Craig] would read the English text of Hamlet, discuss his interpretation of it, analyze the psychology of the characters, and then by means of wooden figurines he had roughly cut out would act out a given scene [moving them with a long stick with a hole at the end] . . . We, that is Stanislavsky, Sulerzhitsky and myself, were supposed to grasp all this, master it and then prepare the actors along these lines for performance. We began with the main characters . . . Craig was working on *Hamlet* for the second year now, but one peculiarity of this clever artist was his inability to set a stopping point, to break off and move on to a realized concept — and this brought us no nearer to production.[3]

Craig's sequestration and his aloofness from most of the members of the theatre led to unnecessary mystification. He could be glimpsed in the corri-

9. A frontal view of the model stage as set up in Craig's workshop at the Moscow Art Theatre, 1910. The cardboard figures for the duel were later used for woodcuts in Craig's German edition of the play. (Humanities Research Center, University of Texas at Austin, Austin, Texas.)

dors wearing a cable-knit sweater with a white linen collar sticking out at the top, a black silk tie, and a loose jacket covered in pockets, a costume at variance with the sober dress of the MAT's administration; his long white hair reminded some of Liszt. Moreover, his rapid movements, impulsive gestures and brisk stride were not consonant with the deliberate and considered rhythm of the Art Theatre. Even Stanislavsky thought he worked "like a hermit," and this excess of privacy got on the nerves of the actors who might be cast in *Hamlet* but had no idea of the demands that would be made of them.[4] Their feelings were summed up by a new member of the troupe, Konstantin Khokhlov, who was to play Guildenstern and then Horatio:

What is he cooking up in there? A few persons tried to steal in, reconnoiter, peep through the keyhole. But Craig was shuffling his dolls and screens in there and had absolutely no interest in those who had to act in the production and incarnate his concepts. He worked in total isolation from us, the actors, and behaved like a conspirator.[5]

Another young member of the company, Serafima Birman, surmised, "We may not have understood Gordon Craig because he never talked to us personally. . . . We had to deal with his demands and not with his dreams."[6] Certainly there was no way for any of them to know how highly personal his interpretation was. At best they could read his published statements and worry about being metamorphosed into Übermarionetten.

Only Alisa Koonen was exempt from Craig's alienating hauteur. After work, he would invite her to take tea and apple tarts in the Metropole Café. Or, more daring, she would accompany him up to his hotel room, piled high with a mountain of sawdust and wood shavings and listen as he invoked the wrath of the gods on the MAT administration.

Resting in his room, he would love to sit at the enormous window on a low window-seat and watch the square. He sat me in the armchair opposite and was much amused that we seemed to be the same height. Sipping tea with milk, he would say, laughingly:
"Eat, eat. Don't stint yourself. The Art Theatre is paying."
He loved the churches, belfries, ancient buildings, was in love with the Novo-Devichy Convent. "If I were asked to be architect, I would build a house in Moscow out of red and pink bricks, and not upwards but sideways. Moscow doesn't soar aloft like Petersburg, it is stocky and hugs the ground."[7]

The privacy of Craig's sanctum in the theatre was occasionally violated when Stanislavsky brought privileged guests to view the genius at work. One of these visitors was a svelte and elegant blonde, Olga Gzovskaya, who had been playing lead roles at the Maly Theatre for some years, and whom Stanislavsky was courting to join the MAT. Craig had seen her as Chérubin in *The Marriage of Figaro*, a performance he enjoyed, but she had avoided meeting him because "he struck me as wondrous and unnatural."

Her diffidence was, if anything, confirmed when Stanislavsky issued his usual warning not to fall in love with Craig the Bohemian.[8]

On March 21, the Theatre held its annual "cabbage-party," an elaborate rag carefully rehearsed for weeks, at which the staid members of the company let their hair down and performed parodies, circus acts and similar absurd skits. Theatrical Moscow vied for tickets to this lupercalia, and when Olga Gzovskaya arrived at her seat in the first row of the dress circle on a ticket procured her by Stanislavsky she was startled to discover Craig in the neighboring seat "who gives me a note from K.S. in which he asked me to translate everything to Craig . . ."[9] For this public appearance he was impressively got up in a fashionable tailcoat with a huge white chrysanthemum in his lapel, and at the curtain call for an excerpt from *La Belle Hélène*, he handed up a bouquet of red roses to Olga Knipper, while a somewhat Chaplinesque Suler in a matching tailcoat handed her a single rose. Arm in arm, the two friends passed before the audience, but Craig grew bored by the antics and in the intermission took Gzovskaya by the hand and escorted her to his workshop.

I was delighted . . . At the time it was all so new, curiously and endlessly interesting, but he never said a word about the images, merely pointed out everything to me like a director, a master of stagecraft, yet said of actors that the only actor was Irving and the only actress Ellen Terry, his mother, and all the rest rubbish, and he would like to turn them all into puppets.[10]

Delivering a well-worn setpiece, he professed misanthropy and refused to talk art with her. Gzovskaya was moderately charmed but her enchantment turned to alarm when he launched his standard amorous Blitzkrieg at her. Passionately declaring his invincible affinity, he inundated her flat with baskets of flowers, staged stormy scenes of jealousy (she was a married woman), and on one occasion when he failed to find either her or her husband at home, broke into their bedroom and ripped open a few pillows. As a member of the Maly company, Gzovskaya had perforce to be highly respectable but in any case her own temperament was alien to such outlandish behavior. When Craig made peace with a puerile apology and more baskets of flowers, she relented but kept on her guard, remembering Stanislavsky's warning. This would merely have been a silly romantic interlude, unrelated to the work of the theatre, except that Gzovskaya was shortly to become a leading participant in *Hamlet* and a serious cause of dissension among its directors. Stanislavsky had enlisted her, partly for her talent, partly as a disciple of his system, and partly as a wealthy woman who might become a shareholder. The rejected Craig began to contemn her as "pretty pretty," "a fat little blonde," and decided that "the rather receptive heart of Stanislavsky" was "enamoured" of her. Years later he uncharitably attributed Stanislavsky's physical collapse in 1911 to sexual exhaustion brought on by Gzovskaya.[11]

While Craig barraged Gzovskaya with flowers and tantrums, Suler and Mardzhanov were initiating work on the set. On March 21, they ordered six trial frames for the screens, and experimented with a bronze backing for them. The experiments were so successful that Stanislavsky allowed them to order more. Working with two screens of four panels each, nineteen feet high, they tried out different kinds of bronzing and modelling: one had all its leaves equally dark bronze and green, another became variegated when lit differently. Swatches of brocade and samples of chainmail were procured from the costume shop for the same purpose. When the finished screens were displayed on March 23, it was decided that the modelling was too finicky, and that large patches and stripes should be tried on the next models. Mardzhanov gave orders for two metal screens with vertical lines, two bronzed screens, one screen with at least one parchment leaf, and one canvas-colored leaf.[12]

The revised cast list for *Hamlet* was finally posted on March 28 and all the actors were called to hear a discussion of the basic principles of the production by Stanislavsky. The distribution of roles held some surprises. To begin with, there were as before few veteran players represented: Vishnevsky was still the King, Luzhsky Polonius, Gribunin the First Gravedigger, Burdzhalov was assigned the insignificant role of Reynaldo and the brilliant comic actor Moskvin was wasted on the Second Gravedigger, in keeping with the rule, "lead in one play, walk-on in the next." The Queen was to be shared by Butova and Savitskaya, neither of them very distinguished. The First Player was bestowed on Leonidov, who desperately wanted to play Hamlet; Horatio on Massalitinov, a budding character actor; and the rest of the secondary characters on students from the MAT school or brand-new members of the company. The promising Gorev, badly afflicted by the tuberculosis that would kill him the next year, ceded the part of Laertes to Ryszard Boleslawski, a Polish amateur. The greatest surprise was that Ophelia did not go to Alisa Koonen but to Olga Gzovskaya who was still not officially a member of the company, although she would become one in August.[13]

It would seem, from the casting, that the strength of the troupe was being reserved for other productions, or, more likely, that Craig's methods were considered so novel that younger actors would respond to them more readily. Nevertheless the absence of MAT "stars" like Stanislavsky, Lilina and Knipper proved a major disappointment to Craig, who was also displeased that his "ideal Ophelia" had been passed over for a woman who rebuffed his advances.

At any rate, the actors assembled in the stalls at noon on March 30, and for the first time Craig addressed them as a body, in a session that went on until three o'clock. He began awkwardly by declaring that a stage director "is a man who can do everything except any useful thing," at which one actress laughingly whispered, "You mustn't say that here." But Craig was not abrogating his principles; he went on to say that the director's forte was ideas, whereas the actor had not only to have ideas but to give them shape, voice and motion.

Hamlet is the most important person in the theatre. He is more important than the director. He is the play. He is the play, and everything depends on how he is played . . . For the director the sole right is in staging the idea, the sole understanding of the play as a whole. But the most important thing in the theatre, I repeat, is Hamlet. How does Kachalov imagine Hamlet?[14]

Startled by the direct question and flattered to be solicited for an opinion, Kachalov replied in embarrassment, "Up to now I've not given much serious thought to the image of Hamlet . . . I am empty. I can grasp whatever Craig will put into it. I want to know how you interpret Hamlet." Craig, amused by the irony that the actor on whom he had just bestowed a modicum of responsibility was willing to return it, reassured him. "I will not give instructions all the time. I give full freedom to the artist . . . You have to unearth your own material . . . The very fact that you know you are empty contains Hamlet . . . You must pour Hamlet into yourself, become a part of him." But he warned the actor to eschew the "melancholy Dane," the gloomy Hamlet in black and go for "the ideal of man. To attain tragedy, one must be joyful." He began to expound his personal views of the play: "Hamlet is the triumph of love. It is a beautiful song, a wonderful song, through which one figure passes, who surmounts all obstacles. Love is music. It is difficult to talk about this in words . . . The triumph of love, all-embracing love, fantasy and music." Paraphrasing Walt Whitman, Craig admitted that "I contradict myself at every moment, as everyone does in life . . . Even Shakespeare himself is contradiction . . . ." "and Hamlet is total contradiction . . . In the course of a single month he ennobled Denmark and Napoleon didn't do that in a lifetime." "Only if the actor thinks less of the content and more of the music of the verse will Shakespeare be possible for him," and at that he requested the actors not to be *thinkative.*[15]

Back in Florence in November, he had sketched out some preliminary notes for this address; vague and highfalutin, they informed the actors that Craig would bring them to a state of ecstasy, of "emotion with all its impurity burnt away," and urged them to experience *Hamlet* through their senses, to court madness. In the notes he interpreted the Prince as a saint and dimly illustrated his point with a Chinese parable. But in the auditorium, "seeing their kind faces and wrinkled brows I had not the heart to add one more wrinkle, I had at least the wit to abstain once more; . . . and I made one more design for an Über-Marionette."[16] In point of fact these notes never were delivered, although Craig published them intact in the May 1915 issue of *The Mask* (see Appendix I). Mulling over the reception of the impromptu remarks he had substituted for them, he had misgivings about the cast's reactions. "My feelings towards all these actors here are those of affection. . . . & I am a little inclined to think that the stage managers here have taught the actors to rely less on themselves than on the stage management. The actors lack initiative — I dislike this although I am in favour of utter subordination. Only an Übermarionette can rise to utter subordination."[17]

Stanislavsky, however, inspirited by the admixture of the actors to the creative process, wrote to Isadora on April 2,

> Today we began work in earnest on "Hamlet" under the direction of Gordon Craig . . . Everything he does is beautiful. We are trying to carry out his slightest wish, and he seems satisfied with us, because we are on his side . . . I am working with a few actors in detail on scenes from "Hamlet" in order to understand this experiment that Craig wants. When we imitate his conception properly, he will go back to Florence and we shall work alone, without him.[18]

Craig had rejected that method of work when Reinhardt had proposed it in 1905, but Stanislavsky sanguinely foresaw rehearsing until August when Craig would return to Moscow to put the finishing touches on the production, and *Hamlet* would open in November.

REHEARSAL DIARY

APRIL 2

Craig and Stanislavsky discussed Act III, Scenes 3 and 4, and Act IV, Scene 1. Craig saw the king's attempt to pray as the point from which the play must accelerate to its conclusion. Stanislavsky noted, "Craig gives the

10. The Queen's closet as set up on the miniature stage at the Arena Goldoni. (Edward A. Craig.)

starting signal, and then lets the actor do what he pleases . . . Here Hamlet displays little reflection, and all in all he reflects little throughout the play. He acts by instinct."[19]

In the closet scene the restless queen is to fling herself into Hamlet's arms and "the play leaps forward like a horse." But at the pharase "Thunders in the index," Craig's enthusiasm was cooled by the incessant note-taking of the amanuenses: "Why? What? How? All of them write it down to study for the sake of psychology." When Craig reached the line "Your bedded hair like life in excrements/Starts up and stand on end," he pettishly commented on Stanislavsky's fear of theatricality:

& yet they attempt to play it realistically/naturalistically. If this isn't *"theatrical"* in the best sense of the word I wonder what is — the use of *this* (as well as any other) word depends upon the lips and brain of the speaker — "Theatrical" may become once again a word with a noble sense attached to it.[20]

Of Hamlet at the scene's end, he remarked, "Here's an example of as wise, active and as powerful a man as ever lived. He is caught in no trap — He's not unlike Ulysses."[21]

APRIL 3

This discussion continued. In IV, 1, the King and Queen are together for the first time since Hamlet's scene with his mother, and the King must be like a wolf in a cage. "The servants must be seen continually spying all over the next scenes."[22] Rising from the table, at last, Craig had the actors dressed in tights to examine their silhouettes in motion. "Let each costume reveal the form under it! . . . until I have seen and studied the movements of the actors I cannot decide on their costumes." "The faces and hands or arms of the actors must all appear waxen — like a fairly coloured waxen (or polished marble) bust appears."[23] Although Alisa Koonen was no longer slated to play Ophelia, Craig requested that she participate in the rehearsals at least until Gzovskaya joined the company in August; consequently the young actress found herself dressed in a chiton and made to dance in and out of the screens set up in the experimental stage. In breaks, she would help him by reading the roles of Ophelia, Hamlet, the Queen and even Polonius, as he shunted the wooden figures back and forth on the model stage. She conscientiously kept a notebook of the table-discussions and the movement rehearsals, but began to be glad that she would not have to play the part. "I could never play Ophelia according [to the role breakdown made by Stanislavsky], because I could probably not make a single step, if I had to remember all the different nerves and muscles that go into motion to make that very step."[24] Between Stanislavsky's anatomizing of the psychology and Craig's insistence on monumental gestures, the actors felt stymied.

APRIL 4

Stanislavsky requested Mardzhanov to set up all the screens that had been ordered the previous month. Craig began to discuss the music for the production, for "the quality of Shakespeare is the quality of Bach"; it must be "bright and valiant to help Kachalov find not the usual gloomy skeptic but a bright, valiant man." He preferred Ilya Sats' compositions because they have "no beginning nor end, but move like waves," "like my production." The music is meant to provide a heightened sense "by easy gradual stages, yet unswervingly upwards." The lighting and music would combine synaesthetically to compose a symphony.[25]

APRIL 5

A means of lighting was sought to shroud the base of each screen with a semicircular shadow when necessary, and to narrow the beam of the projectors to send shafts of light between and behind the screens with sharp definition — in other words, to realize the characteristic lighting patterns of Craig's sketches. At one o'clock, in the main lobby, Stanislavsky and Nemirovich continued the discussion of the play. *Hamlet* was to beat the record for table-rehearsals at the MAT up to that time, though not subsequently. One hundred and fifty-nine were held in all, and after one of them, Craig commented, "It's all very nice, except for one thing: there's no Shakespeare."[26] And to his Daybook he confided, "As the preparations for Hamlet advance I see more and more clearly that the production will in all probability appeal to very few people . . . it tends to show that shortly no one will be *permitted to "produce"* these plays. Victory!"[27] Stanislavsky would have been disquieted to learn that even as he was tying himself in knots to find ways of realizing Craig's ideas, Craig was rejoicing in their very resistance to realization.

APRIL 6

At one o'clock Stanislavsky lectured to the cast about work on the roles.

APRIL 8

Craig went on expounding his fantasies about *Hamlet*, possibly out of boredom. He wanted a thin gold thread, invisible to the other characters in the court scene to bind Hamlet to the Queen, as a symbol of her innate closeness to him. Stanislavsky protested, "But how are they to move?"[28]

APRIL 9-20

Craig grew increasingly frustrated with the acting.

We are at rehearsal — it is not coming out at all satisfactorily — what is wrong? *The whole thing* — . . .

The scenic detail is right but the mood of actor is not in harmony with it not in this nor his actions.
How bring them into harmony
Ah how — that the actor alone can do.[29]

While Craig threw up his hands and longed for geniuses to solve the problems for themselves, Stanislavsky plugged away at finding technical means to perfect the acting. The vocal requirements for blank verse concerned him, for he feared the actors would fall into a singsong rhythm.

Not a single sound on stage must be without meaning.
My method is to take the newspaper and read an article so that I understand it clearly, what is written in it. The reader must have a clear goal as to why he says something. Not so he can practice sounds, but so he can make me clearly understand that there is a SALE on beds.[30]

This was a technical matter. More basic problems of acting were also exercising Stanislavsky at this time, and as he describes it in *My Life in Art*, one evening after tea, he and Craig, with Lilina as interpreter, thrashed out the dilemma. Stanislavsky played various passages in different styles of acting — French conventional, German, Italian, Russian declamatory, Russian realistic, modern impressionistic — none of them to Craig's liking.

With all his strength he protested on the one hand against the old conventionality of the theatre, and on the other hand he would not accept the humdrum naturalness and simplicity which robbed my interpretations of all poetry. Craig wanted perfection, the ideal, that is, simple, strong, deep, uplifting, artistic and beautiful expression of living human emotion. I had failed before Craig, and I was very much confused.[31]

The following day, Stanislavsky and Suler withdrew to a rehearsal room. Stanislavsky began to act a part, having asked Suler to stop him whenever the emotion did not seem sincere or the means of expression became stilted. The director was severely upset when the hypercritical Suler stopped him at almost every word. He began to lose confidence in his own abilities.

APRIL 14

Mardzhanov, delegated by Stanislavsky to carry on technical work on *Hamlet* in Moscow while the company played its annual tour in Petersburg at the end of April, drew up a memorandum: by May 28 the following chores were to be completed by the technical staff.

1. Get the screens on wheels to stop wrinkling and listing to one side and make sure that they don't cause splits at the joints and dark depressions at the corners.

2. Make portable gantries from which the screens must be set up.

3. Write out a plot for the whole play and teach the stagehands how to shift the screens' positions quickly.

4. Devise the lighting for each act.

5. Come up with the costumes.[32]

To accomplish this ambitious agenda, all the stage crews and workshop staffs, as well as the technical administration, were put under Mardzhanov's control. The designer Egorov, swallowing his pride, volunteered to lend aid, and Suler "amiably agreed to join in and help me in performing all these tasks."[33] By April 17, the staff was to have cleared the main stage of all scenery irrelevant to *Hamlet* and to set up all the screens and setpieces that had been made the previous year. More recent experimental screens were to be set up on a platform in the small theatre to act as the model. All costume materials, sketches, sewing tables and clothes racks were to be conveyed into the main lobby by the same date. Suler was specially charged with preparing the lighting, refurbishing equipment and hanging in place an extralarge soffit that had been made for *Hamlet*.

Suggestively the memo ended: "By Vladimir Ivanovich [Nemirovich-Danchenko]'s instructions I will ask L. A. [Suler] not to comply with orders for *Hamlet* that do not bear my signature."[34] The management was anxious to get the show going, without further interference from Craig.

APRIL 18-19

Ophelia's madness was discussed, and a ground-plan for her movements provided by Craig. Ophelia

must give flowers to an imaginary Hamlet. Maybe she doesn't even have any flowers . . . she takes them out of herself depending on the meaning of the flowers, — of course this must be very subtle. The flower of innocence she gently takes out of herself, from the center of her belly, and drops it as she gives it away."[35]

Alisa Koonen recalled that Craig's plan required extraordinary acrobatic ability of the actress playing the part.

The insane Ophelia would suddenly appear on the upper platform. She would be wearing a wet, torn dress, the river weeds would drag along with the long train. She would be barely recognizable. Severe and fettered by the iron laws of court etiquette at the tragedy's beginning, she would now be like a coarse trull off the streets. In a strange, sharp voice she would sing her ballad . . . and suddenly with an abrupt outcry, as if driven by demented fear, roll head over heels down the stairs.[36]

Carried away by his monodramatic interpretation, Craig even forgot his view of Ophelia as booby and suggested that "in moments of spiritual en-

lightenment, she must stand before the spectators in an aureole of that cap-
tivating spiritual beauty, which always struck the prince's imagination."[37]

APRIL 21

The newspaper *Early Morning (Rannee Utro)*, with journalistic overstate-
ment, reported that "the theatre stints no resources, and at the slightest
hesitation, rejects mercilessly everything, often very painstaking and long-
standing work."[38] It was Suler who bore the brunt of this chopping and
changing: he was kept busy compiling notebooks of props, ornaments, patterns of embroidery, sketching headdresses, sorting out dozens of brocades
for the royal raiment, looking out material for chain mail (loops of coarsely-
woven linen rope proved best), selecting varieties of pear, oak and linden
wood for the frames of the screens, and noting down where it can be
bought, translating for actors, directors and technical staff, and recording
the daily discussions.

On this average day, he worked from eleven to one on plans for a new
scene, preparing set-pieces and props. At one o'clock, he and the directors
began to make notes on the "Hamlet's room" scene in Act II, and Craig decided to redo it, this time as a garden suggested by three screens and a practicable fountain. The fountain spray was to symbolize Hamlet's moods,
gentle and playful at the start, but gradually spurting higher and higher,
until the end of his tirade on Man. This orgasmic new idea failed to work
out and was scrapped. They broke at five, and the stage-hand Kichin was
assigned the task of building the new model. Work resumed and continued
until eight o'clock on the scene with Horatio and the seaman, then began on
the conspiracy scene between Claudius and Laertes. From eleven to twelve,
Suler went over the lighting and tried out an arc-lamp as the unique source
of illumination for that scene. And so to bed.[39]

APRIL 22

The Moscow Art Theatre ended its season. Craig's entry in his Daybook
for this date recorded his doubts about the acting.

After two years experience of this Moscow Theatre I find in it a man who has an
even worse opinion of the actors than I have . . . Stanislavsky. He uses them as one
uses bookbinding tools or needles & threads —

Can he *make* an actor this or that. If yes — then he considers him a good actor. It
was this I feared.

This point of view I have always tried to steer clear of. It is a practical one & valuable but quite inhuman —

How to conjure a Hamlet out of Kachalov — an Ophelia out of Koonen or
Gzovskaya — Stanislavsky's answer is with his hands — his left hand closes tight —
he inserts a finger into it & then pretended to hammer it in with his right palm.

Bang bang bang.

"We three regisseurs" he says "can do it" & he laughs his jolly yet grim laugh.

There is much sense in what he says yet he dooms the actor to everlasting servitude — an impossibility if great things are to pass from actor to spectator.[40]

APRIL 23

A dinner party was given at the Hermitage Restaurant by General Stakhovich, chairman of the MAT Board, for Craig, the Stanislavskys, the Nemirovich-Danchenkos, and several actors of the Moscow Art and Maly Theatre companies. As always in social situations, Craig was charmed and charming, and felt especially fond of the actor Moskvin. "Cut Moskvin up into large or small pieces — every piece would be found good." But again the question rose in his mind as to why the leading actors in the company were not playing in *Hamlet*. After all, they played cameo roles in *Woe from Wit*. Privately, he made a memorandum that Moskvin must be promoted to First Gravedigger, Lilina must appear as the Player Queen and Knipper as Gertrude, and that Stanislavsky has to play Hamlet at least once a week.[41]

APRIL 23-26

Stanislavsky looked over all the costume work to date — fabrics, sketches, patterns. Each costume was analyzed in detail as to cut, material, pattern for individual features, methods of dyeing, all based on Craig's concepts. The golden cloth for the court costumes will be specially woven in his own textile mills.[42]

APRIL 27

Craig finally decided to eliminate the round windows from the "Hamlet's room" model. By so doing, Suler noted, he "obviates the most cumbersome element of the staging. What Craig did is beautiful. Beautifully resolved this difficult problem."[43]

On this note of approval and good feeling, Craig left Moscow on April 28, convinced that he had provided the theatre with sufficient materials to realize if not his ideal production at least a reasonable facsimile of it. The technical departments of the theatre were working efficiently on the external aspects of *Hamlet*, and the actors, though somewhat at sea, could be trusted to Stanislavsky's experienced guidance. There was nothing to stop the play from opening in November. Meanwhile the Fates that overlook theatrical destinies must have been laughing uproariously.

With Craig away, the Art Theatre actors returned to their arduous routines of building a character. The actor Leonidov requested permission from Stanislavsky to rehearse the title role in *Hamlet* as Kachalov's understudy. He had cherished the dream of playing the part for fifteen years and it was agony for him, as First Player, to watch another's performance from the sidelines; but his request was couched humbly with calculated allusion to Stanislavsky's pet theories of acting.

I believe in your artistic impartiality and therefore, if you tell me that a role doesn't suit me, I shall give it up without a murmur and in no way be offended. . . . Your teaching about the circles [of concentration] I think I understand, and if you bring me into the atmosphere you and Craig require, I think the work will go forward with great strides.[44]

Stanislavsky gave his assent, justifying his decision in letter to Craig thus: "There will be times when I shall be obliged to take Kachalov away for a while and study Hamlet with him separately, away from the others. Also Leonidov will act as a kind of whip for working up Kachalov."[45] In practice, the rehearsals with Leonidov were to prove time-consuming and retarded the development of scenes.

The season over, the actors dispersed for vacation, leaving Stanislavsky and Mardzhanov to deal with the problems of costuming. During the Petersburg tour, Stanislavsky had overestimated his strength, performing twenty-nine times in twenty-four days, and had returned to Moscow exhausted and drained of energy. As ordered, Mardzhanov had prepared all the screens, furniture and props during the fortnight the company was in Petersburg.

But the costumes remained a conundrum to be divined from Craig's atmospheric drawings and cut-out figures. He had left volumes of historic costume plates to be consulted, but it was often impossible to reconcile the documentation of Viollet-le-Duc with Craig's fantasies. From June 3 to June 17, Stanislavsky and Mardzhanov spent "morning and evening trying to comprehend fully what you wanted," the director wrote to Craig, "and endeavouring to get in reality those lines and folds in the costumes that we see in your sketches. But, alas, we have not got anything. Perhaps we did not understand you quite clearly, perhaps we are not sufficiently skillful for that, or perhaps our materials do not answer your purposes." There were no well-built actors left in the theatre to model the costumes, so two boys and two girls were recruited. "They are very nice and patient young people, but they do not in the least resemble Apollo or Venus. I am sure you will pull a lot of hair out of your head when we will show you these people in trial costume." The cost of making the costumes out of expensive cloth had proved prohibitive, so cheap material was resorted to, with unsatisfactory results.

You desire a simple, natural cut, that will give a simple natural beautiful sculpturesque line and good sculptural folds, that can be well lighted on the stage and will harmonize with the simplicity of lines of the screens. But everything that is exquisitely simple is always difficult to find. We have tried all the cuts of all the fashions that you gave us, and a lot of our own. But these thin, fine shop stuffs cannot express anything at all. All the costumes hang like dressing gowns or shirts. There is scarcely no difference [sic] between them, they are all like each other, and not one of these cuts, as we have got them on our models has that simple artistic "cachet" that should show on every real work of art. All these costumes when worn by our supernumeraries seem shabby, uninteresting and quite the opposite of exquisite, although all the cuts and drawings have been carefully studied and their essential part fully under-

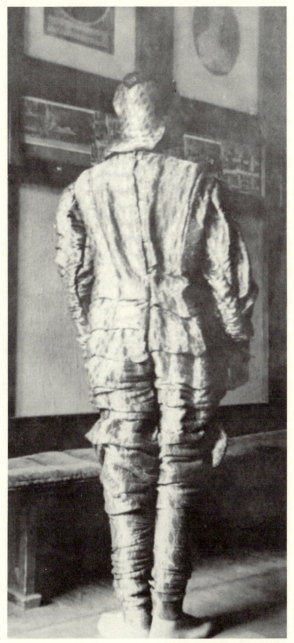

11. An actor standing in the foyer of the Moscow Art Theatre, costumed in a sample of the golden fabric, specially woven in Stanislavsky's textile mill. Although no final costume actually resembled this one, the fabric itself composed the court garb of the King and Queen. (Humanities Research Center, University of Texas at Austin, Austin, Texas.)

stood. In some cases we used our own imagination, we made use of different accidental ideas. I tried to rake up my memory. I reread carefully all that concerned these costumes and their time, and finally I came to the conclusion that a great many of the cuts you have selected are intended to be made out of very thick and dense materials, that give on the drawings such beautiful and deep folds. . . . We have not touched the costumes of the King and the Queen, as we have no ideas at all on them. We have made also a few accidental costumes out of our own imagination. Some of them seem rather good. I wonder if you will like them.[46]

Luckily, things were going smoothly in the other departments. The new soffit light for the proscenium, two side lights and two Fortuny limelights had been ordered, and Mardzhanov was sent abroad to examine the stocks of Berlin electrical firms. And at last Kachalov began to catch fire. Stanislavsky had worked with him in Petersburg, and in Moscow they and Mardzhanov went over the entire role, marking it according to Craig's indications and "to my system that you do not yet like, but that answers better than anything to your purpose."[47]

Blithely unaware of these Herculean labors, Craig sent in a little bill demanding 2000 rubles, on the understanding that his contract implied one last stint in Moscow for August and September. He was answered by Lykiardopoulo who denied his claim, pointing out the error in his interpretation of the phrase "or any other two adjacent months." He reminded Craig that he could be summoned at the Board's pleasure whenever the finishing touches were to be put on the production, and adjudged his financial claims to be "incorrect."[48]

Craig was furious. He scribbled on the Art Theatre's reply, "These fools are leading Stanislavsky a bad time of it" and jotted a reminder to consult a lawyer: "Can Rosselli be *clever* and trick these people — they are too sly for me."[49] The fact was, as usual, that the MAT was holding to the contract and that Craig, wilfully misinterpreting its clauses, was demanding more money with fewer time commitments. Hoping to play Stanislavsky against the Board, he wrote to Lilina, asking her aid in bringing his case before Nemirovich-Danchenko, since Stanislavsky was now vacationing in the Caucasus.

"I am sure your good assistant director M. N. Danchenko is now aware of the action of the Direction towards me, or he would not for a moment permit it in M Stanislavskys absence —

Is there anything I can do for you here [in Paris]. Poiret and his gowns? hats?

Everyone here is excited about my white scene patent — I DO WISH HAMLET WOULD HURRY UP SO AS NOT TO BE *TOO* LATE —

.   .   .

I suppose Stanislavsky never was *without* money — Do you know I sometimes wonder what *wonderful* things he would do were he to suddenly be pennyless [*sic*] — which God forbid for his familys [*sic*] sake but the <u>cost</u> of that kind of effort is terrific.[50]

This stunningly tactless letter, which also announced that Craig had consulted a lawyer to retrieve the money owed him, was responded to on July 2 by Stanislavsky, who addressed him as "Dear sir." He sent a long progress report on the production, avoiding the question of salary entirely. Craig was informed that *Hamlet* must be the opening play of the autumn season, for "If we do not begin with Hamlet, we shall not be able to produce it in the forthcoming season, as it's practically impossible to rehearse such a responsible and difficult play when other performances are going on every night." Consequently Craig had to come back to Moscow on September 2, chiefly because of the work entailed by the costumes, to avoid making two trips in the fall. Then Stanislavsky entered into an extensive description of his work on the costumes, including a numerical listing with notations on those that work, which materials have been ordered, etc. The comments included such despairing remarks as "Do you know what this net will cost for the whole throng — £170. I have not made bold to order it." "Do you know how they are worn." "This costume will fit only on an ideal figure." "Oh oh!" "Quite good, only so heavy that no one will be able to bear the weight." "Has turned out merely as an ordinary theatrical dress for an opera prima donna."[51]

Then Stanislavsky sketched the plans for the imminent work. Suler and Mardzhanov were to return to Moscow on August 2 to work with lights and scenery, testing the screens with the stagehands. On August 14 Mardzhanov would read the notes that Craig and Stanislavsky had made to the company. and the operation of the screens on stage be demonstrated while Suler worked the lights. Craig and Stanislavsky were to arrive simultaneously on September 3, Craig to work exclusively on costumes, Stanislavsky to divide his time between the costumes and the rehearsals. Only at a later stage was Craig to be allowed to polish the roughed-in work of the actors.

Finally, Stanislavsky addressed himself to the ticklish question of casting Olga Knipper in the role of the Queen.

I do not see, and cannot understand how Knipper will play the Queen, the more so, as I do not believe that she really very much wishes to play this part. Anyway, she is now having a jolly good time in Paris. For the meantime, Savitskaya is studying the part. I think and I am sure she will play it well. It is true that she works very slowly and stiffly — but I cannot see any other actress for this part. Of course if you insist we can take Knipper when you come — anyway she will not touch her part at all for the whole summer.[52]

Craig's response to this on July 14 was amazingly submissive. He expressed doubts that the actors could stand still and thus the simple sculptural line of the costumes was bound to be lost in any case, "so I will let myself by ruled by you and shape myself to your wishes."[53] Meanwhile, he continued to send fragments and drawings to Suler, regaling him with "philosophy and feeling." Suler mused about the Englishman's character in a letter to Lilina:

It's wonderful what a strange mixture of polar opposites exists in him — a very tenacious predator of purely English stripe with all the cruelty inherent in that type, and a very noble, tender and gentle artist. But however thin the partition that divides these two within him, one can so manage things as to deal with only one aspect, which is what I do. But earlier, when I was confused, he and I had some run-ins.[54]

Poor Suler's assumption that he finally understood Craig and could cope with him would run up against shocking refutation in the months ahead.

Dutifully, Stanislavsky informed Knipper that Craig wanted her to play Gertrude, but "I thought it didn't interest you, and to tell the truth, I don't see any tender maternal feelings in you. . . . If you want to work — believe me, I'll do everything in my power."[55]

If Stanislavsky was hesitant about promoting one of Craig's favorites to a leading role, he had no qualms about Gzovskaya's entry into the cast. On July 27 he sent her Alisa Koonen's marked copy of the part of Ophelia. "Of course it won't suit you, you would have a different image of her." He advised her to work with Mardzhanov and, to avoid offending the Georgian's vanity, to turn to Suler only in cases of emergency.

The most important thing is to try from the very first to find a good, calm general state in a new scene. . . . It is very important for you to sense the meaning of the whole production and everything that Craig has conceived in all the great plenitude of *Hamlet* in its entirety. Then, on your own, you'll start to understand the part you play in it all.[56]

Surprisingly, Stanislavsky then revealed his private evaluations of the company to this newcomer, no doubt counting on her support in his reforms.

Remember that in our theatre there are only four whose attitude to the work is pure: my wife, Moskvin, Stakhovich and myself (apart from Suler, but he gets depressed). There is one other competent person — Nemirovich. There are decent, honest people who love the theatre, but don't understand its goal very clearly, among them, Knipper, Savitskaya, etc. There are plain ordinary good people — the journeymen of our trade. There are the dear, green youngsters, yet unformed. The rest — the mob — the background — sheep.[57]

At the same time, Stanislavsky wrote to Suler, asking him to take charge of Gzovskaya if Mardzhanov is too busy.

Now that Mardzhanov is in charge of the general rehearsals, you realize there's no point in wounding his vanity. . . . In addition, do something about the costumes. From Craig's letter you realize that he himself hasn't the background. I feel that sooner or later the costumes will become our headache. When I get back, first order of business, we should all stress costumes. Be ready for this in particular, since Mardzhanov who is up to date about the costumes will have to run the crowd scenes.

After costumes you and I ought to focus on Kachalov and Gzovskaya, while Mardzhanov organizes the general ensemble.[58]

Primed by these instructions, Suler returned to Moscow at the beginning of August, only to find that the administration insisted on his postponing *Hamlet* work until the production of Yushkevich's *Miserere* opened. It was a rude yank from the metaphysical heights of Shakespearean tragedy to a dank naturalistic portrayal of the life of the Jewish proletariat. Nemirovich-Danchenko requested him to overhaul the lighting for every play in the repertory, in addition to refurbishing sets and props. As Suler wrote to Stanislavsky, who was still in the Caucasus:

Every day I inspected how the refurbishing was coming along, because I clearly understood that if I didn't finish the refurbishing of the old plays myself before work on *Hamlet* began, there would be the usual slip-ups — the stage would be occupied for repairs, etc.

Now, starting August 16 the stage will be absolutely free of workmen.

. . . Starting August 16, I will light "Hamlet" and put up the set — while Mardzhanov is rehearsing.

I am greatly offended. I would so like to present the actors with everything that I love about "Hamlet," for they have nothing . . . but instead there are the spots, cues, screens and props again . . . Patience.

It is impossible to think that I could touch anything other than sets and lights earlier than August 25-28. Neither costumes nor Gzovskaya. . . .[59]

Time-tables were set, Craig was quiescent, the ordinary rehearsal routines would bring *Hamlet* to fruition, in one form or another, in the fall repertory. And then disaster struck. All of Stanislavsky's carefully laid plans for a speedy opening were set at naught when he came down with typhoid fever in the Crimean resort town of Kislovodsk. The doctors confined him to bed for five to seven weeks, and forbade any exertion before two and a half months had elapsed.

When the news reached Moscow, the Board immediately convened to decide the fate of *Hamlet*. Should it go up as scheduled, produced by Nemirovich, Suler and Mardzhanov under Craig's general direction, or should it be postponed until Stanislavsky's recovery? On August 16, it was resolved that, since Stanislavsky's fondest dreams were bound up with the production, *Hamlet* would therefore be temporarily shelved until he was capable of resuming work. In its place, Nemirovich was to begin rehearsals for his two-part adaptation of *The Brothers Karamazov*, a project which required the full strength of the company and would not permit intermittent rehearsals of *Hamlet*.[60]

Lykiardopoulo informed Craig of Stanislavsky's illness and the Board's decision, and on August 21, the Englishman wired condolences to Lilina, asserting that Stanislavsky "commands the love and thoughts of the whole European theatre and mine."[61] But in his Daybook, he grumbled, "This

HAMLET production for Russia is wasting my time. I seek to know, I do *not* seek a position or success — and this work in Moscow is old work. I have passed it all — gone on into places where I have really seen *something* — a glimpse of something wonderful. And now I have to return and work at this nothing — this 'producing HAMLET.'"[62] So much for the vaunted opportunities offered by the Art Theatre to create the desired masterpiece.

Perhaps the person most strongly affected by the catastrophe was Suler, whose affections were invested in one man remote in Florence, another ill in the Caucasus, and a production that was indefinitely postponed. Craig was pestering him to ask the Board for money, and Stanislavsky failed to answer his letters. His position in the theatre was tenuous, for the Board regarded him merely as Stanislavsky's dogsbody, a higher form of stage carpenter. His first impulse was to rush to Kislovodsk, for he had already had typhoid fever and was immune. As he wrote in his broken English to Craig on August 23:

> I sended your telegram about money to Caucasus to Stanislavsky and I had no answer from him. It was very terrible. I was not able to help you so quick, as was need in it. My poor poor Craig. When Nemirovich came to Moscow I every day said to him to send you money and every day he answered me — "Direction is not coming yet." So when Stakhovich came only then money were sended to you. I feel all this people only as employers, and that I am simply workman. Stanislavsky is ill by typhus. Hamlet is stopped until he will be healthy, or. . . . When I knowed that Hamlet will not go this year, when work for Hamlet was stopped, I said I will go to Caucasus to help Mariya Petrovna, which is very tired because before old Stanislavsky received typhus, his son Igor was ill, and Mariya Petrovna was very tired. Nemirovich said I must not start to Stanislavsky, because I must work. I said, "If Hamlet will not go this year there is not any important work." He said "You must work any work." I said "no," and now I am in a train going to Caucasus. So I don't know if I will receive any money from the theatre. But I off to be with Stanislavsky.[63]

For a poor man with a family to support, it was a remarkable act of reckless loyalty.

This enforced delay proved almost fatal to the *Hamlet* project. The actors, who had little faith in it, threw themselves vigorously into *Karamazov* and later into Tolstoy's *Living Corpse*, Russian material that in subject and treatment was more congenial to them. The Board of Directors, chafed by Craig's insolence and unreasonable demands, grew hostile to a production that wasted money without ever seeing the light. Craig himself, frustrated and depressed, exacerbated their attitude by his intransigence, while Stanislavsky, bedridden in the hinterlands, began to have second thoughts about Craig's more innovative notions. Only Suler, as always, clung to the original vision, insistent that his two heroes complete their collaboration.

7
BREAKING POINT

Idleness was inimical to Stanislavsky. When the doctors allowed him to get up and sit in the Crimean sunshine, his preoccupation with *Hamlet* led him to carve wooden figures, like Craig's, for the model stage.[1] His mood could hardly have improved on receipt of a letter from Olga Gzovskaya, conveying the news that "everything is still in a muddle." Before work on *Hamlet* was called off, the actors had attempted a round-table discussion of the Polonius-Laertes-Ophelia scene but had not yet addressed the directorial interpretation and work on individual speeches. Gzovskaya herself was planning to talk her role over with Alisa Koonen.[2]

A grain of rivalry was bound to enter into the relations between the two actresses. The established leading woman from the Maly Theatre had her own set of preconceptions, which the younger woman, under Craig's spell, could not admire. Later, in 1917, they would be playing rival Salomes; now in 1910 they differed on Ophelia. Schooled in the traditional view of Ophelia as an ingenue with an operatic mad scene, Gzovskaya found Craig's interpretation wilfully eccentric and uncongenial. According to Koonen, "Gzovskaya wanted to play a positive image at all costs, a sort of virtuous Gretchen, and unfailingly beautiful to boot."[3]

Craig sent Stanislavsky a get-well telegram in which he could not refrain from noting that the Russian's major achievement had been realistic productions like the Chekhov plays and *The Lower Depths*; he also kept up communications with Suler, with the refrain of "More money."[4] Jeopardizing his own position, Suler approached Rumyantsev and Stakhovich who agreed to take it up with the Board which eventually doled out a derisory fifty-five rubles. This intercession was not easy on Suler; he quarrelled continuously with his superiors on Craig's behalf. In Stanislavsky's absence, Suler began to direct more and more of his emotional needs at Craig, and his letters were filled with soul-searching and pleading. "Believe," he assured the Englishman, "that you have in Moscow very loving you, always thinking and remembering you, good friend, which always will help you every way he can — this man is *I*."[5] In another letter he admitted, "I am in very bad position in my theatre. They were very bad with me,"[6] and in October, he broke down completely and spoke of his inability to divorce art and life as Craig and Stanislavsky seemed to do.

My splendid Craig!
I don't see, and I'll never see in theatre what you see in it.

Because I am not so artist as you are. You and Stanislavsky — you both are quite and pure artist.

Your organisations, your spirits, your hearts, your minds, are only for artistical life.

I don't say about the talents.

It's at first point.

But if you both had a twice less talents than you have done, it would not change the matter.

You are active artists.

But I am not such a sort man. I am too much man.

I may love the theatre, but the theatre is not all in my life.

I feel the beauty and the arts. I like it, I can get excitement of it, to be full of it, but I am passive artist, if any way I'm artist.

I don't know if I can do anything in art by myself. It is the question.

So!

My heart is too much open for humanity, I never forget the "douleur" of life, dark-ness of life and feel the life of present moment, and it keeps me much lower than must be real artist.

Oh my dear, very often I think that my work in art is something like opium (hashhish) smoke in my life. This way, by arts I am like a drunk man, and don't feel the painful of life. . . .

> Your half a artist and half a man
> (terrible composition) but full
> friend to you[7]

These doubts did not prevent Suler from trying to cheer up his friend: "What is the matter with you? Be more light and happy! I believe every-thing'll be all right."[8]

Craig refused to be jollied into optimism. By now he was convinced that *Hamlet* would never open and that, consequently, the MAT would renege on its financial agreement. On receiving 500 rubles, instead of being grate-ful, he demanded of the Board another 2000 to make up the amount ear-marked for his trip in the fall. The work may be postponed, he asserted, but he has earned the money by remaining at the theatre's disposal. "In making this claim I am entirely correct from the business point of view which the Direction always so admirably keeps before it."[9]

Although Stanislavsky was kept from knowledge of these developments, distance and anxiety filled his mind with fears for the future. For all his statements that the opinions of press and public had no bearing on the work of the MAT, he was in fact highly sensitive to criticism and to reports that his theatre was conservative or regressive. The postponement of *Hamlet* was a blow to his vanity, and in a letter to Suler, he voiced his worry that his competitors in Moscow, the State-supported Maly and the private Nezlobin Theatre (which he believed bribed the critics for good notices) would bear off the palms:

You know I'm starting to get worried: will they recognize Craig's genius or will they take him simply as a crackpot? It seems to me that the Maly and the Nezlobin have so worked on the public and the decadents have so pestered it with their novelties that the corrupted audience will want a production with good sets and when it sees *Hamlet* will say, "What a pity they didn't stage it in the old-fashioned way with Uralov as the King! . . ." Shouldn't we (seeing that the Hamlet sets are ready) put on something stunning with sets by Dobuzhinsky?[10]

Craig would have been furious to hear that Dobuzhinsky, the elegant designer of ballet whose pastel settings for the MAT *Month in the Country* had met with great acclaim, was a preferred artist.

Nor would he have been pleased to learn that shortly before this, Nemirovich-Danchenko had written to Dobuzhinsky requesting him to redo Craig's work on one of the central features of the design: Hamlet's costume.

We have a great favor to ask you.

Craig, for all his talent, turned out to be very helpless when it came to costumes. The theatre has had to create them itself, surmising, as far as possible, his artistic ideas. And on the whole it has succeeded. Only the main costumes have not been worked out — Hamlet, King and Queen. *Hamlet* in particular.

My request is this — help.

The costume must be black or rather — dark (dark grey). We are thinking of something narrow, long. Not what people expect in "Hamlet." Dreadfully modest (but not poor). It's easy enough to manage a cloak, but what goes under the cloak?

You are very well informed about the principles of Craig's stagecraft: simplicity of screens, no specific period. Can't you help?[11]

Whether Dobuzhinsky designed the finished costume or not, this letter clarifies why Craig, on seeing the final rehearsals, protested that the costumes had nothing in common with the sketches he claimed to have left behind. And Hamlet's modernistic cassock, so often cited in histories of stage design as one of Craig's master-strokes, may in fact owe more to Dobuzhinsky's imagination. In any case, it hardly resembled the doublet and tights in which Hamlet appears in most of Craig's sketches.

By 1911, Stanislavsky's health had mended sufficiently for him to travel to western Europe, partly for recuperation, partly to keep an eye on Sulerzhitsky's activities. The previous year, the French actresses Réjane and Georgette Leblanc (Maeterlinck's common-law wife) had been so impressed by the MAT production of *The Blue Bird* that they requested Stanislavsky to reproduce it for Paris; the urgency of *Hamlet* and ill health had prevented Stanislavsky's acceptance, but he dispatched Suler, his young pupil Evgeny Vakhtangov and the designer Egorov to reconstruct it on the stage of the Théâtre Réjane, where it was to open in March. But, by travelling to Europe, Stanislavsky was also putting himself within reach of Craig, whose continual exigencies as to payment were straining their relationship to breaking-point. On January 2, the Englishman had wired Lykiardopoulo who had already sent him 533 lire: when can he expect the rest?[12] Then, hearing that Stanislavsky was to be in Italy, he apologized to Lilina on January 13:

> . . . What a pity I am leaving Italy [for a jaunt to Paris] when Stanislavsky is coming — I waited as I promised but I had no news so decided I could not wait long.
> I never hear from Moscow.
> I write often — but I get no answer.
> Is it a new custom?
> *If Stanislavsky wants to see me I shall be glad to get back to Italy — but he must write and let me know*
> If I were a rich man I would wait about four years for the pleasure of seeing him —
> He is ill — it is too bad — so am I —
>
> Edward Edwardovich[13]

This lack of commiseration was compounded when Craig got to Paris and, in a telegram of January 29, insisted that Stanislavsky have the MAT management send him 300 pounds at once, ostensibly in accord with his contract.[14] But he did turn his mind to the actual production, and made a note that the ellipsoidal proscenium arch of the theatre be painted cream and that the prompter's box must go.[15]

Despite Craig's absence, Stanislavsky proceeded to Rome via Berlin, where he dropped in on Reinhardt's production of *Hamlet* at the Deutsches Theater. It had originally opened in 1909 with a design by Ernst Stern that featured a monumental framework for the acting, suggestive of Craig's linear forms. But it was also embellished with gaudy colors and cluttered with elaborate props. The cleverest aspect of the design was the *Kuppelhorizont*, a cyclorama that supplied a sense of grandeur and expanse in the exterior scenes. Stanislavsky had eyes only for the acting, which he was relieved to find "beneath any indulgent criticism," except for Albert Basserman who played Hamlet very well.[16]

Once settled in Rome at the Hotel Hassler, Stanislavsky could take a deep breath and consider the Craig problem; between February 1 and 5, he drafted a lengthy letter to Suler in Paris, outlining the difficulties and proposing approaches to solutions:

> . . . Now, to get down to Craig, I hope you know that he is in Paris now. I want to and ought to meet with him. . . . I can't go to Florence, because there's no suitable diet there and that's the most important thing for me. . . . So where can I meet Craig? Cannes, but it's the season there and very expensive. Berlin. That would be best and here's why. In Dresden there's a Dalcroze school of plastic movement and eurhythmics. I'll go there because they say it's marvellous. Craig should find it interesting too. So

this is what we'll do. We'll leave Cannes or wherever the same day Craig leaves Paris, we'll travel to Berlin and then on to Dresden. Meanwhile we'll talk over some of the things we have to talk over, *i.e.*

1) Whether he will permit us to find arrangements for the screens on the stage itself, looking for a general mood and not scrupulously reproducing his models.

2) Whether he will permit us, while preserving the general concept of King, court, Ophelia, Laertes, *i.e.*, their caricatural aspect, to depict or present them to the audience in a somewhat different form, *i.e.*, more subtly and therefore not so naively. You realize that to present *Hamlet* as Craig demands is dangerous. It (*i.e.* not Hamlet himself, who is superb à la Craig, but the treatment of the other roles) will not be accepted by Moscow in the form Craig gives it. We must do as Craig would, *i.e.* the King is a Herod, a barbarian, the court is mindless in its absurd protocol, and Ophelia and Laertes are offspring of its environment, yet we must show this not by those puppet-like devices that Craig has given them. Personally, that's really all I have to talk to him about, the rest relates to a simple desire to see him and arrange for his coming to Moscow.

Here are my ideas on that score. I'll get back to Moscow around February 25. There will be a cabbage party on the 28th. Then rehearsals for *Uncle Vanya* (new scenery) − and directly afterwards, *Hamlet*. So that there will be no delay, I've sent my notes to Muratova (for the actors) and Gzovskaya (for the youngsters). They will read them before our arrival, and then will be able to go straight to work. The school and colleagues who need not only to read but have my notes explained are left to you; as soon as you arrive, take up this matter at once. You and I shall work with the main characters, Ophelia, Hamlet, King, Queen, Polonius and Laertes, while Mardzhanov takes charge of the rest. Beforehand we shall all explain things to one another together and reach an understanding on analysis, psychological moments, wants, etc.

Parallel to this we must adjust the general details of the staging, the lighting and rehearse the arrangement.

Finally costumes.

Have Craig clarify, with this time-table in hand, when it will be most convenient for him to come: now or May?

If he has to see the action on stage, we'll have to set him down for the 4th, 5th and 6th weeks of Lent (Lent begins on Feb. 21). Let him bear in mind that before that time, perhaps, he may have to come to Moscow. If you decide on another time, write. Write me whether Craig wants or has to go to Berlin. Of course, his way there and back will be paid. Tell him, dear Suler, that I have tried to write him a letter in German. To explain all the complicated confusion of my proposals set forth in this letter I cannot. That's why I have been so long silent.[17]

Suler's reply was succinct:

I visited Craig and this is what he indicated: he doesn't want to go to Dresden, he says that rhythmical dancing doesn't interest him, and doesn't think it will interest you either. He doesn't want to go to Berlin which he hates. He declares that you summoned him by telegram to Cannes, and he is going there at once.

So now he wants to meet you in Cannes or Capri (depending on your where-abouts), where you will summon him by telegram.

To all your questions about the staging of *Hamlet* and the treatment of the roles, he replies, that he trusts you in all of this to work it out so that it is good. You know best. Therefore do what you think best.

He thinks it best to come to Moscow in May.

These are the answers to your questions.

To tell the truth, as to his coming in May I spoke my mind too — I think it's better if he come later, when at least something will be ready. Otherwise he will hamper the work and construct screens of bronze, oak and so forth.[18]

Annoyed by Craig's elusiveness and nonchalance, Stanislavsky wrote back to Suler on February 6:

I haven't finished with Craig. Ask him if we can adapt his sets, that is, the arrange-ment of screens, and, in devising costumes, eliminate the tone of the South and Italy? . . .

Once you get back to Moscow, find out from Nemirovich, Kachalov, Leonidov, Gzovskaya what translation they want to use? If the old one, the roles have to be copied out again, because they've been lost; if the new one, we have to buy texts of KR [*i.e.*, the translation by Grand Duke Konstantin Romanov. In the event, they used the old-fashioned translation of A. I. Kroneberg.] This has absolutely got to be done before I arrive. Then set up the stage, screens and lighting. We have to find new arrangements for the screens.[19]

Obviously Stanislavsky had reached the decision that if *Hamlet* was to be mounted, it would have to be done despite Craig, not with him. This suspi-cion must have been confirmed when the first communication he received from the Englishman was another telegram (on February 11) asking for money: "Prière arranger que vos directeurs m'envoyer 300 livres immédiate-ment selon contract affectionately Craig."[20] This was followed up by a letter that, in its materialism and patent insincerity, could not have reassured Stanislavsky:

Dear Friend. I have today seen Sulerzhitsky. He tells me that your *Direction* of Art Theatre has written to you saying that I have changed my mind about the matter of payment etc. I have made no change whatever. I asked them to send me what is owing to me according own agreement for the *2nd* year.

I wrote them *very clearly very exactly* — many times.

And I got *no answer*.

I do not know why they should trouble *you* in this matter — all they have to do is to carry out their contract.

There seems to be some slight doubt in their minds as to what their contract consists of — if this is the case I shall be glad to remind them by copying out their own letter to me.

Meantime I cannot say I am happy that I should *be made* the cause for the direction troubling *you*. And may I say here that with money or without money, fine weather

or rainy, it would and will always give me great pleasure to work with you personally, but to be subject to the complicated management of the Direction gives me no
pleasure at all and I am not prepared to put up with their way of behaving towards
me.

I

Am

Affectionately and,

to you, loyally,

Gordon Craig[21]

Stanislavsky still refused to communicate directly with Craig, but again
forced Suler, who was overburdened with *Blue Bird* chores, to act as inter-
mediary in Paris. From Rome on February 12, the director wrote:

As to Craig, this is what we've decided. He is not right on any score whatever, and
do you advise him not to take such a high-and-mighty tone with the theatre, or else
he will spoil everything for me. It makes no difference if he gets paid a part rather
than the whole. It would be best if he were to come to Moscow at the beginning of
the third week in Lent. On his arrival, *i.e.* February 16/29, Stakhovich will send
Craig 300-500 rubles. This is what I'm asking the theatre and hope it will grant my
request. . . .

Explain to Craig that I cannot send him money from here, because I hardly have
enough for my own return trip. You can do nothing by telegram, because the string
is stretched to the breaking-point, and one must be cautious with the Board of Directors. The quickest thing is to act through Stakhovich, who is leaving for Moscow
today.

Explain to Craig that what I write is my plan of action and not a promise; he can
accept it and trust in my promise. That shouldn't keep Craig from writing, because
the question of costumes is very important. I don't understand Craig's concepts. In
addition, let him bring the *mise-en-scène* for Act V.[22]

Apparently, Craig's reaction to this was a refusal to cooperate and a
determination to take matters into his own hands. Stanislavsky, now in
Capri, wrote in exasperation to Suler on February 19:

Thanks for your letter. Now that Craig renounces everything, I have no need to
meet him. *Do not tell him of this.* I shall broach the question and leave ostensibly
urgently, without having seen him. He is now in a Western European mood and
thinks only of getting money from the theatre for doing nothing. Help is ready for
him, if he would act not with bravado but with gentleness. As he is now I don't like
him. *Do not tell him of this,* but say, offhand, on your own or explain that the theatre, not yet having seen any results, has already paid for *Hamlet* (plus experiments)
nearly 25,000 rubles. Can he demand more of foreigners and strangers? Now you
know how foreigners treat us Russians. If we were to find abroad such generous
people as ourselves, the management of the Moscow Art Theatre, we would shout it
from the rooftops and glorify their name. Let Craig understand this. He had better.
. . . Remind him: I arranged for him a guaranteed annual salary of 6000 rubles. He

went on a spree and squandered it all. Now the devil himself doesn't know how much he gets. In autumn he was ill — he couldn't come; he brushed aside costumes and production. Naturally the Board sends to me and asks for an explanation of what Craig's salary is paid for. Now he's beginning to act uppity. What can I do? It'll end with the Board turning him down. Talk as if on your own — don't embroil him and me. . . .

In short, things are at the breaking-point, and one false move will do it.[23]

Craig seemed either unaware of this tension or was seeking to intensify it, for the very next day he sent Stanislavsky a telegram asking him to found a school in Florence in which to study movement, voice and improvisation. There was no mention of *Hamlet* or finances.[24] But the final word belonged to Sulerzhitsky, who fired off a letter to Stanislavsky on February 21 in which he walked a narrow tightrope between his loyalty to the Art Theatre's founder and his personal affection for Craig: the humanity of the document is touching.

Craig still isn't chastened. He is in a dreadful state of poverty. He borrowed 20 francs from me yesterday because he hadn't a penny. Where does he throw all this money? If I had got so much, I would now be living in my own villa and working in the theatre as a patron. However he has no money, and he asked me to wire you to send him at least something on the part of the theatre. He says he was told that they would send him a given amount twice a year, and he agreed, proposing that those be the two times he was to be summoned in the course of a given year. Meanwhile the second of his trips is now set beyond the bounds of the year for which the conditions were made, and therefore he considers he has to be paid afresh for his trip in a new year, because last year's contract has run out. That's why he asks for an advance. Obviously he now wants to remake his contract into an annual stipend. He is travelling and needs money badly. But, who knows, maybe he's saving it and putting it aside? I just cannot understand where he throws his money away in a life like this. I do know that he took 20 francs from me and asked me to wire you, because he didn't have a penny left.

.   .   .

Craig just stopped by and says that he would be much happier if had been called in for a given date, finished the work, been paid and that's that.

But the work has been dragged out *sine die*, they change the dates of his trip, and he himself doesn't know when he will be needed. And, of course, he would be much happier having an annual salary. Now his family hasn't had a penny for two weeks. Nor has he. There was no signed contract which he and the theatre would have signed; he never resented this so long as the theatre kept to its promises, but the theatre is constantly reneging on its promises!!

Those are his words! Devil take the dunderhead! But obviously he is in great need and lives only on what he gets from us. . . .

In the theatre's place I wouldn't reject such an artist without assistance, I would protect him as you did Gorev. I should send him a bit of money, at more frequent intervals. Because, however much he gets, he squanders it all. He must be supported at all times, but not paid off.

He is now sitting on a chair at my place, wearing a round hat, stroking his chin, looking at the ceiling, there's a vellum book under his arm, in which a new system is sketched out, which he will show to no one but you, and a stick with an ivory pommel — he knits his brows, tugs at his chin and does not know what's to become of him, what to say, where to telegraph and what to do in general.

An unhappy, lost figure, which evokes in me both compassion and a smile.

We must support him. I know that at once on instinct. What's to be done if he is simultaneously a child, after all, and an artist? No contracts will hold for him, and the whole business angle will always be in a muddle. Yet, all the same, he must somehow be supported. That's my opinion.[25]

There had been a time when Stanislavsky might have toyed with the idea of an artist-in-residence and, had Craig's working habits been more efficient, he might have become the subsidized genius that Suler envisaged. But Craig had awakened all of Stanislavsky's middle-class distrust of bohemianism; he had offended his sense of honor, fair dealing and discipline, and, what's worse, made him look like a fool before Nemirovich and the Board. The Moscow Art Theatre's inability to mount Shakespeare and to deal with this production in particular was becoming a joke in the Russian art world. Preparing to leave Italy, Stanislavsky had made up his mind. From now on, *Hamlet* would be solely his responsibility.

Stanislavsky returned to work anxious not only to see *Hamlet* come to fruition, but also to make its rehearsals the testing-ground for his newly developed system. The previous months of inactivity had left him with immense reserves of energy with which to promulgate the ideas he had been incubating. On February 27, he had written from Italy to Olga Gzovskaya, asking that the players in *Hamlet* "become well acquainted" with the notes on his system before his return to Moscow. "HAMLET rehearsals are to begin, and then it will be too late to get involved in theory. If they are not prepared we will certainly fail to understand one another."[26]

They, in this case, were an almost entirely new cast, selected by Nemirovich, "as is best for the theatre, without consulting any of the actors' selfish wishes."[27] Kachalov and Luzhsky, although caught up in their new roles as Ivan and Fyodor Karamazov, remained the Hamlet and Polonius, Vishnevsky continued as Player King and Gribunin as First Gravedigger. Of the theatre's old guard, Knipper had agreed to take on the Queen and Massalitinov had been promoted from Horatio to Claudius. Gorev the Laertes having retired to a sanitarium in Davos with terminal tuberculosis, his part was ceded to the Polish apprentice Ryszard Bołeslawski. The rest of the company was composed of newcomers and students, Stanislavsky's "dear green youngsters," whose openness to the "system" made them preferable to old stagers. Among them were the promising actor Mikhail Chekhov, nephew of the playwright; Serafima Birman, later to become one of the Soviet Union's finest character actresses, and a brilliant directing candidate Evgeny Vakhtangov. At his first lecture about the new principles of work

on the roles in *Hamlet*, based on the system, Stanislavsky's eye was caught
by Vakhtangov's ardent note-taking. Afterwards, examining the notebook,
he complimented him, "Attaboy! How did you have the time to do so
much? You're a regular stenographer." Vakhtangov was enlisted on the spot
as the production amanuensis, assigned to carry out experiments in the
system.[28]

"Stanislavsky came in full of energy and is ceaselessly incensed that we
are like worn-out jades," wrote one actress to a friend.[29] As he took control
of the production, he gradually began to limit Craig's *mise-en-scène* to the
realm of design. The play's interpretation, its inner life, now became the
province of Stanislavsky's quest for a deeper reality.

Craig did not assist his own cause by his recalcitrance. On March 30, in a
letter to the Board, he claimed to have received no definite instructions,
refused to accept indefinite postponements, continued to demand 1500
rubles, and would not set a date for his next coming until he had received a
satisfactory answer. A copy of this in French, addressed "Cher ami", he sent
to Stanislavsky with the complaint "Hélas! vous n'avez jamais repondu à
mes lettres!!!! — ! — !!"[30] His mood was exacerbated when the wife of his
neighbor, the Estonian poet Jurgis Baltrushaitis, told him that the Moscow
papers had announced that his concept of *Hamlet* was too incomprehensible
for the public and therefore only his scene designs were to be used. From the
same source he learned that Koonen had given up Ophelia, purportedly
because the concept was beyond the public. His comment was doleful: "It
would be natural if 'Hamlet' should fail — yet why does Stanislavsky ask
me if I will permit him to change this & that a little when all the time (if
report is true) he intends to change so much."[31]

REHEARSAL DIARY

APRIL 5

The extent and nature of these changes were rapidly made manifest.
Stanislavsky and Nemirovich led a discussion of *Hamlet*, which showed
how Craig's ideas were being diluted by Stanislavsky's positivist, psychological approach. Stanislavsky explained, "I picture the court as a whole
world of lies, intrigue, depravity, in short, the same as our macrocosm. As
Christ came to purify the world, so Hamlet passed through all the palace
halls and purified them of their accretions of vileness." Hamlet must not be
played as "some sort of gloomy punitive bureaucrat" or neurotic, for "he is so
full of love, joie de vivre, he is the best of men. A sour neurotic cannot be
the best of men. Fond of life, he wants to live, to build, to believe he seeks in
everyone the human being. This interpretation is very close to Craig and I
feel it very strongly. . . .[32] Yet Craig would hardly have recognized his

thanatophilic aesthete in this, and he would have been outraged to hear Stanislavsky continue:

Further on Craig falls into exaggeration, caricature, audacity, talented naiveté. Because of his love for Hamlet, he shades everyone in dark colors, he makes all the rest of the characters into toads, buffoons, allows them nothing human. . . . Craig, with his naive understanding of the theatre, borders on the fairground booth, in the best sense of that term. His theatre is almost a puppet-show with pure, lofty feelings, we have not yet grown up to it. He is superior to us and our generation has barely grown up to him. There's no room for all of this in my head.[33]

If Stanislavsky tried to exonerate Craig even as he undermined him, Nemirovich, with his worldly common-sense, was more dismissive. "There is an obvious danger in Stanislavsky's interpretation — I don't know, maybe it's Craig's — that the theatre might become a commentator" and muddy the crystalline clarity of the play. "I am terrified of ideologies: Hamlet = Christ. This may uplift or inspire the actor, but it is alarming." According to Nemirovich who had once claimed he understood the play better than anyone because he had *been* Hamlet in the early years of his life, "one must start with the period. Seek from the first rehearsals that horrid roughness and bestiality. For me the whole play comes down to barbarians vs an enlightened man."[34]

As for the denigration of Ophelia,

Mankind, having made Ophelia into an image of purity over the last three hundred years, has guarded this crystallinely pure maiden. And suddenly overnight, somewhere on this street, they want to deprive people of this. She is not a co-ed of the 1860s, she is not the Maid of Orleans, it's not in her. She is simply the most beautiful, purest femininity, an eidolon of the beautiful. And they are shamefully, horribly polluting this beauty. And most important, there's no reason for it.[35]

Gzovskaya must have been reassured to hear this.

On the matter of the play's supernatural aspects, Stanislavsky suggested that the Ghost be made an unseen facet of Hamlet's personality. In the production of *The Brothers Karamazov*, in a twenty-seven-minute monologue, Kachalov already acted out both Ivan and the Devil simply by changing the tone of voice, conducting a monodramatic colloquy with himself. He was heartened by Stanislavsky's suggestion. "As an actor, I was excited and enthused that the Ghost would be invisible. Hamlet sees him only in his mind, as an inner vision, an hallucination . . . feels him within himself, hears his voice perhaps echoing in his soul. I wanted to speak the Ghost's lines myself."[36] But Nemirovich cast cold water on the problem of the apparition as well. "We must reject that question, because it is a convention of Shakespeare's tragedy, and we must not eradicate it from contemporary sight by explaining it as Hamlet's fantasy or Fate."[37] The production was slipping back into traditional grooves.

APRIL 7

Stanislavsky and Nemirovich continued the discussion of the design concept and the staging from one o'clock to 5.30.

APRIL 10

Stanislavsky went over Act I, Scene 1, with the actors, and considered taking the role of the Ghost himself. Nemirovich noted, "Once Stanislavsky plays the Ghost, there'll be no holding either him or Kachalov!!"[38] But, in the event, it was assigned to the actor Znamensky.

APRIL 12

Further discussion of roles. Stanislavsky's method was to break down each scene into sections and assign tasks or "inner wants" for each scene. The actors were to write in these internal desires next to the lines, and these would become the scoring of the role which was to be learned by heart after each rehearsal. It has since become standard operating procedure for "method acting," but this may be the first occasion on which it was compulsory.

With Gzovskaya, Stanislavsky reinterpreted Ophelia as truly pure, the only character to understand Hamlet's grief and to try to solace him. She is not Craig's little booby, but knows full well the court's hypocrisy and her brother's libertine behavior in Paris, she regards the world with inquisitive and open eyes. His image for her was of a not-fully-blown rose-bud which blossoms only in the mad scene. As to the mad scene, the usual clichés — a vacant stare, an unsteady gait, outstretched hands — were to be avoided, but she was not to run to the other extreme of clinical authenticity. The inner logic of her behavior, its sanity and not its madness, was to be sought. He also chided Gzovskaya for her genteel mannerisms, brought over from the Maly Theatre. "Get rid of that Guardsman's young lady, that drawing-room idiot, throw away that society tone."[39]

APRIL 20

With rehearsals well under way, Stanislavsky sat down at his desk to deal with the Craig problem. Stiffly, alleging his illness to excuse his long silence, he wrote to "Mr Craig":

I do not understand your intentions. You have done everything to spoil those good relations that I contrived to establish between you and the Board of Directors of our theatre. The Board of Directors is seriously offended and insulted and considers your demands as derision, although you yourself have fixed the conditions.

As you remember I declined to regulate the money matters because even then I did not understand your wishes. . . . I know that in money matters you can never reconcile people unless they themselves make such a reconciliation, and you always regarded rather illfavouredly and lately by your letter you have quite destroyed the good relations of the Direction for you. To dispel this misunderstanding I will ask the Board of Directors to comply with your request and send you 1500 rubles. But I am afraid that after that the Direction will put an end to our further work together. I will be your ardent solicitor but I have great doubts as to the success of my mission. . . .

My situation is awful. I had just begun to understand your intentions in the mounting of Hamlet and I foresee an enormous lot of doubts and questions, that it will be very difficult for me to solve even with Suler. The question of costumes remains quite unsolved and quite obscure for me. We have not received from you any definite designs and I am obliged to mount Hamlet with such incomplete materials only being able to guess your intentions. I feel that such work is difficult and inadequate to my forces. I thought of returning to Egorov's project, but I cannot do that now as I am too much infected with your beautiful plan of mounting Hamlet and because the Direction demands from me the justification of those considerable sums already spent on "Hamlet" and that were expended by my personal demand and on my responsibility. And now I suffer doubly, for myself and for you.

I grieve greatly about all that has occurred, because I know that you will never find again any institution that, in spite of all its defects, would so ardently answer your call and your artistic aspiration and so sincerely want to work together with you.

Personally I always remain your invariable admirer and friend and will be sincerely grieved if I shall not be able to finish the work begun together with you.[40]

When Craig received this letter, he was irritated and jotted on it, "Now that you are personally Almighty and Just in your theatre what happens will be what you personally command. I leave all in your hands."[41] He also dashed off a petulant reply.

Dear Friend
Your letter is not at all a surprise — I am a poor man — I ask for money from rich men — I expect to be refused — They are only rich enough to pay other rich men — I am an artist — I deal with a direction at whose head sits a Nemirovich Danchenko who has praised exaggeratedly my work without understanding it all and I therefore expect to be dealt with as though I was a butcher offering meat for sale.
Nothing surprises me in all this — It has been my good fortune to travel round Europe *testing* theatres.
— I always believed that modern theatres were like most other institutions cursed by association with business men who were without generosity. — I desired to test this.
— I found every theatre management poor, mean and cruel —
— I also believed that in the modern theatre intrigue reigned supreme.
— I desired to test this also.
— I found every theatre ruled by small men who only desired by intrigue to destroy their own home —

I came to Moscow believing all the theatres were the same — As you will remember I distrusted everything I saw — I could not believe in an honest modern theatre.
There was only *one* thing I believed would redeem a modern theatre *A man.* I thought I had found one in you. I was deceived. Your theatre I have tested and it now sinks to the level of all the other theatres of Europe.[42]

After getting this off his chest, Craig thought better of it and did not send this self-righteous message. Instead, he and Baltrushaitis composed a more reasoned, if equally self-exonerating letter, which was mailed on May 2 from the Savoy Hotel on the Riviera.

I have to . . . regret some few . . . things which you tell me in your letter.

1st that you do not understand my intentions — for they have always been so far as your theatre is concerned to act towards you and your family as a friend, towards the work as an artist — and to be as exact as possible in my dealings with your direction.

If I have done anything to spoil the business relations between the *board* of Directors and myself it has yet to be made much more clear to me than your letter makes it, before I can blame myself for anything.

You tell me you will act as my ardent solicitor.

I cannot only congratulate myself on such good fortune but I can also congratulate you on a good and easy case.

It is the old case of artist *versus* businessman — it is as old as the hills — the world tires of it . . . because it is an unnecessary càse always brought about by the businessmen:

An artist wants but few things — a little money — a great deal of material for his art — and the sympathetic and faithful cooperation of his *crafts*men until the work is finished.

Then they separate having had an enjoyable time and everyone is contented.

The businessmen always succeed in making difficulties between the artist and his fellow workers the craftsmen for they fear that these jolly people will spend too much money . . . besides as they do not understand the <u>nature</u> of the artist they mistrust simple ideals.

I have no quarrel with anyone in your theatre — I do not notice them individually — I look on them one and all collectively as servants of yours (faithful and affectionate servants I hoped — and still hope) who are prepared to obey — and who had learnt their lesson thoroughly. I understand that you desire to exaggerate a little when you write "my situation is awful." I'd say that everything is not yet quite clear to you concerning my *Hamlet* — excuse me speaking of Shakespeare's play as mine.

I allude to the production.

But, my dear Mr Stanislavsky, how can you or anyone else understand entirely my production till you see it finished.

All I ask for is obedient and enthusiastic assistance & I hope the two things are possible. I do not ask that my plan for production shall meet the approval of anyone. I am responsible for that — it is enough if I approve.

That which I am not able to understand in your Russian productions does not upset me, nor prevent me from appreciating with enthusiasm the part which *is* comprehensible to me. — Art is not judged the same as anything else.

We know that, do we not? Therefore do not be worried nor imagine difficulties where none exist — I shall now come to the actual facts of the differences which the Direction finds exists between us.

Our whole disagreement and the whole mistake of the Direction consists in that they have departed from the only correct & logical standpoint of facts from which the contract was made.

These facts are that Hamlet should be produced within the year 1910.

i.e., that I would in any case give 4 months work & receive for it 6000 rubles in all. Any other material conditions I could not agree to — because as you know I have brought to your theatre the work and experience of a lifetime. There I can only express surprise and very much deplore that the Direction drags into our contract a new securance not anticipated by the Contractor.

i.e.: the *postponement* of the production beyond the year 1910. Such are the facts, moral & logical of the case.

It therefore follows that if there is anyone who has just cause to speak of being offended, insulted or *derided*, it is I: because I have been obliged to listen to accusations of being incorrect made to me in a tone, which to say the least of it, is very arrogant and must appear more so to anyone as independent as myself who seek only to obtain that to which he is entitled.

I hope now that I may hear from you less *despondently* than you appeared in your last letter and that we may be united again shortly.[43]

This exchange can hardly be said to have cleared the air, but it did manage to re-establish communications between the two directors.

MAY 4

Vakhtangov worked with the technical crew on Act II, Scene 1.

MAY 9

Sulerzhitsky led a discussion with the actors with Vakhtangov taking notes.

MAY 12

Suler was interviewed by S. Spiro of *The Russian Word (Russkoe Slovo)*. He indicated that when the theatre first met Craig, it was passionately attracted by his theories, "but then over the course of continuous and persistent work, both the theatre and Craig himself realized that they were impossible." "Our theatre, having learnt from Craig, is trying to bring to fruition everything that it considers feasible."[44] This trimming was a hint of the abandonment of much of Craig's concept. Meanwhile, the newspapers had a field-day, mocking the length of time the production was taking and the frequent shifts in interpretation. One piece by the popular journalist Doroshevich is typical (see Appendix 2).

MAY 16

At a meeting of the MAT Board, Nemirovich resolved to put *Hamlet* into the Fall season "as far as is possible 'according to Craig's concept.'"[45] So far as they were concerned, Craig had been paid everything owing to him.

MAY 17

Stanislavsky directed a memo to the Board: "To avoid fresh misunderstanding I advise the following to be made clear: whether or not Craig is to work on it. I advise that he be clearly, bluntly and pointedly written about this."[46] Meanwhile Suler, mediating for more money for Craig, had a great fight with General Stakhovich, during which Suler was blamed for being a bad influence.[47]

JUNE 2

As if to rehabilitate himself and Craig, Suler demonstrated for the first time the arrangements of the screens and the lighting for Act 1. The actors and the Board were greatly excited by it, exclaiming that the theatre had never done anything similar. To this, Suler replied proudly but nonchalantly, "Now you know what a Craig is all about — now you understand you must give him money."[48] Stanislavsky found the demonstration "splendid, magnificent and grand. If they manage to realize Craig's concept of the costumes as well, something great will come of it. Now it's all up to the actors."[49]

But, spoiling this effect for Suler, news of his interview had filtered back to Craig who was angry at having his ideas described as impractical. Managers all over Europe mouthed that commonplace, and Craig had hoped that *Hamlet* would prove his efficacy in the theatre. Suler was in despair at Craig's recriminations and in a very painful letter tried to mend their broken fences.

You know, you must know, you *cannot* forget that I am, was, and will be always your faithful friend. But I feel that you are not good to me now. Why?

What had I done against you?

How it is painful for me, if you would be able understand that!

And it is now, — now, when I am with broken heart, when I so need one man who would be able, and would *wish* to understand me, my misfortune.

Are you as all? — Oh no!

Is the reason for your coldness with me this interview in newspaper, which about, I am sure, had say you Lykiardopoulo, that I said, that your decoration are good, but not practical?

I said nothing like that — all interview was given only for to make all people understand what a great artist you are, how you are right in your position against our theatre. You know my opinion about that — and must at last believe me, my love to you, more than words of anybody about me, about my love too, and about what I can able to say about you.

In words of Lykiardopoulo (his specialty to make a doubt among people) was part of truth because I said: That you are *so great artist of theatre, staging so much forward of contemporary theatre that practically we cannot realize you, we are not able do it, we must grown up for it. And it is a reason, why we cannot make all you want. But it is not your fault, but our. And you gived all you can* — *and said: "Take from this all you can take,* — *you know better, what you can realise, what not* — *and I can do only all."* Our theatre understand — but great is all you give, and will *try realise so much, as it can, able realise.*

It was the sense of my interview.

It is bad? heh?

It was written for you, for . . .

I don't want say any more about it.

Believe my feeling to you, and you will be always right.

I am working now on your Hamlet.

All theatre is working for it.

How it is hard!

.   .   .

That you are not here now it is good. It would be too much hard for you to see this operation with your child. Only believe that operators: — Stanislavsky and me — do all with a great love and great consideration to you and your work, and we are trying to do so much near to your wishings as we understand that, and so much as it is possible for our theatre. Two months yet, and you will come to us. Don't be angry with Stanislavsky. He is not able to do anything for anybody. And he is rich and don't understand, don't feel what is need of money.

Do you know, that Hamlet is my last work in theatre? Oh! what they did with me! Now, when I gived all my force, all my heart to a theatre, when I am weak and ill, when I feel old, I must break my life, and go to another theatre, among other people for make money for my family because here in my theatre, which I like, which I love where is all my heart I cannot receive no one penny more than 2400 in a year. And Stanislavsky does not anything to keep me, and what is more terrible — he first will say, that I am bad man because I am going off from the theatre to another.[50]

Suler went on for another three pages in this complaining vein, annoyed that he had not been offered shares in the MAT, that Gzovskaya's wealth had made her a stockholder, that Mardzhanov got 4200 rubles a year and so on. However much Craig might have agreed with Suler's grievances, he could hardly have enjoyed hearing someone else crying poor for a change. In fact, Lykiardopoulo sent Craig 1500 rubles on June 19 as the final installment of his pay, intended to bring him to Moscow for the last stage of rehearsals.

JUNE 19

Stanislavsky made final decisions about the costumes from sketches drawn not by Craig but by Sapunov.

8
CROSS-PURPOSES

Ironically, just at the moment when the MAT was preparing to jettison many of Craig's innovations, Craig's London friends decided to honor him with a banquet, to celebrate his importance to the modern stage. Two hundred guests from the world of painting, music, literature and the stage attended; the poet Yeats was to be in the chair but his reluctance to drink the King's health put Will Rothenstein in that position instead. At the Café Royal on July 16, 1911, Ellen Terry and Mrs. Patrick Campbell, John Martin Harvey and Alma-Tadema, Yeats and Roger Fry and many others gathered over Darne de saumon au beurre de Montpellier and Ris de veau aux champignons to pay tribute to a prophet without honor in his own country.[1]

Seated at the main table, but at the farthest remove from Craig's eye- and earshot were Mikhail Lykiardopoulo and K. P. Khokhlov, the actor who played Horatio, as the deputation from the Moscow Art Theatre. Despite the recent acrimony, the former rose to speak of the MAT's pride in being midwife to Craig's brainchild, as

the first European stage on whose boards Mr Gordon Craig was able to materialise his artistic vision and to realize on the completest scale possible those ideals, which born in England were cradled in Moscow . . . It was the privilege of the Moscow Art Theatre to provide that alchemist with the materials by which the philosopher's stone may be found.[2]

Stanislavsky had already congratulated Craig in a letter that wished him the "patience and energy to produce the beautiful things that you create," and a similar monitory clause appeared in the telegram from him read at the banquet. "May you have further perseverance to fulfill your mission of beauty . . . The beauty which is too subtle and too strange to be appreciated immediately by the throng of ordinary theatre goers, over which your genius hovers."[3]

These felicitations served also as self-gratulation, a useful tool of publicity, for as Lykiardopoulo wrote to Stanislavsky the next day, to honor Craig was virtually to honor the MAT, "because all the speakers remembered the Art Theatre in their speeches as the only theatre in the world to be worthy of the name of theatre."[4]

REHEARSAL DIARY

AUGUST 14-16

Nemirovich and Stanislavsky rehearsed Act I, Scene 2. Nemirovich was impressed by the achievements of the technical staff. Vakhtangov was officially asked to keep a stenographic record of the proceedings, and the antiquated Kroneberg translation was finally approved as the script for *Hamlet.*

Stanislavsky, Nemirovich and Suler discussed Polonius.

SULER. Craig wanted this to be a swamp. A toad squatting in it. . .

NEMIROVICH. Even toads have their own great desires.

STANISLAVSKY. If I get a feeling that a toad will emerge, that's all that's needed. There's no need to play a toad. A toad is a harmonization of feelings which will produce a toad.[5]

Stanislavsky saw the queen as "someone beaten down by conventions, an affectionate mother. A silly female. Afraid of the king. She wants peace and quiet."[6]

AUGUST 17

Working on new methods of creating a role, Stanislavsky pointed out that all his suggested devices were needed to force oneself to feel. But if the feelings already existed, the grammar could be ignored. He recommended that Vakhtangov set up problem exercises for the *Hamlet* actors.[7]

AUGUST 18

More work with the "system" in performing Act II, Scene 1, with Kachalov and Luzhsky as Stanislavsky's chief adherents. Stanislavsky complained privately that his time on the production was eaten into by work in the office or at his factory or by the approaching première of *The Living Corpse.*[8]

In the afternoon he examined the completed sets and costumes. "Beautiful costumes. More motley perhaps than according to Craig's specifications, but nevertheless according to Craig and beautiful. The second scene, *i.e.,* the king on the throne and all one mass of gold is above all praise. For the first time, our company understood Craig's genius."[9]

AUGUST 20

During rehearsal Stanislavsky charged Vakhtangov to supervise exercises for the actors playing Osric and Fortinbras.

AUGUST 22

More exercises with the system. Analysis of Polonius, Hamlet, the Queen. For an hour Nemirovich discussed Hamlet as the first enlightened man in an age of Vikings, the concept originally broached with Egorov's designs back in 1909.[10]

Hamlet rehearsals were halted temporarily to make way for *The Living Corpse*, but resumed again on August 27.

AUGUST 27

Rehearsal of Act I, Scenes 1 and 2, with Leonidov standing in as Hamlet. At one point, Stanislavsky took over the role and acted it out with great economy of gesture: for the scene with the Ghost, two or three exclamations, the eyes turning madly upwards; scene with Ophelia, a cold contemptuous mask of horror at life; after the Mousetrap, frenzied jubilation. Suler noted, "According to Stanislavsky, Hamlet is of an active nature, but according to Shakespeare, he is of a weak-willed and reactive nature . . . He is the same superfluous man as Rudin, the same singer of universal grief as Manfred."[11]

SEPTEMBER 10

At an evening meeting the Board came to a decision: in view of the urgency of getting *Hamlet* on stage, Nemirovich was entrusted with scheduling rehearsals and even rehearsing some of the scenes. Up to September 21, Stanislavsky was to pay full attention to his role in *The Living Corpse* and to aid Suler only in his leisure time. After the Tolstoy play opened, Stanislavsky would be able to devote full time to *Hamlet*, which must go up in early December. Kachalov was still allowed to perform in the evenings, but all his daytime rehearsals were to be given over to *Hamlet*. By November Kachalov was to be removed from performances, which would entail striking from the repertory *Woe from Wit*, *At the Gates of the Kingdom*, *Enough Stupidity for Every Sage* and *Brand*, all money-spinners for the company.[12]

Kachalov had been living at Stanislavsky's flat until the family returned from holiday and there rehearsed in his free time. "To my mind," wrote Stanislavsky, "he has fallen on the right foot. . . beginning to love the work."[13]

SEPTEMBER 23

Craig took out a patent on his "one scene with a changeable face," the self-standing screens with reversible joints. Simultaneously, he gave an exhibition of his models in London, which was received, for the most part, with acclaim. The *Times* spoke of the "obvious advantages . . . the ease and quickness with which these things can be handled and the simplicity of the manipulation ... the light can be directed from almost any point; and a change of light makes a change of mood, or even of place ... It is certainly of wonderful effect in the suggestion of place and mood, and experiment with the moods only whets the appetite to see a stage equipped with the new scenery on the full scale."[14]

One dissenter from this opinion was the stage reformer William Poël who seemed distressed by the wrongheadedness of it all.

Mr. Gordon Craig seems to think that Shakespearean representation at the present moment is unsatisfactory, because of our miserable theatres, with their low proscenium and unimaginative scenery, which cannot suggest immensity! Shakespeare would tell us that the fault lies in our big scenic stages and our voiceless, dreary acting. Now, two men with such different ideas about the theatre are not likely to prove successful in collaboration.[15]

Had Poël substituted Stanislavsky's name for Shakespeare's, the statement would have been equally telling.

SEPTEMBER 27

Stanislavsky and Suler rehearsed the Rosencrantz-Guildenstern scenes.

EARLY OCTOBER

Performing in the evenings, Stanislavsky rehearsed *Hamlet* every day. "Hamlet will be interesting," he wrote to the critic Lyubov Gurevich, "at least those of its parts done by Craig."[16]

OCTOBER 20

On Stanislavsky's initiative, the MAT began work on rhythmic gymnastics along Dalcroze lines, with sessions held at 10 to 11.30 in the morning. One of the directing students recalled, "In the mornings we youngsters would watch with curiosity as Stanislavsky, Kachalov, Moskvin, Gribunin, Knipper, Germanova, Lilina and other actors of the older generation, dressed in shorts and singlets, would painfully go through the rhythmic exercises in the lobby."[17]

Hamlet rehearsal from 12 to 4.20.

OCTOBER 29

Rehearsal of Act I.

STANISLAVSKY. Human nature is subtle. It is cunning in its manifestations. It doesn't like to depict black as black, it prefers to extract white from black. Therefore nature does not present grief, for instance, as grief. There isn't enough contrast in that. To intensify the power of grief, one should have recourse to brighter, livelier feelings. As a matter of fact, laughter during grief is horrifying. More horrifying than tears.

So Hamlet, in hiding his sorrow from Marcellus and Horatio, may shout, laugh, joke, fool around.[18]

OCTOBER 30 - NOVEMBER 1

Stanislavsky rehearsed scenes with Ophelia, Laertes and the King, both at the table and on their feet.

Lilina informed Craig for the first time that Knipper was playing Gertrude. He was delighted to hear it and dropped "Mrs Temple-Queensky" a postcard. "I cannot say how happy I am that you are to act the Queen. *You know how much I wished for that* and now *I have my wish!* . . . say to Kachalov that I will not disturb him until the work is done. I am sure he will *be noble* and that he will be *the first* STRONG HAMLET the world has seen."[19]

OCTOBER 31

Suler rehearsed the closet scene and insisted that

there's no need for Hamlet to howl, shout, get excited . . . he must enter calmly, only to talk things over. The most important thing is to refrain from shouting. A shout breaks out in a couple of places, no more. Ordinarily shouting derails an actor off sincerity and on to theatricality and cliché. Every Hamlet has always come on in this scene intending to punish and pardon his mother. And they do so because in a stagey sense it's effective. But it is not true. It is a cheap effect.

The basic problem in the scene is *"Hamlet has come not to punish but to save his mother."* To Suler's mind, this scene manifested the energy and will-power of Hamlet asserted by Craig and Stanislavsky, in contrast to the German critics who stressed his passivity.[20]

END OF OCTOBER - DECEMBER

Continuous rehearsals with Stanislavsky. Kachalov often interrupted the work, saying "Sorry for stopping. It isn't right . . . not right . . . it's not coming out the way I want. Let's go over it again."[21] From the rehearsal notes:

Soliloquies. "In costume drama it is hard to force the audience to listen and understand, and not simply look and admire the soliloquies."[22]

The Mousetrap scene. "Kachalov was puffed up, tried to be subtle, merry, cunning, ironical. In short, he played results — was in despair that he had no tragic quality." Stanislavsky's advice:

Sort out bead by bead the heap of pearls that makes up the contents of this scene, and you will find 1) First bead. Hamlet is energetic and therefore wants to cross the stage valiantly and well; 2) Hamlet wants to slap the king in the face, but without revealing that it is a slap in the face; 3) ditto to Polonius, 4) ditto to Ophelia, 5) Hamlet wants to watch the King unobserved (but you show that you are watching).

Hamlet is afraid of alarming the King too soon; 6) the King has risen. Hamlet runs and leaps on the throne, trying to see the King; 7) Hamlet shouts to the King, "Why, let the strucken deer go weep" and wants him very much to hear him; 8) Hamlet runs downstage to keep the fleeing King in sight; 9) Hamlet wants well and quickly to don the mantle (because he has had an upsurge of energy and at such times a man does everything well and quickly); 10) Hamlet wants to declaim well; 11) Hamlet wants to force Horatio to see what he has seen. The tragic quality will emerge from a series of mechanical tasks of extreme simplicity.[23]

Act V. "Kachalov took the last scene at rehearsal at a horribly slow tempo. When he started speeding up, he garbled the words with no time to live them through (words outstrip feelings). Have to give him a general task for the whole act."[24]

Act III, Scene 2. Displeased with the advice to the players scene, Stanislavsky dashed on to the stage and played Hamlet. Said Gzovskaya, watching from the stalls, "This was a brilliant Hamlet. Hamlet the artist, teacher and preacher, who knew more than anyone around him . . . This was not Craig's abstract Hamlet, illuminated by death lights, striving to overcome his despised earthly existence . . . Stanislavsky showed Hamlet to be virile, full of human nobility and restrained passion." Another actor stated that "Stanislavsky showed Hamlet to be passionate, emotional, full of contrasting shifts from tenderness and love for mankind to angry sarcasm and hatred." Playing the scene with Rosencrantz and Guildenstern and the recorders, "he moved back and forth, forcing them to chase him like foxhounds. He led this 'chase' at a hectic tempo and then suddenly stopped short, tossing them a line, so that Rosencrantz and Guildenstern with no time to halt crashed into him."[25]

NOVEMBER 6-7

Stanislavsky worked with Massalitinov (Claudius) on the mad scene and the prayer scene. In the former,

Concealment of a boorish smile. An Oriental pasha. A law unto himself. Eyes somewhat squinting. An intelligent, appraising glance. A smug villain. This sort of sovereign is told that there's an uprising. In a twinkling he's a new man: he does everything confidently, Napoleonically . . . When he isn't imperious, he talks to God and Fate. He makes deals with them. What's going on inside him during the prayer scene? Curses. A chained dog. He doesn't know what to do. Wants to be shriven. Pounds the table. Gnaws his hands.

MASSALITINOV. *Pray can I not.*

STANISLAVSKY. You got down on the ground so conventionally in so cliché a pose that it can only result in stagey conventionality and not life-like truth. Don't you feel how this pose produces clichés of mime, rhythm, voice, speech, diction . . .

Try to find for this mood — a tormented prayer — another simpler pose, far from any theatrical picturesqueness, and you'll see it will result in life-like mime and a tone of voice and a way of speaking usually associated with such a pose in real life.

Massalitinov tried.

STANISLAVSKY. You see how much closer you are to truth. There are still traces of cliché left — rip them out too. Besides, you still don't live for the reason Shakespeare wrote the king's words, but rather for the words themselves, you inventory their direct meaning. You illustrate "smells to heaven," "offense" with impeccable mimicry and this generally keeps you from feeling the truth. Don't live "smells" or "offense" but the impossibility of praying to God, the helplessness, the despair. . . . Find truth in inner realization — then you can worry about outward truth. [26]

NOVEMBER 8

Stanislavsky and Suler did a rough blocking of the first five scenes on the main stage, working on groupings, but without the extras. Nemirovich attended and wrote to his wife, "Perhaps I'm carping at Stanislavsky, but today I got upset at the way he apportions time at rehearsals. It puts *Hamlet* in danger of postponement. But perhaps I am carping. The same old story. He shows off for the bystanders, wallows in their thinking his instructions wonderful, while the actors and the production itself are no better off for it." [27]

NOVEMBER 11

The banquet and the exhibition had suddenly thrust Craig in the public eye, and he was frequently interviewed at this time. To the London *Daily Chronicle*, he claimed that Sarah Bernhardt had commissioned him to do the designs for her own production of *Hamlet* and boasted of his successes at the MAT.

When, two years ago, I was asked to design a production of "Hamlet" for the Moscow Art Theatre, my methods, my ideas, were diametrically at variance with the traditions of the theatre, which had been realistic. But were my beliefs flouted? Were my designs returned as infeasible? Not a bit of it! For two years Mr Stanislavsky and his colleagues have been working at my plans, and only yesterday I received a most cordial and enthusiastic letter from Mr Stanislavsky, telling me of their successes and hopes at rehearsals." [28]

This letter, if it ever existed, has proved elusive.

NOVEMBER 13

Stanislavsky noted in the rehearsal diary,

If they want *Hamlet* to go up in December, the whole theatre will have to be set to work at once . . . At the moment utter chaos reigns . . . Absolutely necessary: 1)

Sulerzhitsky must be taken off construction work, because he must be totally involved in the directing, the arrangement of screens and the lighting. 2) Indispensable for November 20, a makeup and costume parade for all five scenes of Act I. 3) Indispensable, organize during performance of *Living Corpse* practice makeups for the courtiers and guards.[29]

He also asked Nemirovich to judge whether Craig should be sent for or not and on what conditions. "I can only remember that at the present time Craig is the greatest talent in our art. It would be a mistake to break off relations with him."[30]

NOVEMBER 17

Stanislavsky went over the music for Act I with Sats the composer. The MAT Board met and decided not to summon Craig so long as the production was unfinished, "because, in the Board's opinion, *Hamlet* with Craig's participation will not be ready by December." Not wishing, however, to break off relations, it recommended bringing him to the dress rehearsals or ordering a new production from him. It also suggested that Stanislavsky not refuse Nemirovich's help in "*organizing* all the work."[31] Stanislavsky's reaction: "I have never refused, on the contrary, I expect the whole theatre to work. If Craig is to come to the finished product, he had better be informed now. He cannot come at his own expense."[32] Craig was, accordingly, sent the money to make the final trip to observe the dress rehearsals.

DECEMBER 5

Stanislavsky instructed Kachalov to penetrate through the eye to the soul.

For a long time I forced him to scrutinize and familiarize himself with the faces and souls of the living persons who play Rosencrantz and Guildenstern. When he felt their living spirit, he began to relate not to the material of the objective, but to its spirit, and began to experience it, although five minutes before he had fallen into despair and declared that nothing would work.[33]

Falling into despair was not uncommon for Kachalov at this stage of rehearsals. Exhausted and enervated, he complained that he was oscillating between Stanislavsky's interpretation and Craig's concept. He had never really wanted to play Hamlet, he protested, and would just as soon relinquish the role to Leonidov who was dying to play it.[34]

DECEMBER 6

Craig, interviewed by the London *Evening Standard*, was asked if he had any new ideas about Hamlet as a character.

No, I don't think so, except that I take an entirely commonsense view of the man and his motives. [Stanislavsky would have blanched to hear that.] He simply succeeded in performing in two months a task that has been tried in every Court in Europe for centuries. He set out to cleanse social and official life of its moral grime and its degeneracy. He set about his task with direct purpose, and with the full enthusiasm of a young, virile and cruelly wronged man. His ideas were logical, and he reasoned and thought out every movement and act during that brief time of storm and stress that ended in tragedy.[35]

MID-DECEMBER - JANUARY

With Christmas set as a deadline, there is persistent, incessant work on *Hamlet*. One young actress related, "Stanislavsky could never make up his mind to release Hamlet, he kept wanting to realize something unborn. But it was terrifying; Kachalov and everyone working on *Hamlet* were exhausted."[36]

DECEMBER 15

Nemirovich assisted at rehearsals and went over the scene with the players.

DECEMBER 18

Nemirovich, Stanislavsky and Suler rehearsed the second half of Act II, Scene 3, and then Act III, Scene 1.

DECEMBER 21

Nemirovich went over the closet scene with Kachalov.

Reaching the last lap of rehearsals, the MAT Board cancelled all performances from December 25 to January 4 so that *Hamlet* could rehearse on the main stage day and night and open on time. The first runthrough began at 11 A.M. on December 26 on the main stage and had reached the middle of the Mousetrap scene, and Hamlet's line "Go let the strucken deer go weep" when something unheard-of in the history of the Art Theatre occurred. In the auditorium where no one had ever before raised his voice during a rehearsal, the word "Stupid" was shouted in English. Gordon Craig, come to the theatre directly from the railway station, lost his temper to find they had begun without him and raised a mighty uproar. Diplomatically, he was asked to leave and not to return until the final dress rehearsals. The actors, who had thought some accident had occurred and who had remained in their circles of concentration, carried on the scene without a break.

The rehearsal concluded at 5 P.M. The actors grabbed a bite at the buffet and moved to the small stage to continue working the same scenes over and over. Finally, Kachalov, pale under his makeup, announced, "I can't go on any longer." Stanislavsky was surprised to see by his watch that the time was 2:30 A.M. and ended the rehearsal, he and Kachalov being the last to leave. This was the only time Kachalov ever called off a rehearsal.[37]

The next day, Craig, as usual domiciled at the Hotel Metropole, sent Lilina some roses and requested Lykiardopoulo to inform him when the last rehearsals were to be held. Stanislavsky sent round a tactful card — "Ich binn sehr glücklich dir zu sehen — Ich liebe dich sehr — Kommen sie zu uns."[38] Thinking this meant an invitation to a rehearsal, Craig went round to the theatre, where he found Lilina, but discovered that Stanislavsky was at home rehearsing three of the actors. He left a note to say that he had no intention of disturbing the work, but did hope to see a final rehearsal. "For why see too often what cannot be corrected and are the faults of conciet [*sic*] — if it be faulty," he confided to his Daybook. "I fully expect this fault of faults to veil the whole spirit of 'Art.'"[39] In the evening, Craig dined with Prince Volkonsky, Director of the Russian State Theatres, his nephew and Lykiardopoulo. After chatting of Appia and Dalcroze,

Volkonsky also spoke of my production "Hamlet" — he had seen 3 acts rehearsed yesterday.
That's more than I have seen!
(Nemirovich Danchenko I shall not forget you — be sure)
V. said that much was bad — in fact he was not enthusiastic about it. It is hard to remain patient & silent while my imaginings are being messed about.
Afterward . . . Prince Lyovin . . . most cordial but regretted the performance he saw of Hamlet at rehearsal yesterday.
I said I like Stanislavsky & that that was my only answer — He agreed but said he alone was a man in the theatre & asked me not to repeat what he said about Hamlet. I assured him I would be silent because I no longer had anything I care to say.[40]

The following day, Suler came to report progress and Stanislavsky invited Craig to dinner, "happy at the thought he can have a good talk with you," Lilina averred.[41] Craig's impressions of the dinner were that

They are all talking here in Moscow about Craig's way & Stanislavsky's way of producing 'Hamlet' & there is fighting & arguments & all the truth is lost in dust & noise —
Stan is getting very sore —
for the truth is concerned with *Shakespeare's* way.[42]

The adverse publicity Craig had been fed could not have reassured him about the production, and when at last a general rehearsal was held in his presence on January 1, all hell broke loose. He was aghast at the costumes, blocking and lighting, most of which was radically different from what he had sketched or worked out the previous year. He protested that he had left forty or fifty costumes designs with swatches attached, although Suler asserted that this was not the case. Craig began to suspect "sabotage" and deduced that Suler destroyed the designs and Craig's part of the concept in order to aggrandize his master Stanislavsky.[43] He sat hunched up in his seat, grinding his teeth. Things again came to a head in the Mousetrap scene, when Craig insisted that the lighting must be more subdued. Serafima Birman, one of the court ladies, recalled, "The rehearsal ground to a halt — so vehemently were they arguing at the directors' desk about the stage lighting. We who were on stage at the time heard Craig demand something persistently of Stanislavsky in French and Stanislavsky no less ardently and also in French refuse him."[44] Simov, the designer for *The Living Corpse*, was also in the auditorium and recollected that Craig wanted

the lighting to fall in shafts from high windows to create darkness beneath the ceiling and thus increase the height and massiveness of the palace. Instead, the soffits gave diffused light while the conical projectors were off. Craig's expression, I can recall it now, shifted nervously. He paid no attention to Kachalov's acting as Hamlet, he leaped from seat to seat and rapidly withdrew from the stalls. Confusion reigned. The rehearsal was broken off. The English gentleman had turned into a raging lion.[45]

To resolve these difficulties, Stanislavsky called an evening meeting with Suler, Moskvin, Craig and Kachalov to effect the desired changes. But the climax came when Craig spilled an ink-well on the stage and demanded to have his name removed from the poster.[46] Alisa Koonen, anxious to know what was going on,

slipped into the office, hoping from there to penetrate the auditorium. I could not, the door was locked from inside. Then, despite the cruel frost, I decided to wait outside. The meeting went on endlessly. I was numb with cold and had already made up my mind to run home, when suddenly Craig burst out of the office in just his suit, his scarf flying, and tore along the alley. Behind him ran Suler, holding Craig's coat and shouting, "Wait, Mister Craig, wait!"[47]

The next day Craig failed to show up at the theatre, but Suler dismissed the problem with a wave of his hand, insisting "Don't worry, everything'll work out, everything'll work out." The lighting of the Mousetrap scene was redone to Craig's specifications, and notes on the general rehearsal were read to the cast. By chance Koonen ran into Craig who was "downcast and malicious" and declared "If Stanislavsky wanted to turn Shakespeare into Gorky, why did he invite me and put up my screens?"[48] He then insisted to Stanislavsky that Suler's name be removed from the programme. Many years later, he tried to justify his motives for this incredibly callous demand.

Why should I have another name except Stanislav: as part producer on the programme except Stans perhaps — & only perhaps since it was my production & St had assured me & others that he was my assistant.

Produced by EGC said I thats all right, assisted by Stan and uncle Tom Cobbler & all But even then why give this bit of fat to Suler
Suler was well paid by the theatre —
Suler was assisting with 20 others — but none of these were really my assistant . . . & the other assistants were not to be named by St: now I see why St wanted that — He wanted to make Suler feel that he was responsible if anything went wrong.[49]

This egoistic and incorrect analysis may have soothed Craig's conscience, but it traumatized Suler who, when he heard that Stanislavsky had acceded to Craig's request, also refused to come to rehearsals. On January 4, Stanislavsky wrote to him.

Today you were not in the theatre, yesterday you didn't come by . . .
Either you are ill, in which case write a little note about the state of your health, or you are demonstratively protesting and getting angry, and so I begin to get depressed that the work, begun joyously, is ending so sadly.
When I confront such surmises, I feel stupid and don't understand. I feel I need to do something to understand, and I don't know and don't understand what's going on. You got angry with Craig for changing the lighting? I don't believe it and I don't understand it. The whole design and concept were created by Craig . . . don't you think he's the best one to know what he envisages . . . It would be as absurd for Hansen [the Ibsen translator] to consider "Brand" his own work as for me to accept the success and concept of the "Hamlet" production as my own creation. Nobody criticizes a winner, and really "The Mousetrap" had an enormous success yesterday.
Moreover, didn't you really feel the day before yesterday, when Kachalov was rehearsing acting in the darkness just set up by Craig, that it (the darkness) is the salvation of our whole show. For actually, yesterday's darkness hid all the unfinished bits. And Lord, how Boleslawski's flaws showed up when he was lit by light from all the reflectors! And the last scene worked precisely because the lighting concealed all the operatic garishness of the costumes.
It has been suggested that you are offended on account of the playbill. But aren't I as well?
Craig is beginning to be capricious, refusing all suggestions. The theatre requires that Craig's name be on it, because the scandal he created is now notorious throughout the city. Craig demands my name on the playbill, because he's afraid of responsibility and hides behind me as a scapegoat. Amid all these stratagems I have to reconcile Craig with you or you with Craig, because I can't stand alone on the playbill. I can never figure out what to do at such moments, I go to you for advice and you start talking about "The Blue Bird." And then I don't understand anything. Is this to be the end of work so well, so amicably begun? If so, then one would have to reject the best thing in life — art, — and run from its temple, which has become suffocating.
It is impossible to live and live — and suddenly take offense, without explaining why. That Craig has offended you I understand, at least I'm sorry for it. But . . . Craig is a great artist, our guest, and Europe is now watching how we deal with his creativity. I don't want to be embarrassed, and as for schooling Craig — really, I don't care to. Isn't it best to finish what is begun, especially with only one day to go.

Turn your anger to graciousness and do not spoil a good beginning by a bad ending.

Tomorrow at 2 we shall arrange the apparition of the Ghost in the closet scene.[50]

Suler's reply the next day was heart-rending.

Craig is a great artist and remains and shall remain so for me forever. That he is our guest I also know and I think that in the course of two years' work with him I have proved that I know how to put up with the rudeness and irascibility and muddleheadedness of this man, and, despite that, love him sincerely.

That Europe is watching him makes absolutely no difference to me, this cannot change my attitude to him or to anybody else.

He can light it any way he chooses — that's his right and I have nothing against it and have helped him and will work today on the lighting of the closet scene, because in the closet scene as in the whole play, it's not just screens, but your work and mine and the work of the theatre, and if something has to be done over, I will do it over, if that is the wish of the director-in-chief of the play — you.

Besides, until "Hamlet" is finished, I am ready to carry out Craig's directions, even if they don't gibe with my opinions, now that you have decided that Craig is right.

In the realm of artistic work I cannot be offended — you know that very well and you know why: because I don't have enough faith in myself and my abilities, especially when I'm dealing with you — it would be preposterous and absurd.

Things are not quite the same with Craig.

When he talks about lines, designs, composition and even lighting, I feel that this is the real Craig, but when it's a question of directing, then I don't trust him: he may be absolutely right, but he is too uninterested in acting.

And from that standpoint I find that "The Mousetrap" is lit unsuccessfully. Even if it did come off at the dress rehearsal, it wasn't *thanks to* the lighting, but *in spite of* it. Everyone complained that he couldn't see Hamlet, and the audience at the premiere will not forgive the theatre for that.

But even this change does not and cannot offend me. I may regret that this lighting injures the production and Kachalov, but there's no point in taking offence at that, because, after all, with little faith in my own powers, I readily assent in thinking that I'm wrong, although I am offended that you so quickly joined the general opinion, for you yourself were quarreling with Craig for almost ten minutes, saying that it was impossible to act in such darkness, that it was good for the screens and bad for the actors and the production.

But I repeat — there is no offence in that.

Craig didn't want me to be on the playbill — after two years of hard, arduous work, after many, I may say, sacrifices for Craig, realizing that without me he would hardly have managed to bring his affairs in our theatre even this far. — It caught me offguard.

And that's all.

But I am not offended.

Craig the artist will survive for me, Craig the friend is totally destroyed — forever.

This type of Englishman is very familiar to me from the days of my work in England and America.

He and I can never have anything in common. There is no offense in it, but I will never be able to have any dealings with him — I simply am not interested in dealing with such a man — and that's that.

But his work, whatever it be, I shall observe with pleasure as before.

The only moment in this whole time when I had a feeling of momentary offense, a rather keen one, was when you began to ask me how I would feel at Craig's, quote, not wanting me to be on the playbill.

It was offensive that a few days ago not I (I think otherwise), but you yourself said that my name ought to be on the playbill, because in your opinion it was important to me, seeing that I work on the sidelines.

But no sooner does Craig, not Craig the artist but Craig the adventurer, the insolent confidence-man that lurks in him and is revealed in this incident, wish this, than you, even realizing that he is unfair to me and thinking that it is important for me, are immediately ready to rush to betray me on his account, and then you ask me my opinion of it.

I could not help but remember how, always, whenever I was right, but when I had to be defended, you were ready, at the slightest side attack or even from the very possibility of an attack, to rush to betray both me and my, not only imaginary as in this case, but real interests.

And you always did betray me.

And meanwhile I see that with your other friends, you know how to act and act subtly, so that their interests never suffer unjustly.

And when I recall all this together, as I recalled it the last time, then I began to be very offended and ask the question — are our good relations still standing firm?

This is very soon forgotten, but the mark of every such occasion involuntarily remains on my soul and produces a slight pinprick on my relationship to you.

And that is all.

There was offense, I felt it for a few hours, and then it went away, and there's an end.

You say a good beginning must have a good ending. Don't tell this to me but to Craig.

In conclusion:

I am not offended by Craig for his actions, but people capable of such things do not interest me — they are not my colleagues, I simply avoid meeting such people and I certainly have no intention of teaching them or reforming them, — there are too many of them — I simply avoid them, I find them tiresome and unpleasant.

But I am not offended by you, for heaven's sake — for neither the first nor the last time.

It will always be that way. There is nothing in me that would sever your relations with me.

Especially since you do not even notice such matters. There's nothing to be done about it.

But if one meets with too many such pinpricks, so many that they combine into one whole, then probably our good relations will cool off.

But life is short, and such occurrences are infrequent, so there is enough room for pinpricks and to spare, and this means that everything will go on as before.[51]

During this backstage drama, Craig continued to sulk like Achilles at the Metropole, where he carved a medallion for Kachalov to wear and fashioned a headdress to suit his ideas. He was in to nobody and wrote to Olga Knipper,

Please Miss Temple-Knipper-Queensky do not send anyone to see me.
    I think they would scarcely find me either — for I have only just found myself.
    And you will understand that sometimes one does not want to see strangers on business.
    I wish to be as much alone as possible like the White-Owl who sits warming his five wits in the belfry tower.
    But I hope I shall see *you.* That would be a pleasure. but I do not ask you. You will come or not as you wish —
    I am pleased about all I hear of *Hamlet* — and I shall applaud the work of the actors.
    I only beg one thing — one little request — it is that you should speak an affectionate word to *Kachalov* and a word to King, Polonius, *Laertes and even to Ghost and whisper to them all*
    "Speak a *little quicker*
    Do the Shauspielerei [*sic*] *quicker."*
    It seems good to begin slowly and to *hasten* as flames *hasten* — as they increase, and as water *hastens* as it increases — [52]

Meanwhile the general rehearsals continued, and Alisa Koonen spent whole days in the auditorium, comparing the differences between Craig's concept and the actual performance. The division between the two was palpable. Kachalov was convincing and moving in the lyrical passages, but seemed to lack drive in the more impassioned scenes. He felt this himself and once asked her, "Tell me honestly, am I a very boring Hamlet?"[53]
    On January 5, the day of the opening, Stanislavsky and Suler worked out the lighting for the closet scene, hoping to effect last-minute improvements. But one more catastrophe was in store. One hour before the performance, Stanislavsky was rehearsing the shifting of the screens with the stagehands. Everything went smoothly and after setting up Act I, Scene 1, they were let off for a tea-break. Suddenly,

one of the screens began to lean sideways more and more, then fell on the screen next to it, and the entire set of scenery fell to the floor like a house of cards. There was a crack of splintering wood frames, the sound of ripping canvas, and then the shapeless mass of broken and torn screens all over the stage.[54]

Desperately, behind the closed curtains, the stagehands repaired the breakage (similar falls had been a not uncommon occurrence at rehearsals). To steady each screen a weighted tray of ballast was affixed to its base. This of course would necessitate changing the sets behind the curtains, slowing down the performance and obviating Craig's notion of kinetic scenery.
    Craig had not been in the theatre during this accident and Stanislavsky made a point of not telling him about it. And so, when *My Life in Art*

appeared in 1923, Craig regarded the story as a fabrication. To the *Morning Post* in 1926, he proclaimed "My screens did not fall over and anyone who says that they did is inventing merely to give me pleasure."[55] In 1935, he threatened to sue Stanislavsky, on the grounds that the canard was ruining his reputation, and Stanislavsky secured an affidavit from the master carpenter and stagehands attesting to the actual occurrence of the mishap.[56]

Knowing that Kachalov came to the theatre long before curtain-time, Alisa Koonen decided that his first congratulatory flowers would be hers, three blue roses, at the time a sensational novelty, from a fashionable florist. It was not considered seemly for an actress to appear in the men's dressing-rooms, so she slipped in just as he was uncapping his makeup, deposited the roses on the table, and ran out, only to collide with General Stakhovich who read her a stern lecture on "inadmissible behavior." She had just enough time to run home and change and return to watch the performance breathlessly from the students' gallery.[57]

9
UNFINISHED PRODUCT

The curtains parted at 7:30 before a sold-out house. Even the standing room was completely filled. The playbill read, as a compromise:

HAMLET, a tragedy in 5 acts
by W. Shakespeare
Translated by A. Kroneberg
Production by G. Craig and K. S. Stanislavsky
Regisseur L. A. Sulerzhitsky
Designers G. Craig and K. N. Sapunov (costumes)
Music by I. A. Sats

CLAUDIUS, King of Denmark	N.O. Massalitinov
HAMLET, his nephew	V. I. Kachalov
POLONIUS, a dignitary	V. V. Luzhsky
LAERTES, his son	R. V. Boleslawski
HORATIO, friend to Hamlet	K. P. Khokhlov
VOLTIMAND	A. A. Barov
CORNELIUS	Boltin
ROSENCRANTZ	S. N. Voronov
GUILDENSTERN	B. M. Sushkevich
OSRIC	V. V. Tezavrovsky
MARCELLUS	P. A. Baksheev
FRANCISCO	N. A. Podgorny
BERNARDO	B. M. Afonin
1st ACTOR (PLAYER KING)	A. L. Vishnevsky
2nd ACTOR (PLAYER QUEEN)	P. P. Zharikov
3rd ACTOR (LUCIANUS)	B. M. Afonin
4th ACTOR (PROLOGUE)	A. P. Bondyrev
PRIEST	I. V. Lazarev
1st GRAVEDIGGER	V. F. Gribunin
2nd GRAVEDIGGER	P. A. Pavlov
GHOST OF HAMLET'S FATHER	N. A. Znamensky
FORTINBRAS, Prince of Norway	I. N. Bersenev
GERTRUDE, Queen of Denmark, Hamlet's Mother	O. L. Knipper
OPHELIA, daughter to Polonius	O. V. Gzovskaya

Courtiers, ladies, officers, soldiers, actors, servants.

Among the extras appeared such celebrities-to-be as Evgeny Vakhtangov (who played Lucianus later in the run), Mikhail Chekhov and Serafima Birman.

ACT I, SCENE 1.   A GUARD PLATFORM OF THE CASTLE.

Before the curtains part, the audience hears a women's choir singing a wordless hymn, mingled with sound effects of raging wind and roaring sea. The intended effect is of an "harmonic wind" and, to cover the human quality of the voices, the melody is played by first and second violas, cello and bass viol. This hymn and the sound effects continue long after the set is revealed and are punctuated intermittently by the doleful sound of a gong.[1]

High grey screens set far downstage suggest the castle walls; they are lost in shadow, so that, in the dim pale blue moonlight, no one can discern clearly where entrances and exits begin or end or what lurks in the space between them. The soldiers, silhouetted against the screens, wear shallow

12. The first scene of *Hamlet,* sketch by A. Lyubimov. The ghost enters *left,* as Horatio and the guard cower at *right.* (*Theatre and Art,* 1912.)

helmets with noseguards, hoods and sleeves of knitted chain-mail, capelets overlapped like shingles on a roof, gauntlets, carry short swords and spears, and are shod with what appears to be ski-boots, Before the dialogue commences, the Ghost, costumed to match the walls in color in a long grey winding-sheet over its armor and crowned by a dome-like cap, creeps in unseen, hauling the train of its cerements behind it. It is suddenly picked out by a projector-lamp, but vanishes just as suddenly, startled by the shouted watch-words of Bernardo and Francisco. Horatio (in black fur-lined mantle and cap) and his comrades later huddle together stage left as the Ghost stalks towards them.[2] For the critics, it was characteristic of Craig to start the play with the Ghost, and effective in thrusting the spectator into a "fairytale, phantasmagorical world." The nonspecific locale lent credence to the supernatural.[3]

ACT I, SCENE 2.   THE CASTLE.

The curtains had closed at the end of the previous scene, since the changes could no longer be effected in full view of the audience. Before they part again, trumpets sound, "impertinent, sinister, insolent fanfares with improbable assonances and dissonances, which blare to all the world the criminal majesty and arrogance of the newly crowned king."[4] The curtains draw apart to reveal a tableau so successful that it called forth a round of applause in a theatre where clapping was traditionally relegated to the end of the performance.[5]

The stage picture supported Craig's concept of *Hamlet* as monodrama: everything that took place within the scene until the exit of the Court was Hamlet's nightmare. At back, arranged in a semicircle stand the high screens covered with gilt paper, and up center a raised platform, approached by steps, surmounted by the gold half-moon of a throne. There sit Claudius and Gertrude: the King in a long golden mantle, with a collar overlaid with rectangular flaps, a high conical crown, and a golden kirtle with belt and wallet; the Queen in similar garb, with a coronet, a highnecked collar, a plain chain of office, and her wallet slung lower. From their shoulders spreads a cloak of gold brocade that fans out to occupy the whole width of the stage, before dropping into a trap behind the apron. Out of this shimmering expanse jut the heads of the courtiers, in golden caps like narrowbrimmed derbies with earlaps, and with hypocritical smirks on their faces. This effect was not achieved as Craig had wished, by one vast piece of cloth with holes cut in it. As Serafima Birman, one of the court ladies, describes it,

the people were arranged on wooden platforms so as to represent symbolically the feudal ladder: at the top the King and Queen, the courtiers below; at the feet of Claudius and Gertrude assemble their more intimate henchmen, with the less honored below. The court ladies were dressed in golden mantles as were the men, but with plated stomachers. From the slits in the golden skullcaps hung long, almost knee-length braided brocade ribbons. . . . The actors were distributed on various levels, their mantles flowed out and gave the impression of a monolithic golden pyramid.[6]

To sustain the effect, the courtiers were required to remain in a static position for almost the entire scene, and since the ladies' costumes weighed thirty-five pounds, some lost consciousness from excessive kneeling.

(The young actors recruited to play courtiers were wretched. "We came on stage as if to prison," recalled Birman. There was the danger of a contagious laugh breaking out and when certain tardy actors later in the run forgot to apply their deathlike pallor, their contrasting florid complexions not only spoiled the harmony of the picture but caused surreptitious hilarity.)[7]

To Stanislavsky the tableau resembles a "golden sea with golden waves"; to the Japanese observer Kaoru Osanai "an almost perfect sculpture"; to Kachalov as Hamlet "a phantasmagorical, many-headed hydra."[8] The whole was bathed in a diagonal beam of light, extending from upstage left down center. The reflections cast from the gold costumes on to the dulled reflector of the gilt walls produced for one critic the semblance of "a splendrous church Mass blazing with brand-new gilding and bright 'electricity.'" For him, the profussion of gilt was reminiscent of Christmas crackers, and most of his colleagues commented on the garishness of the lighting.[9]

Before the court is a low cream-colored barricade, made up of cubes to represent a stone balustrade. Semi-recumbent on a bench and leaning back on the barrier, Hamlet sits facing the audience, lost in a revery, isolated from the image of molten gold behind him. His costume is not the traditional suit of sables, but a long garment of greyish blue with plain dark geometric ornaments embroidered on the chest and with long buttoned sleeves; a square medallion hangs on his breast and a dagger at his side. The costume as well as Kachalov's wig, lank, black and center-parted, suggested to most Russians a monk in a cassock. ("Grigory Otrepev but without the impulsiveness of Pushkin's hero," said one. Yet another was reminded of Alyosha Karamazov.)[10] The silver trim contrasts with the gold of the court to emphasize Hamlet's alienation from the world in which he moves; the court's gaudiness bespeaks its vulgarity and ostentation as it appears to Hamlet's mind's eye.

The scene begins with the King's harangue, spoken as by an automaton, jaws snapping. Only occasionally does Hamlet glance up at the court. When the Queen addresses him, he sits motionless, almost turning his back to her, and answers as if to himself. On the King's line, "Come away," the royal party and its suite remain in place, as a light black tulle curtain falls between it and Hamlet, blacking out the upstage area and signalling Hamlet's awakening. It reminds Osanai of fog rolling in.[11]

With the fading of the "vision," Kachalov launches into the "Sullied flesh" soliloquy, or perhaps glides into it would be more exact. It is spoken simply and quietly, not for the audience but for himself, as a private, long mulled cogitation. Tears are hinted at but not expressed; at moments a sob rises in his throat. "Heaven and earth! Must I remember?" is almost a whisper uttered in bitter wonderment, rather than an angry outburst.[12] This reflective tone in the soliloquies is one of the elements of Kachalov's performance that most bemuses an audience accustomed to romantic ranting. "Hamlet's soliloquies sound on Kachalov's lips like mournful but already fully formed reflections . . . and not the torments of a spiritual *struggle* breaking into flashes of articulated thought."[13] Sats' "Hamlet's Solitude" theme is intoned by a wordless choir of male and female voices under the soliloquy, and after the scene with Horatio and Marcellus the fanfares blare out once more, providing an ironic commentary on what is to follow.

This is the first of the three scenes in the play that Craig approved of (the other two are the "Mousetrap" and the finale), for it corresponded closely to his sketches and plans, and was one of those least broken up by movement. He did, however, object to the King's performance and to the sharpness and clarity of the light.[14] In later performances, the light would be softened and diffused.

ACT I, SCENE 3.   A ROOM.

The stage, narrowed to a cream-colored interior, with a high square object that might be a bed at left, is brightly lit by sharply defined streaks of sunlight dappling the walls. The critics misconstrue Craig's desire for sharp-edged beams here and suggest that the lighting should be toned down.[15] Polonius' frog motif is manifest in his long quilted mantle and cap, spottled with irregular lozenges and squares; straggling white hair and a sparse beard, heavy-lidded eyes with dense white lashes and a large beak-like nose lend a cunning and cynical expression to his face. His speeches are incredibly slow in tempo. For all that, Luzhsky's acting is considered to be extremely naturalistic and, though good, out of keeping with the general conception.[16]

Laertes, as portrayed by Boleslawski, seems uncharacteristically flaccid and simple-minded, in short too "Russian."[17] Gzovskaya's Ophelia is docile and timid, her flitting across the stage reminding one critic of "one of those slender girls with a lily in their hands whom the Pre-Raphaelites are so fond of."[18] The resemblance is aided by the straight dark hair held by a fillet and the long-sleeved, high-bosomed neck, cinctured with a narrow belt forming a V in front, a costume the actress claimed to have designed herself. Efros in *Rech'* found her "quite the little girl with a child-like phiz, child-like voice, child-like intonations and child-like grievances. And she apprehends her

13. Kachalov as Hamlet, holding the ubiquitous book. This photograph gives a good idea of the monk-like nature of his costume and makeup. (N.N. Chushkin, *Gamlet-Kachalov* [Moscow: Iskusstvo, 1966].)

14. Gzovskaya as Ophelia and Luzhsky as Polonius. Sketches by A. Lyubimov. (*Theatre and Art,* 1912.)

grievances like a child, as undeserved reproofs. And that is moving and poetical."[19]

ACT I, SCENE 4.   A GUARD PLATFORM.

The setting reverts to Scene 1, with Hamlet, Horatio and Marcellus hidden in one deep embrasure, while the Ghost slinks along the wall. The lighting is so managed that Hamlet and the spectator become aware of the Ghost's presence simultaneously. At that point, asserts Aleksandr Koiransky, "there begins another Hamlet, another Kachalov. The slicked-down, smooth, monk-like hair fans out disobediently around the lofty brow."[20] Kachalov makes one of his rare gestures at "Angels and ministers of grace, defend us!", suddenly flinging his arm aloft. "My fate cries out,/And makes each petty artery in this body/As hardy as the Nemean lion's nerve" is the cue for his rushing out behind the vanishing Ghost.[21]

ACT I, SCENE 5.   THE BATTLEMENTS.

A shallow stage and cream-colored screens, with a step-unit extending stage right to stage left at a 45° angle, another similar step-unit continuing back to stage right, and a triangular expanse of sky above it. The lighting aims for moonlight, the upper portion of the sky deep blue from a spotlight directed from the sidelines, the lower portion purple; and as the scene progresses, the blue shifts to blue-green and then to the red of dawning.[22] The Ghost moves to the very highest point on the platform, with Hamlet congealed in attention on the lower level, and there they play the scene in silhouette. It makes an impressive picture, but is a torment to Kachalov. Hampered in movement by a heavy hooded cloak lined in grey fur, kneeling in discomfort on the narrow causeway, his myopic eyes watering from the sharply focussed lights, he finds any attempt at intimacy impossible. The lighting has been so aimed that the Ghost in its translucent cerements will seem ethereal and Hamlet in his cumbersome garments earthbound; but this symbolism requires the actor to stare straight into the glare.[23]

For one critic the whole effect was misguided:

Thanks in most part to the lighting, it must be said that one has seldom seen anything more tasteless than Hamlet's interview with the ghost at the top of a flight of stairs against a background of violet curtain with the most powerful bluish beam from an electric spotlight on the side. The wooden cut-out figure of Hamlet on his knees, making a very ugly profile on the topmost step, and beside him the wooden and at the same time flabby ghost (can that be the "realism of a phantom"?), each of whose movements was crudely and realistically seconded by a movement of the thick shadows it cast.[24]

Kachalov's Hamlet has entered as if on fire. Stationary throughout the Ghost's tirade, he leaps up at last in a frenzy. His voice is emotional, velvety and sonorous on "O all you host of heaven!/O earth! What else?/And shall I couple hell?", then almost a plaintive whimpering whisper on "Oh fie!

15. Khokhlov as Horatio; Kachalov as Hamlet and Knipper as Gertrude in the closet scene; and Boleslawski as Laertes. (*Theatre and Art*, 1912.)

— /Hold, hold, my heart;/And you, my sinews, grow not instant old." This was the scene which, for Stanislavsky, "began the important part of the play."[25] Here Hamlet's duplicity begins, and it is manifest that Kachalov's prince consciously chooses his mask of madness at this point. During the scene of the oath, the musical theme of "Hamlet's Solitude" swells up again under the action. At the Ghost's last "Swear!", Hamlet kneels, kisses the place whence the voice issues and speaks the final lines kneeling. On the words "The time is out of joint!" he looks up to heaven, imploringly, and mutters an unheard prayer, before completing the couplet.[26] At that moment, Kachalov's Hamlet seems an avenging angel.

The end of the act was greeted with "friendly applause," and inaugurated the first of four intermissions, one after each act.[27]

ACT II, SCENE 1.   A ROOM.

This replicates Act I, Scene 3. The passage with Reynaldo was cut.

ACT II, SCENE 2.   THE CASTLE.

The tall gold screens, lit from upstage left, form a background for the King and Queen, again in gold, surrounded by their golden court. Rosencrantz and Guildenstern in dark cloaks and overdrapes are played as cringing and obsequious, seldom straightening up from their servile bows.

ACT II, SCENE 3.

This is an attempt to fulfill Craig's wishes. Since neither Hamlet's room nor a garden had proved feasible, this extra scene-change creates a new locale by juxtaposing the cream-colored screens with the golden ones, thus producing a wide corridor that extends in an arc from the furthest downstage wing to the furthest upstage wing opposite. To those familiar with Craig's work, it resembled his design for *The Hour Glass*. The tops of the screens were lost above the proscenium arch. The reddish lighting, reflected off the gilt paper that covers the screens, gives a quivering, glittering effect. The previous scene has ended with the King's "We will try it." This one begins with a dumbshow: Hamlet, the one dark figure in this shimmering ambience, enters at the upstage end of the corridor and slowly passes along it, immersed in his book, surreptitiously watched from the corners by the King and Court.

This mute scene makes a tremendous sensation. "How eloquent, how revealing was the Hamletian silence, how much this scene conveyed," asserts Efros.[28] Rossov of the *Saratovskie Vedomosti* feels that the scene is totally successful in communicating the atmosphere of Hamlet's estrangement, "so alone amidst those enormous walls, so dark amidst the gold, so alien to everything."[29] Even Kachalov found this set extremely helpful in establishing the proper mood, and, perhaps because he could here identify more closely with the character, the critics consider his performance in Act II the high-water mark in its penetration and excitement.[30]

Hamlet crosses downstage and exits, Kachalov's subtext here to flee people. The golden King and Queen move up the corridor and make their exit. Hamlet returns to the deserted stage and plays with his book, pretending to read as he looks round in distrust, anxious that none of the King's spies is behind him. It becomes clear that his madness is self-preservation. In the dialogue with Polonius, Kachalov, following Craig's and Stanislavsky's instructions, is neither scornful nor vicious; instead, he tries to elude his unwished-for interlocutor, to turn the conversation into a joke, warn him with a laugh away from his dishonorable games. The book becomes a refuge. "What do you read, my lord?" Hamlet points to the book and calmly, sorrowfully, ironically, says, "Words." A pause, then he turns to walk along the curved wall and then "Words . . ." A brief moment of silence to find a new stratagem, and, as if passing judgement on all earthly knowledge, ". . . Words."[31]

Rosencrantz and Guildenstern enter timorously, shoulder to shoulder, eyeing each other askance, suspicious of one another, the King, Hamlet,

16. Voronov as Rosencrantz and Sushkevich as Guildenstern. (*Theatre and Art*, 1912.)

everyone. Hamlet, on the other hand, greets them warmly as old friends; but after the first few lines, he begins to have his doubts, cools off and conceals his real feelings behind feigned affection. A lady in the audience recalled how his gestures figured forth his inner state:

the palms of his hands, softly lying on his sword's hilt, gradually squeezed it to prevent his scorn from erupting outwardly, a shadow of a smile said that the cunning of his companions was revealed. When Hamlet-Kachalov conjured his dear friends to say frankly who had sent for them, his feeling of contradiction burst forth sincerely not only in the coloration of his voice but even in the barely seen tremor, the lightning-charged quaver that ran from his shoulder to the palm of his hand, conveying the quaver to the sword-hilt.[32]

Standing between them, he pinches Rosencrantz and Guildenstern and they jump up as if stung. The scene becomes filled with inner tension as he casts uneasy glances at them. Once he is convinced they are spies, he wishes to be rid of them and makes abrupt, rapid crosses.

Suddenly something searing blazed in Kachalov's eye, hidden malice rang forth in his voice, and the rage of wounded affection. With curt convulsive movements he casts from him in different directions the courtiers whom earlier he had wooed, plays a cat-and-mouse game with them. At that moment, one could feel in Kachalov's Hamlet a kind of madness, something of repressed inner frenzy.[33]

After these abrupt crosses and poisonous sarcasm, the line "So shall my anticipation prevent your discovery and your secrecy to the King and Queen moult no feather" is delivered quietly, sternly, with a blend of sorrow and anger. From this point on, Hamlet's speech becomes an inner monologue, ignoring them. He sits beside them, but speaks turned away, head thrown back, eyes cast upwards, his right palm on his forehead. "What a piece of work is a man!" is spoken almost in a whisper.[34]

Craig had hoped that the Players could fly in through windows, like the Chinese jugglers he had seen in Paris who slid down a tightrope by their queues to the sound of bird whistles.[35] This had, not surprisingly, proved to be impossible, but even so, the arrival of the Players changes the mood effectually. Sats had composed delicate fanfares in the style of Lully and Rameau; it is the lightest music so far heard in the production, played by flutes, cymbals, oboes, piccolos and tabors. The Players enter with panache, swaggering and colorful, bearing gaudy wardrobe trunks and property trees: a splendid genre picture, but somewhat out of kilter with the rest of the production.[36] Hamlet lights up with joy and greets them heartily and enthusiastically. Vishnevsky's First Player lacks plasticity, but seems truly Elizabethan in his "spontaneity, expansiveness, power of gesture and voice, and the excitement of a grown-up child."[37] He performs the speech about Pyrrhus with real pathos in his declamation. This act ends without applause.

ACT III, SCENE 1.   THE CASTLE.

The previous set is used, now bathed in yellow light and with the addition of a step-unit at one end. Before Hamlet's entrance, Polonius leads Ophelia to the top of the stairs.

Since Craig's notion of a spectral Death figure had been negated early on, the scene lacks character, and all the critics are disappointed by Kachalov's rendering of "To be or not to be." He enters with head bowed, eyes aglow, staring fixedly ahead, prey to his terrifying thoughts. But there is a kind of strain in the intonation and acting: it is intelligent, subtle, clever in conveying meaning, but it does not work for the audience as the thrilling aria it expects. The spectators are hard put to exonerate Kachalov and conjecture ranges from the belief that he does not share Hamlet's pessimism to the fact that there is nowhere for him to sit down! Kachalov may also be somewhat upstaged. On the line "For in that sleep of death what dreams may come," Polonius forcefully pushes Ophelia down a few steps. There she halts in a ray of light, as the tears stream, unchecked, down her face. On the lines, "But that the dread of something after death,/The undiscovered country, from whose bourn/No traveller returns," she walks down, out of the strip of light into shadow and stands pressed up against the wall. Then, towards the end of the soliloquy, she steps back into the light, so that Kachalov, his head down, practically bumps into her.[38]

The general impression is that Kachalov's Hamlet does not love Ophelia, but either admires some Platonic ideal or is half in love with easeful death. Consequently the critics find him too insipid and unimpassioned in this scene and object to its positioning along the walls. They demand more action, more physical intensity to correspond to Hamlet's state of mind.[39]

Kachalov's subtext in his encounter with Ophelia is "They are poisoning you. I should reveal to you what monstrous thing is tormenting me, but I cannot and will not. If you are like them, it means there is nothing holy in the world." So, he imbues his voice with pity and understanding, not revulsion and contempt. His subtext for "Are you honest?" is "I want to show her to her face that I know all." On "Where's your father?", Gzovskaya pauses briefly and makes an almost imperceptible movement towards the eavesdroppers, hoping to warn him, before answering quietly, "At home, my lord."[40] Throughout this scene, from the moment she returns his tokens, Gzovskaya's Ophelia is drowned in tears. Hamlet observes them and, barely raising his voice, speaks to her out of hopelessness. He moves very close to her ("as if about to bite her," thinks Osanai) and in an undertone says, "Get thee to a nunnery."[41]

ACT III, SCENE 2.   THE CASTLE.

Actually, this is an interlude in the Players' dressing-room, formed by the cream-colored screens simply opened at wide angles. Stanislavsky and

Craig were able to indulge their love of backstage activity by depicting the players putting on make-up and costumes, practising vocal exercises and gestures, and tuning up the instruments. Hamlet delivers the speech on acting with real zeal and conviction, for it certainly corresponded with the Moscow Art Theatre's aesthetic program.

ACT III, SCENE 3.

Most observers felt that this scene was the climax of the production, both in the realization of Craig's concept and in Kachalov's performance. The great hall is, to some degree, a replica of the first court scene, shimmering with gold, with the King and Queen on the throne upstage, high above the action; the courtiers stand in rows along the walls on either side of them. But here the screens are withdrawn to the back, the stage opened up to its full length and depth, and the trap which runs the full width of center-stage opened, so that an actor may descend stairs behind the apron and reveal no more than his head. Other stairs lead upward from the trap to the foot of the throne up center, and there are passageways into the wings from either side of the throne. Thus, the audience of courtiers remains upstage, looking out at the play-within-the-play, which is performed on the apron area, delimited by two huge screen-columns. The deep trap becomes Hamlet's turf. [42]

Although the grandeur of this scene impresses the spectators, it irks Kachalov by forcing him to shuttle back and forth between the two extremes of the stage, and to broaden his gestures and force his voice. "I had the feeling of being in a town square," he was to complain. "And I suddenly noticed in myself, in my own actor's state of being, that it was pushing me into theatricality, conventional stage expressions of animation." [43]

The King and Court enter to a dull and dismal march, which Sats entitles "Power" and which is meant to evoke the tramping of boots. After they take their places, they are lit by a "lilac-greenish gloaming," [44] and some critics moan that in this dim penumbra the King and Queen are so far upstage that they can be seen only with binoculars. [45] The play-within-the-play is performed in brighter lilac and sunny yellow hues, which highlight the motley costumes of the Players.

Hamlet begins upstage at Ophelia's feet, after placing Horatio, who bears the Prince's sword in his folded arms, on the very front edge of the apron, to peer out from behind a column at the King. During the dumbshow (which is performed to music, Lucianus singled out by the critics for his skillful mime), Hamlet leaps up and rushes into the trap to view it more closely. Khokhlov (Horatio) remembered,

Hamlet's crosses were rapid and impetuous. Sometimes he approached me (that is Horatio) making signs for me to watch the King. We were like two conspirators. When Kachalov went down into the trap, he could be seen by the audience only down to the waist. Standing below, as if cut in half, he leaned his elbows on the edge of the Players' area and watched the play. At those moments his face and arms were quite visible. The King's face was barely discernible in the shadows. Kachalov's Hamlet had his back to the king almost the entire time. The only way for Kachalov to look into Claudius' face or to toss him a line was to turn around, his back three-quarters to the audience. As a result, *only* Horatio could watch the King, and Hamlet received what took place through him, a reflection of it. It was difficult and tiring for Kachalov to play this scene, for he had to move around a good deal, cross from place to place, run, cover too much ground.[46]

Hamlet's seeming nonchalance to the King's reactions was a result of the subtext: he had no doubt of his uncle's guilt and although the Court was horrified by the coincidence in the murder of Gonzago, Hamlet retained his outward calm. (To make Hamlet visible in the trap, a blinding spotlight was used which prevented Kachalov from being able to see Claudius — another reason for his reliance on Horatio.)

After the dumbshow, on Ophelia's "What means this, my lord?" Hamlet moves back up to her with the subtext, "I want to interest the King through Ophelia" and sits beside her on a low bench. At the question, "Madam, how like you this play?" he moves up to the Queen and addresses her in a soothing, facetious tone. When Lucianus prepares to commit the murder, Hamlet moves back down past Ophelia, almost as far as Horatio, and in a hectic, impatient temper, runs to the front of the trap with "Begin, murderer; leave thy damnable faces, and begin." During the rest of the play, he moves back up and behind the throne, his hands on its back, advancing his face closer and closer to the King's until at the climax, his head is level with the chair-back; his glance and voice hypnotize Claudius. His tone gradually rises to a shout for the first time in the evening, topped by his uncle's panicky "Give me some light!" In great perturbation the Court flurries off; the King, by a series of ludicrous leaps, flies forward in animal fear into the bright light of the apron, leaving his robes on the throne, as Hamlet, in the trap, pursues him. As the King disappears offstage along a narrow side passage, Hamlet in a delirium of triumph bestrides the Players' stage, enwraps himself in a yellow cloak left by the Player King, capering and electrifying the house with "Go let the strucken deer go weep,/The hart ungallèd play."[47] Almost every commentator on the performance mentions that line as the single most thrilling moment of Kachalov's interpretation — a kind of antic mummery whose hysteria concealed horror. "This moment is worth the whole performance," declared the critic for *Yuzhny Kray*.[48] Kachalov "forced the spectator to shudder with his long-drawn-out cry . . . The audience was overwhelmed by a powerful and luminously refined point of interpretation, much aided by Kachalov's rich voice."[49] Hamlet dances a predatory victory dance, flapping his yellow cloak about him.

Craig at a general rehearsal had told the dubious Kachalov that in the Mousetrap scene, "Hamlet's movement must be like lightning cutting across the stage. The actor's temperament must here be revealed with maximum intensity in strong gusts of fury, despair, irony and finally triumph."[50] The actor had feared that this would destroy the integrity of his subdued interpretation but finally, throwing restraint to the winds, he gave full play to his voice and movement, and became the powerful masculine figure of Craig's imagination. The scene caught fire, and, significantly, here Craig's intention and the audience's expectation were fully in accord.

Yet even this powerful episode is effaced for some by the scene with the recorders, "where mummery and indignation, heartbreak and sarcasm reached a zenith."[51] Hamlet irritably pokes the recorder in Guildenstern's chest and finally flings it in his face.

The scene has been followed with breath-bated attention and its excitement and success are so great that Craig is called before the curtain at its conclusion — another unheard-of occurrence in this temple of art. Calls for Stanislavsky and Sulerzhitsky allow them to join him in receiving an accolade.[52]

The scene of the King's prayer had been cut at the final dress rehearsal to keep the production from running overtime.[53] This may be no great loss in view of Massalitinov's uninspired performance, but certainly conduces to the idea of Hamlet as a monodrama.

ACT III, SCENE 4.   THE QUEEN'S CLOSET.

Coming as it does after such a spectacular episode, the scene in the Queen's bedchamber could not fail to be an anticlimax, particularly since the spectators looked forward to the customary vituperative, *Angst*-ridden portrayals.

Here the cream-colored screens are arranged much as in Act I, Scene 3, with a recess center, and a square white bed, the tone of the lighting yellowish-grey: the impression was of a "sailcloth summerhouse," "the most ordinary Moscow suburban villa."[54] And even worse was the Ghost's appearance, squeezed up against the folds of the canvas where "it is reminiscent of a garment on a hook, a hung-up sheet."[55]

The critics find the scene too even and monotonous. Hamlet expresses only "quiet love" for his mother, using the middle register of his voice, after the unwonted shouting in the previous scene. The one outstanding moment is said to be when he lays his head in his mother's lap. Knipper as Queen, no longer in her golden raiment but in a dark beige Mother Hubbard, wimple and close-fitting cap with earlaps, falls naturally into a "Chekhovian" tone which seems out of keeping. Even so, the act ends with an ovation.[56]

ACT IV.   THE CASTLE.

Scenes 1, 2 and 3 are all cut, following both traditional stage practice and the need to abbreviate the evening. The Queen's throne is placed upstage center, flanked below by two square cream-colored column/screens. The

17. The Queen's closet, sketch by A. Lyubimov. (*Theatre and Art,* 1912.)

stage is hemmed into a semi-circle by golden screens, reproducing the corridor in Act II, but backed by open space, so that the impression is not of a room but of a garden with blue sky above. The scene begins with the Queen seated; on either side, in a diagonal line, stand four ladies of the court in white costumes marked off into squares. Two more ladies stand at the end of each line facing the audience. These extras hold music-books and sing a madrigal, which is interrupted by the entrance of Ophelia, who flies on to the stage and hides behind the ladies. Her silver dress is now covered by a faded, tattered garment of black silk gauze, with bits of grass and straw clinging to it. According to Gzovskaya, she, Lilina and Stanislavsky had designed it, following Dürer and Holbein drawings, with no reference to Craig's wishes.[57]

The ladies make their exit on the King's line "Follow her close" but return again when Laertes' mutineers begin storming the castle and stand around the Queen in postures of alarm, themselves protected by impassive guards. Stanislavskian realism takes over at this point. The iron doors (offstage) are staved in and a life-like crash accompanied by assorted crowd noise is heard; in rushes a horde of insurgent plebeians in picturesque rags. The unruly mob, composed of MAT apprentices, includes young Mikhail Chekhov as a "ragamuffin." "I pounded my property axe on the iron doors with such inspiration that you might have thought the whole production revolved around me."[58] Whatever Craigian atmosphere had been produced was utterly dispelled by this moment.

The mad scene is played without real flowers, a touch which is felt to increase the pathos. (Ellen Terry and Helena Modjeska had already used that piece of business in Europe and America but it was new to Russia.) Ophelia plaits an imaginary wreath of rue and addresses all her remarks to a Hamlet only she can see. Her songs are patched together from vagrant snatches of medieval Danish folksongs, accompanied by the composer Sats at the piano.[59] Of the scene in general, Efros writes,

It is done superbly, not at all in the stereotypical way with distinct "points." But here the acting begins to become externalized, a shell without a kernel. One may admire Ophelia and her performer, but one wants more, one wants it to be, if not shocking, at least deeply moving. The actress succeeds in this only to a small degree. Very great and subtle technique, but no strength and sincerity of feeling.[60]

Others also complain that it is all pose and no suffering or poetry.[61] Still, the scene is met with applause.

ACT V, SCENE 1.   A CHURCHYARD.

Craig loathed Stanislavsky's realization of this scene, which he considered "banal and cheap."[62] In place of his conceptions of a crater into which the court peers from a great height, or a low torchlit catacomb, the stage is cluttered with cream-colored cubes and step-units and a plain rectangular downstage trap for the grave. The screens suggest the inside of a church, which makes no sense of the gravediggers, and one reviewer gets the impression that the scene takes place at the coping of a well.[63] Nevertheless, the French observer Jacques Rouché finds it to be the most moving scene he has ever witnessed.[64]

As the gravediggers toss out bones, they fall into a small rectangular basket, which is carried off by the Second Gravedigger. Gribunin's First Gravedigger is played in a tone of realistic, good-natured vulgarity, and is praised in the reviews, with the demur that his is the easiest role in the play.[65]

Hamlet returns to Denmark swathed in a black toga-like cape. Most of his remarks on the corruptibility of human flesh are cut, as has been the Queen's description of Ophelia's suicide, which makes the girl's death as great a surprise to an uninformed spectator as it is to Hamlet. The funeral cortège enters through five column-like screens of grey canvas: the King and Queen, Horatio and the Priest, followed by six supernumeraries, two of them bearing torches. The Queen tosses three small white flowers on to the

18. The graveyard, sketch by A. Lyubimov. (*Theatre and Art,* 1912.)

coffin ("maimèd rites" indeed) and the entire scene is permeated with a pungent sadness (Chekhovian gloom, one wonders?). Hamlet's line, "Forty thousand brothers / Could not, with their quantity of love / Make up my sum" suddenly thrills and startles the audience as if the suit of mourning were thrown aside and Kachalov is, for the first time, revealing Hamlet the lover.[66]

ACT V, SCENE 2.   THE CASTLE.

The gold screens recede on either side of the stage in a zigzag, leaving an empty expanse of blue sky up center. Below it is a platform for the throne, with two step-units of five steps each leading down to the stage floor. (In later performances, the center gap will be filled with black.) Craig is displeased with both the overly bright lighting and the cluttered aspect of the stage.[67]

Osric's costume is elaborately fanciful: he wears a vaguely Moorish cap with long plaited ornaments ending in flowers, and chain-mail covered with a tabard of concentric squares and rectangles. No courtiers are present at the duel, which compels Hamlet to address the line "You that look pale and tremble at this chance" to Horatio and Osric alone. Hamlet and Laertes fight

19. Detail of the stage picture of the end of *Hamlet*. Gertrude, Hamlet and Claudius lie dead on the steps, as Fortinbras, in his archangelic guise, gazes down at them, and banners are draped over their bodies. At back, the waving sheaves of spears that attracted ridicule. (N.N. Chushkin, *Gamlet-Kachalov* [Moscow: Iskusstvo, 1966].)

it out in heavy gauntlets and encumbered by their overdrapes, but both are singled out for their agility. (Kachalov fences better than Rossi, according to some.)[68] Hamlet's body is laid out on the center steps on a black cloth, the dead queen directly above him, and Laertes below on the stage floor. The King has, suitably, died at the foot of the throne. To quote Stanislavsky,

Far beyond the arch a virtual forest of spears moving back and forth and the banners of the approaching Fortinbras; he himself, like an Archangel, ascending the throne at whose foot lie the bodies of King and Queen; the solemn and triumphant sounds of a soul-stirring funeral march; the huge, slowly descending banners that covered the dead but smiling face of the great purifier of the earth who had finally discovered the secret of earthly life in the arms of death. So did Craig picture the court that had become Hamlet's Golgotha.[69]

Craig is in fact greatly pleased with the finale, although he has misgivings about the stagey trick of the moving spears (meant to suggest an innumerable army) and thinks they looked like sheaves of waving grain. The critics agree, finding the device laughable and smacking of the pantomime.[70] The archangel motif of Fortinbras is carried out in his costume, which bears a golden cross on a white tabard and a nimbus-like shield behind him. As Fortinbras' soldiers fill up the stage like a rising tide, they bear on their shoulders banners of white, black and indigo-blue which are laid on Hamlet, until the black body is covered by a mound of white. But the element most conducive to the solemn ending is Ilya Sats's wild and majestic funeral march, which chimes in on the line "Let four captains / Bear Hamlet, like a soldier, to the stage." This march was to become so popular that when the MAT actor Burdzhalov died, it was played during his funeral procession through the Moscow streets.[71]

10
REACTION

It was almost one o'clock in the morning when the performance ended, and yet the curtain call met with another loud ovation. Craig came on stage once more, with Stanislavsky and Kachalov; the appearance of this last was in response to repeated insistence from the audience, for the Moscow Art Theatre had a rule of no separate calls for actors. When the curtains finally closed, Craig found the entire company, technical staff and orchestra ranged behind him, congratulating and applauding, as a fanfare blared. The audience, reluctant to depart and overhearing the celebration, insisted on the curtains opening and renewed its applause.

The two managers, Stanislavsky and Nemirovich, then presented Craig with an enormous wreath, inscribed in English "To the noble poet of the theatre." Nemirovich made a brief address, wistfully asserting that no differences, political, racial or geographical, can "ever divide those who are joined by one common aspiration — the perfection of their art."[1] For days Craig had been making a list of conventional phrases to use on such an occasion — "Amazing what they have done," "They have surpassed themselves," "Shakespeare would be astounded" (this last rather ambiguous), and had even used one of these, "One of the best things you have done," after the final rehearsal.[2] But in the furore of the moment, he was gratified at being lionized and thought the evening an overwhelming success. He wrote to his sister the next day, "I won't say it will equal the touch of 'Masque of Love' or 'Acis,' but it will do its best under the disadvantage of having cost the management over £14,000." He appended a sketch of himself jumping through Stanislavsky's hoop.[3]

Not everyone had been so carried away by momentary enthusiasm. At home, Kachalov noted in his diary, "Dubious success of Hamlet. A difficult season, but an interesting one."[4] The least satisfied was Alisa Koonen. Watching the performance from the students' gallery and knowing all the dreams and projects that had gone into the production, she had been upset at not understanding what was going on on stage. The usual electric contact between audience and stage at the MAT seemed to be lacking, and the performance to drag on forever. Chilled by this she had stayed in her seat during the intermissions and at the play's end the applause struck her as meager. Without joining in the on-stage celebration, she ran home. She began to recognize that something important had happened on stage but could not get over the coldness of it all. She remembered Stanislavsky's words, "Some failures in the theatre are more important than the most touted success."[5]

As Stanislavsky had foretold, the critics were anxious to show off their learning, and all sorts of names were dropped in the reviews, from Beardsley and Nicholson to Terborch and Gourmont, from *Kunst und Dekoration* to the *Archidoxis Magnia*. Craig's *Hamlet* was a touchstone by which the erudition and timeliness of connoisseurs might be tested. It was also a shibboleth that divided its appraisers into two armed camps.

The conservatives, not unexpectedly, were unfavorable, placing the blame for the production's flaws squarely on the design concept. Their favorite image was of "stifling." *Hamlet* was said to be

smothered by Craig's screens. They imprisoned air and light [and] interested the audience only as a stunt. Then they began to weigh on it, became a nuisance in their monotony and suffocated it . . . it is very difficult for the actor to perform. He is a kind of afterthought. First come the gimmicks of Gordon Craig, the screens and cubes. And only then the actor. Tacked on . . . Stanislavsky and Nemirovich are head and shoulders above this swell-headed Englishman. Let him learn from them, not they from him.[6]

An impression of stylization which could more accurately be termed sterilization.[7]

What sort of glorious genius is this, who over the course of three years cannot cope with Hamlet! . . . The monotony of the screens eventually begins to bring the spectator to the verge of illness and despair. You want to cry out and run away. No light, no air, it's stifling. Screens, screens, and more screens. Screens without end.[8]

It was an evil day for the theatre world when Craig's screens appeared and were apportioned more space in the reporting than the performers themselves . . . without these screens, it would be greeted as a poorly performed tragedy and nothing more.[9]

The critic Aleksandr Koiransky (who was later to emigrate to the United States and translate Chekhov's *Three Sisters* for Katherine Cornell) spoke of sitting in the auditorium for five hours and, on leaving, finding himself unable to communicate with the occasional beauties of the production because they were blocked from his mind by "the sharp corners of the desolate cardboard constructions, the endless space, the nauseating gold paper, the right-angled intersection of lines, worthy sketches for some elevator or other technical structure, modernistic cubes for some ultra-modern smoking-room, marmalade-colored effects from a confectioner's shop-window."[10]

Some of the more reflective Moscow commentators were willing, with reservations, to accept the underlying principles of the production. One correspondent to a provincial paper thought the Spartan décor aided the tragedy in creating a proper environment and giving "centrality" to the hero.[11] The MAT's pre-eminent publicist and analyst Nikolay Efros observed,

In the intermissions there was no dearth of grumbling about the screens. But the architectonic lines and lighting successfully suggested the necessary atmosphere, the spectator was conveyed into the basic character and mood of the given place and moment. And that in abundance. . . . What was the fate of *Hamlet* at the Art Theatre? Does Moscow consider its extraordinary expectations fulfilled? Will it inscribe this production on the active or retired list of its favorite theatre? I cannot answer the first two questions, but the third must boldly be answered in the affirmative. . . . The theatre has, amid extraordinary upheavals and creative pangs, reverentially prepared this production. And anyone who cares about the theatre, who cherishes art, will bow low to it as a result. [12]

If Craig's success for the Muscovites was problematical, Kachalov's was not. Audiences, nourished on legends of the spasmodic, turbulent Hamlet of Mochalov, were taken aback by this contemplative, low-keyed interpretation, but for the most part, accepted it. It was noted that not once in the long evening did he slap his breast or explode with passion, and that Kachalov's personal dislike for rhetoric led him to avoid heroism and to display pensive reasonableness. Lyubov Gurevich observed that he used only the middle register of his voice, even when he shouted, and that much of his performance was obviously not yet set; but for all the restraint and unsureness, this Hamlet reflected the spiritual crisis going on in the souls of Russian intellectuals at that moment. [13] The MAT's most hostile assessor, A. R. Kugel, editor of *Theatre and Art*, was forced to admit:

I have never seen such a Hamlet, although I have seen many times over ten famous actors in this part. Craig's production also made for great attention and, with all its gaffes, I found it brilliant and totally unappreciated by our theatre critics. . . . After Kachalov, all Hamlets will seem made out of theatrical cardboard. [14]

Of the other performers, kudos were meted out to Polonius, the Player King, Rosencrantz and Guildenstern and Osric. Luzhsky's portrayal of the wily old courtier was said to reveal a medieval version of Chekhov's "Man in a Shell." [15] But the King, Horatio and Laertes were unanimously damned. Massalitinov's Claudius looked and sounded like an archdeacon and seemed too drab ever to seduce the Queen; there was no complexity to his motivation and so he seemed a villain out of a melodrama. [16] Young Boleslawski was unable to give definition to Laertes; and despite the sincerity and soulfulness to be found in Khokhlov's rendition, not to mention his beautiful make-up, his Horatio was judged to be "pallid and uninteresting." [17]

Knipper, whom Craig had cajoled into the role of Gertrude, was found to be a "rather pasteboard image, a queen in general and nothing but a queen, neither the transgressing wife nor Hamlet's mother." Some spoke of her "Chekhovian" intonations. [18] Even Craig later admitted that she was a "disaster," while Gzovskaya as Ophelia he condemned as "just nothing but a box of sweets." [19] Gzovskaya, however, was a bone of critical contention.

The conservatives often referred to her as the best thing in the play, while the avant-garde criticized her as "colorless. A sweet exterior and an absence of psychology."[20]

Craig had been very eager to have his work evaluated by Western journalists, for only then could Europe taste his triumph and commissions be forthcoming. While in London, he had tried to persuade Hitchenson to review it for *The Graphic*; but Hitchenson asked too much money from the editors. The Moscow correspondent of the theatrical weekly *The Era* claimed ignorance of the Art Theatre, leading *The Mask* to wonder, "After this, one may indeed ask, *which* Era?"[21] Of British journals, only the *Times* considered the event news, and Terence Philip's report was glowing.

Mr Craig has the singular power of carrying the spiritual significance of words and dramatic situations beyond the actor to the scene in which he moves. By the simplest of means he is able in some mysterious way to evoke almost any sensation of time or space, the scenes even in themselves suggesting variations of human emotion. . . . the production is a remarkable triumph for Mr Craig, and it is impossible to say how wide an effect such a completely realized success of his theories may have on the theatres of Europe.[22]

It was Philip's critique and Craig's own initial reports which convinced the Western world that *Hamlet* had been an unqualified success, and laid the ground for later legend. Jacques Rouché, director of the Théâtre des Arts in Paris, spread word of

that grandiose simplicity, which allows the word to expand over the entire stage, leaves ineradicable impressions: you feel yourself in the presence of a totally original work, whose whole as well as each of its parts is animated by intelligence. Then one understands the form the author wishes to give to the art work of the future, the effort which will lead, after stylization of scenery and character, to the elimination of the actor.[23]

Designers in the theatre were among those most bowled over by the production. Simov, who had witnessed Craig's tantrums at the runthrough, nevertheless declared that for his generation of scenic designers, "the fantastic screening, the bold solution of bothersome problems of color (for instance, the golden mass of the court walls) literally staggered us and knocked us back on our heels."[24]

Among the spectators had been the eighteen-year-old-poet Vladimir Mayakovsky, who, with his friends David and Mariya Burlyuk, had front row seats. (Mayakovsky was the Burlyuks' guest, for he was too poor to attend the theatre unless he received a student pass or a complimentary ticket.) They were struck by the dependence on "the imagination of the onlooker," and the silent, watchful young poet was most taken by Ophelia's frailness and transparency. According to his companions, it was at this performance that the idea for his own imagistic tragedy *Vladimir Mayakovsky* took shape. Hamlet's role-playing and questioning of identity certainly seem to be present in it.[25]

Indeed, it was the individual cultured spectator, untroubled by partisanship or the need to render a verdict, who most appreciated the Art Theatre's achievement. Stanislavsky must have been gratified to receive a most appreciative letter from the literary historian A. E. Gruzinsky:

What a wonderful production. Rumors reached me from various sources that somewhere some people were dissatisfied. I don't know how or why, I only know: I immediately and intuitively accepted the novelty of the staging as something artistically beautiful and interesting in itself; moreover, it all entered my consciousness at once and seduced me without a protest, as something legitimate and natural, and yet, when you think it over, you realize that much in it is really an upheaval, a theatrical revolution. Deliberation brings another argument to bear in favor of such a production: a different production with the usual sets, etc. would obviously threaten to convey the play into the realm of complicated props, the recreation of far away and long ago and run the risk of transforming it into an *historical tragedy*, and this burden would crush the concept of Hamlet. Then as now the psychological lines of Shakespeare's concept are easily and freely kept uppermost, unburdened by the complication of historical real-life embroidery.[26]

The wits, on the other hand, were quick to make hay of *Hamlet's* more controversial features. Back in 1910, the cartoonist Andrey had shown Stanislavsky digging a grave surrounded by skulls numbered for rehearsals and gravestones marked *Twelfth Night, Julius Caesar, Shylock.*[27] Now the caricaturists' mocking suspicions of failure were realized. "A Night in Kammerherr Street" showed "the ghost of Shakespeare among the cubes of Craig"; "Hamlet in Cubes" depicted another graveyard, this one with Craig sourly delving away as Stanislavsky addressed a skull with "Alas, poor Hamlet! So much fuss, work, expectations, hopes — ." Another cartoon exhibited Craig puffing on a pipe and proudly leaning against his screens, while a gigantic Hamlet rose up behind him; the caption: "In vain Craig blows smoke in our eyes; he can't smoke 'Hamlet' off the stage!"[28] On January 21, at The Bat ("Chauve-souris") cabaret run by the MAT's own Nikita Baliev, Vakhtangov performed a skit, parodying Kachalov in a soliloquy which complained of the bitter necessity of having to play Hamlet in the manner of Craig.[29]

The Englishman himself was probably unaware of the mockery. As if to block reality from his mind, Craig plunged into reading *Le Théâtre de l'Âme*, by the French symbolist mystic Edouard Schuré. Now that the production had opened he was willing to let bygones be bygones, and when Alisa Koonen saw him again at Stanislavsky's home, the two men were clearly reconciled. Stanislavsky joked and kept off perilous topics, and Craig chatted away garrulously.[30] He left Moscow on January 28, 1912, sending Lilina a note giving my deepest and most true love to your husband. He has something in him which has no name and which moves me terribly when I stop to think of it. All that he desires shall come to pass and his reward too.

And I have one wish for him which must also come to pass — that in time to come he shall work *alone*. It is the best wish I have to give for he is a great being.[31]

Whether this last clause was a parting shot at Suler and the MAT administration, or a cryptic suggestion that Craig had no further intention of collaborating cannot be determined. But once Craig was back in Florence, he composed another missive for "John Semar":

No more Art Theatres for me. This is in no way to be construed as suggesting dissatisfaction with the Theatre of M. Stanislavsky. On the contrary my enthusiasm for the Moscow Art Theatre is just what it was. There are one or two rats in the building but they don't count; as soon as the ship shows the least sign of sinking, they'll desert, and we shall all see them . . . and their tails. But after such a theatre, other Art Theatres are out of the reckoning . . . and other non-art theatres non-existent.

But the Art of the theatre still calls, and I, feeling refreshed after my late experience at Moscow, turn to the question of the Art with renewed pleasure and determination.[32]

Craig may have turned his back on *Hamlet*, but for Stanislavsky, the most important critical consensus was still to come. In April 1912, the Moscow Art Theatre went on its annual tour to St. Petersburg and included *Hamlet* in its repertory. By that time, the first reports had been disseminated widely and the intelligentsia of the northern capital was eagerly awaiting its chance to pass judgment. Artistically and theatrically, Petersburg fancied itself more avant-garde and sophisticated than Moscow: it was the *locus* of Dyagilev's *World of Art* movement, the mystical and symbolist salons of Vyacheslav Ivanov, Dmitry Merezhkovsky and Zinaida Gippius, the theatrical experimentation of Nikolay Evreinov and Vsevolod Meyerhold. The Moscow Art Theatre had always been regarded with the attitude "What good can come out of Nazareth?" The leading journal of stage criticism, *Theatre and Art*, edited by the astute and waspish A. R. Kugel who wrote under the pseudonym "Homo Novus," mounted periodic attacks on the MAT's dramas of mood and psychological realism. Although the Petersburg climate was favorable to Craig, it looked askance at Stanislavsky.

Consequently, the theatre was uneasy and dreaded the opening. Kachalov had been getting progressively more tired and feared that he would be unable to finish out the season. In Petersburg, he sought medical advice and treated himself with sponge-baths, cold showers and headache powders, while Lilina sent bouillon cubes to every performance. The actor told Koonen that he envied every passerby's freedom, whereas he, Kachalov, was constrained to guard his voice, take care crossing streets and so on.

"Even on days *Hamlet* isn't produced, I can't feel at liberty. I'm compelled to recall that in a day or two I'll go on stage as the Prince of Denmark and that I have to have enough strength for it."[33]

In the main, the reception of *Hamlet* was respectful and the cognoscenti admitted the production's originality, audacity, talent and responsiveness to the philosophic meaning of the play. There were some dissenters, among them the poet Aleksandr Blok who noted in his diary, "Hamlet at the Art Theatre (bad),"[34] and the traditionalist actor Nikolay Rossov, who mocked at the intellectual pretensions of making lilac and pink and straight angles stand for religious symbolism. "Craig's theatre is a laughable appeal for universal harmony; its threats are pale blue symbols, like skimmed milk."[35] The reviewer for *Zvezda* (*The Star*) mourned the "wave of decadence" that had swept over the MAT and found nothing of value in it.[36]

But more perceptive observers were aware that the central flaw in the production was the discrepancy between concept and realization. A. Rostislavov, in an extended critique for *Theatre and Art*, admired the sculptural abstraction of the figures, even as he deplored the shocking contrast between the tinsel paper on the screens and the real brocade of the costumes. He particularly disliked the lighting, for "the powerful contrast between light and shadow disfigures the face and turns it into a kind of crudely carved painted mask with black holes instead of eyes and a black shadow under the nose hiding the mobility of the mouth." In addition to the garishness of the colors and the density of the shadows, the lighting was characterized by provincial ineptitude for "thanks to footlights lower than the level of the floor, in every scene where bright light was not diffused from above, the floor and lower part of the wall were in rather thick shadow and its lights hideously cut off the characters' feet."[37]

But it was the Symbolist poet and polemicist Valery Bryusov, who had worked with Meyerhold at the MAT workshop in Pozharsky Street, who best expressed this central dichotomy, when he stated that the conventionality of the production was only superficial. He noted that the MAT had failed to grasp the principle of the screens and cubes, by using them to construct realistic locales. The real cloth of the costumes, realistic intonations, and even the realistic duel clashed with the design concept.

A conventionalized staging requires conventionalized acting; the Art Theatre failed to understand this. . . . Instead of a court there was a hint of a court; in correspondence with this we should have heard not a shout but a hint of a shout. The platform was indicated by parallelipipeds disappearing aloft; lifelike movements, lifelike gestures should have been indicated by conventionalized gestures, like those we see in old Byzantine icons. A house without windows, doors and ceilings, the monochromatic denuded walls, even the stone graveyard itself with its square pillars would not have seemed strange and inappropriate if we had seen them filled with substantially "conventionalized" creatures, with conventionalized gestures and vocal intonations.[38]

The designer and art critic Aleksandr Benois, a prime mover in the *World of Art*, took the side of the actors, asserting that Craig's idea "of presenting Hamlet outside a definite era, amid 'abstract' sets . . . is not in the nature . . . of actors. They are used to other ways of 'living on stage,' have other ways of gaining definition, and other ways of feeling and understanding." In his view, the Art Theatre was to be blamed for the pretentiousness and taste-lessness of the production, in repudiating its usual goal of truth to life. Stanislavsky, he deduced, had refrained from personally appearing in the play because he instinctively knew that his subtle acting could have none but an ill effect on this "kingdom of cardboard boxes, tinsel and magic lanterns."[39]

More than in Moscow, Kachalov's performance polarized opinion. Some saw his Hamlet as an anemic melancholic, a somnambulist whose gestures were too modern and Russian; or too much in line of descent from Turgenev's "superfluous men" and Chekhov's characters. Others, Bryusov among them, were pleased to see the Danish Prince removed from his pedestal and turned into "one of those whom we daily meet among our dear friends in drawing-rooms, at opening nights and vernissages."[40]

In Petersburg, too, parody had a field-day with the play. At the "theatre of miniatures," the Crooked Mirror, Evreinov staged a divertissement called "The Inspector General," with scenes from Gogol's comedy presented in five ways: as if directed by a traditional director, a student of Stanislavsky's, Max Reinhardt, Mack Sennett, and Craig. In this last, the master of ceremonies introduced the "student of Gordon Craig" as "a young lord, former Oxford student and well-known footballer."

Suffice it to say that the action is played out in some point in infinite interplanetary space. The actual method of staging *The Inspector General*, however, we have decided to keep secret, so that the novelty of the spectacle will impress the audience. I will only allow myself to say with some assurance: the immortal comedy is, in this version, capable of reducing you to real tears.[41]

Gogol's grotesque bureaucrats came on muffled in black cloaks and masks, the Mayor's wife and daughter in shrouds. The constables were garbed as archangels, and they all delivered their farcical lines to the accompaniment of a church organ, tolling bells, a plangent violin and a choir singing a requiem.

Stanislavsky's reaction to these rebukes and jokes was despondent, especially when the critics that season went wild over Reinhardt's *Oedipus* with its massive crowd-scenes. After all, had not the MAT originally wanted Craig to mount *Oedipus and the Sphinx*? "I cannot recall when we've been so insulted as this year," Stanislavsky wrote to a friend. "To cap the climax, Benois abused us and Craig. . . . And Benois was our warmest adherent. On top of this comes 'Oedipus,' that dreadful Berlin 'Oedipus' and creates a furore in Moscow itself, where we have been trying to educate people for 30 years. So I don't know whether to go into a monastery or open a circus."[42]

At the end of the run, Kachalov was ecstatic at his release and proclaimed to Alisa Koonen, "No *Hamlet*? You know what that means? I'm a man again! The most ordinary man! I can walk as much as I like, even run, I can eat what I like, I can drink champagne, I can stand like a fool staring in a shopwindow at the silly things there. To hell with powders, showers, sponge-baths!"[43] But Stanislavsky in his conscientious way set about to perfect the production so that it could play an important role in the next season's repertory and come closer to Craig's original ideas. "To improve and even follow Craig's concept to the end — changing the sets before the spectator's eyes without closing the curtain" more rehearsals would be required. In addition, he proposed replacing Knipper with his sister, recasting Laertes, and altering the costumes.[44] But in early December, Gzovskaya fell ill and both *Hamlet* and the Turgenev comedies, which Stanislavsky called "our bread-and-butter plays" had to be temporarily removed from the repertory. When Shakespeare's tragedy reopened, some minor changes had been effected — there was a new Fortinbras and Voltimand — but the production was much as it had been by the time Isadora Duncan finally beheld it.

Isadora, who had to some degree engineered the entire extravaganza, saw the screens in action on February 22, 1913, in the company of Herbert Beerbohm Tree. Lilina reported in a postcard to Craig,

they both find the screens were beautiful but the actors not quite good. Mr Kachalov was not well and played very slowly; and Mrs Baranovskaya [Gzovskaya's alternate] is not pretty enough to be a nice Ophelia. And the queen also was played by a new actress [Z. S. Sokolova] because Mrs Knipper is ill and lying in her bed with a broken rib. So you see they could not judge quite right and it is rather annoying.[45]

Hamlet remained in the MAT repertory for three seasons in all, with a total of forty-seven performances: 1911/12, fifteen in Moscow, eight in Petersburg; 1912/13, eighteen times; 1913/14, six times with the final performance on March 11, 1914.[46] Not many persons can have seen it. In 1915, Nemirovich-Danchenko who had been longing to co-opt the production, planned a complete overhaul, with very thorough recasting (different Queen and Laertes, for a start), a fresh interpretation of the Ghost, the reinstatement of the King's prayer, and more rehearsals for Kachalov. Writing to Sulerzhitsky, Nemirovich explained:

Of course, Konstantin Sergeevich and you and Craig helped Kachalov in full measure. Maybe you three have already done all that Kachalov needs. But if you take into consideration that I have lived the role of Hamlet in my younger days, that its very image and the role were gestating in my soul continually till recently, that, in addition, I have my own methods of influencing an actor and that, finally, I know Kachalov's potential as well as you and K. S. do, it would be strange not to use all this.[47]

But the time required for the projected changes was more than the theatre could afford, especially during wartime and with the establishment of Sulerzhitsky's Studio workshop (which Nemirovich considered a "pest-house"). Not until 1942 would Nemirovich-Danchenko get the chance to work on his own, unfinished production of *Hamlet*.

11
REPERCUSSIONS

Despite the brief tenure of *Hamlet* in the Art Theatre repertory, the production's influence was profound and far-reaching, and, regardless of critical controversy, outside of Russia the news spread that it had been a full-fledged success. This notion rested in part on the favorable reports of the *Times* and Jacques Rouché. But Craig himself did nothing to belie it, and even indignantly denied rumors that the staging had been expensive. In *The Mask*, under the disguise of "John Semar" he called it an "Era-making event."[1] Will Rothenstein and other friends spoke of it as "a triumph" and "naturally thought that what he had done for the Russian stage he could do for the English stage."[2] This opinion was confirmed when Craig opened an exhibition of his *Hamlet* models in London in September 1912 at the Leicester Galleries. The models, static and carefully lit, were only marginally related to the Moscow production; they better represented Craig's conceptual intention than had the staging realized by Sulerzhitsky and live actors. Craig's catalogue notes were uncharacteristically modest and remarkably generous to the MAT: "I wish publicly to thank my friend, Mr Konstantin Stanislavsky, — the one ideal figure in the Russian theatre, — for his affectionate and loyal support of my work at a time when all other celebrated theatres found it incomprehensible."[3]

All these factors combined to provide Craig with the best press notices his work had yet received in England. Although the *Times* thought the sketch for the court scenes ugly, it regarded the exhibition as a whole "exhilarating" and admired the "serene and mysterious spaciousness which Mr Craig can charge with what emotion he likes." Ignorant of Kachalov's and Massalitinov's performances, the *Times* could say of the sketches "we have never had so Hamlet-like a Hamlet as No 31, and King Claudius is realized in all his crafty sensuality for the first time."[4] All the papers recognized the practical efficiency of the screens and wistfully conjectured at the freshness the Moscow *Hamlet* must have shown. A full-page article with pictures in *The Graphic* concluded, "whether Mr. Craig's interpretation evokes satisfaction or provokes fury in the onlooker, really does not matter in the least. Progress is being made in the right direction."[5] The exhibit toured to Manchester, Liverpool, Leeds and Dublin, no doubt leaving its imprint on the impressionable minds of local *aficionados*.

Slowly, the example was taking hold. In July of that year Lugné-Poë, director of the eclectic Théâtre Antoine in Paris, had written to Stanislavsky asking, in a patronizing manner, for critical and iconographic material on the *Hamlet*: "I intend to stage *Hamlet* in the spring in Paris in a totally new way with Suzanne Dupré. I should very much like to know what that amusing dilettante Craig might come up with. I have read all his writings, but it isn't practical."[6] Lugné-Poë's condescension was not seconded by the Russians. The important Petersburg journal *Theatre and Art* not only published several articles reflective of varying opinions about the MAT *Hamlet*, but ran a three-part translation of Craig's "Actor and Übermarionette," illustrated with many of his sketches and drawings. A production of Goethe's *Faust*, performed at the Nezlobin Theatre in Moscow at the same time, had several sets that reflected a Craigian influence, especially in the use of stairs. Meyerhold was the first to adapt the *Hamlet* model to a modern play in 1914, when he used cubes and rectilinears as the basic structural components in Pinero's *Mid-Channel*, at the Alexandra Theatre, with settings by Golovin. This "cubist" production met with failure, not least because of the dissonance between the play's tone and the conventionalized setting.[7]

Craig and Kachalov had conclusively dispelled, for progressive theatrical practitioners, the nineteenth century vision of *Hamlet* as a romantic costume pageant. When Boleslawski redirected the play in Prague in 1921, using Kachalov, Knipper and Massalitinov in their original roles, the designs by Gremislavsky utilized the portability of Craig's screens and quick scene changes, although the acting was more in the MAT's mode of psychological naturalism.[8] The 1924 *Hamlet* at the Second Moscow Art Theatre, which featured Mikhail Chekhov as the Prince, based many of its "tragic-grotesque" elements on Craig's premises: undifferentiated courtiers in bald, rodent-like make-ups; Claudius as a crystallization of evil; an abstract monumentality, with a golden pyramid of a court; and a ninny Ophelia. Chekhov's Hamlet sought the mystical "invisible world" that Craig had hoped Kachalov would seek, but where Kachalov had been rational and contemplative, Chekhov was morbid and erratic. He saw the play as "the striving of Hamlet's soul towards the light," "the tragedy of a Man who undergoes a cataclysm."[9] The Second MAT had developed out of Sulerzhitsky's studio and Vakhtangov was one of its inspirations: no doubt Craig's teachings had been handed down in modified form. In fact, the *Hamlet* work had spawned the studios that the students working at the MAT as apprentices and supernumeraries developed into hotbeds of experiment and innovation.[10]

Meyerhold, late in life, half-jokingly said "Engrave on my tombstone: 'Here lies an actor and director who never played and never staged *Hamlet*.'"[11] The production of Shakespeare's tragedy was an unfulfilled dream throughout his career; he even envisaged a theatre where that play alone would be performed in the versions of Stanislavsky, Craig, Reinhardt and himself. From 1923 to 1926 *Hamlet* was advanced for the repertory of his theatre, and he hoped to open his new theatre building with it in 1936, with settings by Picasso. But none of his plans were realized. As early as 1915, he had aped Craig in staging "The Mousetrap" and "Ophelia's Madness" as improvised pantomimes during a recital of his studio, but his motive was to get to the heart of the popular stage that had inspired Shakespeare. Heinrich Notman who played Hamlet in those fragments was coached to be the diametric opposite of Kachalov: impulsive, dynamic, musical and buoyant. The Craig/Stanislavsky version had become a standard from which to deviate, and Meyerhold deliberately went after those grossly comic elements in the play that the Art Theatre had just as deliberately eschewed.[12] A similar adversary position was adopted by Nikolay Akimov in his 1932 production of *Hamlet* at the Vakhtangov Theatre; rejecting the Craigian Hamlet's love of death, Akimov, in a wildly caricatural adaptation, made *joie de vivre* the keynote of the Prince's character.[13]

If, in Russia, it was the ideological aspect of the MAT *Hamlet* that directors sought to attenuate or contradict, outside of Russia it was the design aspect, known through the models and the preliminary sketches, that most affected workers in the theatre. The shifting of screens to make easy the multiple settings of a Shakespearean tragedy was first seen in a professional production in the United States and Canada in Livingston Platt's sets for Margaret Anglin's *Anthony and Cleopatra*, which toured in 1914. Wing pieces and sky borders were omitted in favor of screens which "both block the sides and tower up suggestively out of sight, making sky borders needless" and which, when a simple short panel was set at right angles to them, seemed quite solid. Platt, however, also utilized realistic furniture and painted drops; his Craigianism was dictated more by the need for portability than by aesthetic determinism.[14]

John Gielgud has recalled that Craig's unlocalized setting "influenced later productions tremendously. There was a violent reaction against the old-fashioned setting."[15] In 1919 Craigian elements placed behind a curved proscenium could be observed in Eduard Verkade's *Hamlet* in Amsterdam, in settings by H. Th. Wijdeveld.[16] Even Sir John Martin-Harvey, last of the old actor-managers, whose Hamlet was appreciated for its emotionalism, fitted up a fresh production on modified Craigian principles, perhaps with touring in mind. Arthur Hopkins' production of the tragedy in 1922 for John Barrymore cleaved closest to the MAT model visually; Robert Edmond Jones' setting, both in his designs and their realization, were manifestly founded on Craig's published drawings. If one reads Stark Young's description of the set, suppressing the name Jones and replacing it with Craig, the similarity becomes clear:

> Mr. Robert Edmond Jones has created a permanent setting of architectural forms and spaces, bounded across the stage, and down two-thirds to the front line of it, with a play of steps. Within this, easy variations are possible to indicate the changes

of scene. The design of the setting cannot be conveyed in words, of course, but it is princely, austere and monumental. It has no clutter of costumes or elaborate variations in apartments, but instead a central rhythm of images, of light and shade innate to the dramatic moment. The shortcoming of this bold and eloquent setting is that it either goes too far or does not go far enough. In this respect the limit was reached when the time came for the scene of Ophelia's burial, where the setting was at least enough like a palace to make the grave toward the front of the stage — and therefore the whole scene — appear to be incongruous if not absurd.[17]

Apparently neither Sulerzhitsky nor Jones could cope with Craig's vision of a crater, given the rudimentary elements of the design.

Coincidentally, the MAT was playing in New York at this time, and Stanislavsky managed to see the Barrymore performance, which he thought "far from ideal but very fascinating." As to the décor, the Russian director thought his American colleague misused shadows, not only keeping secondary characters in obscurity, which might be admissible, but also blotting out the leading actors.[18] One hears again the dress rehearsal quarrel over "The Mousetrap," with Craig insisting on atmosphere and Stanislavsky demanding that Hamlet's expression be seen.[19]

The same year (1922) Oskar Strnad designed monumental Craig-like pillars for a *Hamlet* in the Vienna Burgtheater. And New York received yet another Craig-inspired *Hamlet* setting in 1925 when Claude Bragton mounted it at Hampden's Theatre.

Of all Craig's designs for *Hamlet*, the most striking was the picture of the golden court. Fyodor Kommissarzhevsky had seen the original production when it toured to Petersburg, and borrowed the image of the courtiers emerging from a single cloak when, as Theodore Komisarjevsky, he directed *The Merchant of Venice* at Stratford-upon-Avon in 1923. Gielgud was similarly attracted by it, though, unaware of the use of separate capes rather than one all-enveloping mantle and of the black scrim that concealed the courtiers when Hamlet began his soliloquy, the English actor thought the drawing infeasible, "an idea rather than a practical stage arrangement. What attracts me most in it is the placing of Hamlet, the contrast of light and shade, and the focusing of attention on the King and Queen at the rise of the curtain."[20] Therefore, in his 1934 *Hamlet*, he reproduced this grouping, though on a diagonal to the audience, with the courtiers ranged in a semi-circle hiding Hamlet from his mother and uncle.

Whether or not they were aware of it, many later directors interpreted facets of the play in ways which Craig had already mooted. When Alisa Koonen saw the Royal Shakespeare Company perform *Hamlet* directed by Peter Brook with Paul Scofield in Russia in 1956, she was startled to find that Mary Ure's Ophelia captured the "aureole of spiritual beauty" which Craig had said existed in the Prince's imagination.[21] Even the Jonathan Pryce *Hamlet* at the Royal Court Theatre in 1980, although visually as far from Craig as can be with its Holbein costumes and Tudor furniture, hinted at monodrama, by having the Prince speak the Ghost's lines almost ventri-loquially. Such ideas as the unlocalized setting, Hamlet's aloofness from the world of the court, Ophelia's fecklessness, became assimilated into twen-tieth century stage tradition.

As time went on, Craig himself became more and more dissatisfied with the Moscow *Hamlet* experience. In his mind, it became a paradigm for the taint his ideas suffered when reduced to tangibles, and confirmed his belief in the folly of practising in the professional theatre. To Count Kessler in 1922 he expressed his refusal to work with Stanislavsky or the Russians ever again. "Even the Russians are nothing but 'clever monkeys,' when they are let loose on the stage. There is nothing genuine behind their optical tricks."[22] Although he appreciated Stanislavsky's fight against obsolete conventions, he continued to condemn what he saw as Stanislavsky's timidity, naïveté and smugness. The publication of the story of the screens falling down in *My Life in Art* infuriated Craig, and in 1935 he launched another acerbic correspondence demanding changes and omissions or else he would sue.[23]

This resurgence in his animosity came so late (the book had been pub-lished in 1923 and Craig's review of it in *The Mask* had been a panegyric)[24] because Craig had returned to Moscow in 1935 to attend an international theatre conference. After seeing Alisa Koonen as leading lady at the Kamerny Theatre, he called her "still the best actress in Russia . . . because she pos-sesses that *something more* which the great artists always had."[25] He even paid a polite call on Nemirovich-Danchenko but, when he sought to visit the other partner, Stanislavsky pleaded ill health. The two men did not meet; Stanislavsky did not appear in the list of friends Craig drew up on his departure.[26] And when a young student named Nikolay Chushkin inter-viewed Craig on the 1912 *Hamlet*, the elderly *enfant terrible* exploded, "They slaughtered me! Kachalov played Hamlet his own way. It was inter-esting, even brilliant, but it wasn't mine, not *my* Hamlet, not at all what I wanted! They took my 'screens,' but discarded the production of my soul!" Returning to his complaints of Russian realism, Stanislavsky's refusal to use the Death figure, and Kachalov's lack of theatricality, he repudiated all of the finished production except for a few "oases" which had "audacity, prin-ciple, impudence."[27]

Although Stanislavsky in a conciliatory letter humbly confessed "my powerlessness to translate fully the manner in which the screens ought to have been used,"[28] Craig continued to nurse a grudge. When *An Actor Prepares* appeared in England, he wrote a damning review, putting down the Stanislavsky system for its encouragement of non-actors and, as a gratuitous jab, praising the former writing-master Artyom as the only "born actor" in the Moscow Art Theatre.[29] Later he cited Jean-Louis Barrault as "many times a better Hamlet."[30] By the time he was nearing death, Craig had so distorted the entire experience that he considered the use of the screens in *Hamlet* totally ill-advised and the whole project like "taking God Almighty into a music-hall."[31]

For all his egocentricity and pigheadedness, however, Craig was not without self-awareness. In that same conversation with Count Kessler in 1922, he had discussed his working methods. "When his imagination is set alight, he cannot stop until suddenly the flames are extinguished, and then he cannot go on at all any more. That is why he is always nervous of undertaking anything, hesitates and makes difficulties for himself and others, because he can never foretell how long the fire of his imagination will keep burning."[32] Under these circumstances, it is astonishing that Craig managed to work with the painstaking, slow-moving, conscientiously backtracking Moscow Art Theatre for as long as he did, and that the achievement was as impressive as it was.

For the *Hamlet* production at the MAT, with all its compromises and mistakes, did indeed constitute, as the historian Gruzinsky had said, "an upheaval, a theatrical revolution."[33] It scraped away the encrustation of antiquarian, veristic stage business that encumbered the Shakespearean canon; it subordinated the star performance to the total intellectual import of the play and, in so doing, revealed a fresh way of approaching tragedy.

When Craig began work on the Moscow *Hamlet* in 1909, the play was still bogged down in Victorian tradition. That same year at the Lyceum Theatre, London, Matheson Lang had impersonated the melancholy Dane against an equally melancholy background of Romanesque arches and supernumeraries who resembled a second-string chorus in *Lohengrin*. It was a décor that went back as far as Charles Kean, as redolent of ham as of Hamlet. The Germans, more progressive in their stagecraft, had made some headway. The 1909 *Hamlet* of Fritz Shumacher at the Dresden Court Theatre used stylized arches that could be reassembled in various combinations to set the scenes. In Munich, Georg Fuchs, one of those closest to Craig in innovative staging, placed his *Hamlet* at the Kuenstlertheater in settings by Fritz Erler that partook of Fuchs' synaesthetic combination of landscape painting and architecture. The effect was not devoid of naturalism but simplified and harmonized it. But for all of Fuchs' insistence that the pictorial elements of theatre be three-dimensional and concrete, his production was still grounded in a specific historical period encumbered by irrelevant detail. As with the sketches Egorov had prepared for the Moscow Art Theatre, there was no suggestion of a meaning beyond the play's action, a deeper significance or a wider intent.

Grigory Kozintsev, the director of the Soviet films of *Hamlet* and *King Lear*, never saw the MAT *Hamlet*, though he heard all the legends and saw all the designs. His glowing appreciation best encapsulates the meaning of Craig's work for later generations.

While I was still only a boy, I was astounded by Craig's sketches; space, devoid of any recognizable landmarks, the unification of emptiness of night and the coldness of ice, sea mist in which anything can be imagined. Lonely figures in the midst of unfamiliar worlds of stone. There is not one detail, not one feature which you can grasp on to in order to find your way to that place, so strongly does the void beckon you. The rhythm of this structure, the shades of grey, the vertical and horizontal lines give it poetry in their own code — it is no longer heard but seen. Next to these engravings and sketches, the theatrical décor seemed mean, insignificant, on the level of provincial Shakespearean productions: wrinkled tights, drawers pulled tightly over them, declaimed speech and howling, and beards made of tow . . . Craig was the first to insist that Shakespeare's tragedies are concerned not only with human passions and the relationships between the main characters in the plays, but first and foremost, with the conflict of some sort of mighty visual powers; you cannot restrict the poetry within the confines of the subject matter, it goes far beyond those bounds — it is a whole universe![34]

For Kozintsev, Craig freed the imagination in a way similar to the methods of the film, a medium admirably suited for the concept of the single artist as master-mind. Intuitively, Stanislavsky was aware of this, and when he was approached by Hollywood in 1923 to use the Moscow Art actors in a feature film, he begged off, saying, "I think the pictures have overlooked the one person who could have given them what they needed — Gordon Craig. He is a great artist, a man of genius with a keen sense of synthetization by the visual line."[35] The monodramatic eye of the designer/director fusing with Hamlet's mind's eye might be best portrayed by a camera lens.

But if the staging of *Hamlet* in Moscow did not fully embody all of this exceptional vision, it did set the seal on Craig's reputation as a potent force in the modern theatre. As Sulerzhitsky observed, the Moscow Art Theatre was "the laboratory in which he revealed his concepts and by this revelation at once became CRAIG! for all of Europe."[36]

Appendix 1

"'HAMLET' IN MOSCOW:
Notes for a Short Address to the Actors of the Moscow Art Theatre,"

by Gordon Craig

(November 19 1909)

I do not want you, when you come to perform this Drama of Kings and Princes, to create the impression of actors acting, for that nearly always means something insincere and which for some shameful reason we have been forced to hear called "theatrical."

But you must not go to the other extreme. If you do so you will create an impression of everyday people who have never seen a court, much less a king, and who have no idea of Royalty.

The Royal is not yet the Theatrical although sometimes the two are confused. You must attempt to move and speak as though you were in an atmosphere which is *rare* . . . for Shakespeare has made it rare.

To do this you must try to think rarely and see all things as rare things. The stage offers nothing more difficult for your talents.

I am of the opinion that no band of actors will succeed in thoroughly representing this sense of Royalty until they become Royal . . . and to do this it will be necessary to live their lives with the object of culture uppermost; for only by this means can they absorb that air which, after it has entered a man, lends him at least a manner which is magnificent and a tone which is sweet.

It is this manner and this tone which we need for the representation of Shakespeare's Dramatic Poems.

I have said culture for I purposely limit our aspirations here to culture; if I went further I should say that we must first get into that spiritual state of ecstacy which we can better imagine than tell about. But for our purpose . . . Shakespeare's purpose . . . a Royal state is enough, . . . nay, it is not half the way to a Religious state; and if we can acquire it one way or another shall we not all be very fortunate, being nearer by a step towards the spiritual state?

From *The Mask*, 7, 2 (May 1915): 110-15.

And how to acquire it?

Now here you bring me face to face with a Riddle at once very difficult and quite easy to solve.

How to make something which is Rounded at each end stand up on either end: . . . the Egg of Columbus.

I can help you but I cannot teach you, for this is a thing which no man can teach. I can tell you some things which, if you will believe them, will unfailingly bring you in time nearer to that state which we have called ecstatic.

Remember that the acme of ecstasy is not apparent excitement, but apparent calm. It is the white heat of emotion; . . . that is to say, it is almost trance. This state has a thousand names and takes a myriad forms. We call it wisdom.

It is pure emotion with all its impurity burnt away.

In order to have the courage to make the attempt to enter such a state, some great promise must be given you that the attempt will not be made in vain.

I will give you that promise. You must believe me, for what I say is true. I promise you that you can reach any state provided you can see beyond it. I know quite well that you have at least ten or twenty times in your life seen or felt things which seemed *mad* to you. You avoided these feelings not because you disliked them but because you saw no *use* to put them to, . . . and so grew frightened. In other words, your Imagination awoke in you and possessed you for a moment or two.

Now I tell you that you must awaken your Imagination and let it possess you entirely. Be less frightened of those moments when they come. Go towards them . . . run the risk: leave yourself free with them; let them possess you. Ecstasy is nothing else than a kind of madness . . . a kind of madness, remember, not any kind of madness.

It is all which is Rapid . . . White . . . Glowing . . . Circular . . . Vast . . . Steady.

It is all that you dare to dream about and fear to go near.

It is the great Danger.

And for this very reason I tell you that you must go to meet it.

(November 20 1909)

You want to be able to understand and interpret one of the greatest works of genius which the world possesses and therefore you must bring yourselves nearer to the state of that genius.

You must become ecstatic. You must lose yourself.

It is impossible to believe that you can interpret so great a work without making use of your own greatness. You cannot do it by your reason, which is your littleness. You can only do it by the power of Imagination.

If you can loosen the bonds which imprison your freedom (and your imagination is your freedom) you will be in a state to receive the communications of my imagination.

We can then advance upon the work and master its secrets.

If you remain tied by your intellect or reason you would never understand me and so we should be unable to achieve anything. And I have only one thing to communicate to you. The ecstasy of Shakespeare.

Under this heading a thousand moments of madness are gathered.

Madness is something which, when it seems to succeed is called Heroic: when it seems to fail is called Folly.

To attempt what is called the Impossible, . . . that is Madness, and that is Good.

On October 20th 480 B.C. was fought the Battle of Salamis. The Greeks had 380 ships, the Persians 2000 ships led by Xerxes.

This is the gist of the words spoken by Themistocles the Greek general, before the battle.

"The argument of it was that in all things that are possible to man's nature and situation, there is always a higher and a lower" and that *they* must stand for the higher. (1)

They did so, . . . and they won the battle; and the madness of the attempt was called Heroic . . . and justified.

You must make this same mad attempt in "Hamlet"; and "if the Muses leave us may we die." (2)

And now that I've told you what I want you to do let me advise you what not to do.

Do not, I beg of you, do not think too much.

Everybody has a habit of thinking, but modern actors think too much.

No one by thinking can see the sky. He sees it and realises it through his senses.

To think when music is playing would be idle . . . one must merely receive it into the soul through the senses.

And it is to be so with our Hamlet. Let your brains rest and absorb the beauty of Hamlet through your eyes and ears and do not forget what is called touch, for it has much to do with your movement.

By means of the brains . . . by thinking, one can act cleverly. A clever man is he who thinks; and you are acknowledged by Europe to be the cleverest company of actors in the west.

By means of the senses and the soul you may become the most profound . . . the most beautiful . . . the most spiritual.

So, my dears, do not think too much . . . and feel more, . . . much more. And let me tell you here that I love you all very much and will do anything I can, and all I can, to be of help to you during this your interpretation of our

Hamlet; but that it is you who have the harder task, . . . that is, to bring yourselves willingly into the simplest state of being possible; and you can only do this by choosing the higher in place of the lower means: *the senses and the soul* instead of the *brain*.

(1) Heroditus. [*sic*]
(2) Euripides.

(November 30, 1909)

It has been proved by experience that the Shakespearian Dramatic Poems cannot be performed in the same manner as we perform modern Plays.

All the colour departs from the Poems when we act them as we act Ibsen, or Chekhov.

One difference between Shakespeare and the modern writers is that whereas they deal in men and women he deals in types. His lover is the type of all lovers, distinguished by nothing but his passion. We know no details about his life; we do not know his character. Shakespeare only shows us his passion. It is the poet's passion. Romeo sighs and floats before us, . . . he does not converse and walk. He loves . . . loves again . . . sickens . . . revives . . . sickens again . . . meets Fate . . . and dies.

And Passion, not Character, stamps its mark on the whole tragedy of Romeo and Juliet. It is only where something comic has to be revealed that Character is made use of. I learnt this from my friend Yeats, our great Irish poet.

Well then . . .

A company of actors who would perform this play must weigh all this very thoroughly.

It is because modern stage managers and actors attempt to turn Shakespeare's Dramatic Poems into Plays of Character that they produce to lamentable results.

Hamlet is made up of Passion . . . Style . . . Music . . . and Vision: but not Character.

Character appears incidentally in the figures of the two Grave-diggers, and even they have something of that strange mystic *appearance*, that strange and magic expression of face which arrests our attention in many of the Greek portraits and in the Pompeian frescoes.

On looking at them we are startled by what they appear to see . . . or what they have seen long ago and is reflected in their eyes and mouth. A gravity which lends a rare beauty to the staring eyes and slightly opened mouth. (In Greek Tragedy or Comedy masks the mouth was indicated as open. It is the passionate state. The closed mouth is the intellectual state). Character appears also in Osric . . . and in Polonius.

And now . . . how shall a company of actors who have trained themselves to represent Plays of Character as you have done, who have based your methods of representation upon actuality instead of Poetry and Imagination, how shall they wrestle with Hamlet?

Shall they do better than treat it as a *Romance* . . . a thing of fancy, . . . or an *actuality*? Dare they face the thing as it is?

To me the secret of performing the play lies in the capacity of the actor to understand Passion, . . . the white heat of Passion, the calm of Passion, its ecstasy, and in having given his life to the creation of a technique which shall convey ecstasy to those who look on.

Were Grasso, our stunning Giovanni, to interpret Hamlet we should expect and ask for red heat. That is another story.

Hamlet is a saint, . . . yet loves Ophelia . . . in that he is a saint; yet kills Polonius . . . in that a saint. . .

How so? you ask. Because he is the creation of Imagination, because a Poet gave birth to him. He is no reality.

Remember Gioconda's smile which is Leonardo's smile . . . Hamlet has that smile.

Yet Hamlet talks much?

Well, we must not touch on that dread matter, for it is, alas, too true. Can the actor nowadays understand this state of being created through the Imagination? . . . can he attain to it?

To the point then. This is a question which slowly and unwillingly thrusts forwards for an answer . . .

It is as Tragic as the Tragedy of Hamlet.

If the reply is "No", then why is it he cannot understand it?

Because . . . .

NO! . . . No man but only angels may answer this question.

When Love by luck returns to the Theatre the Theatre will be reborn.

When it returns to Earth It will enter the Theatre.

Come, Chuang Tzu, come to my help; tell them what I mean, . . . or rather tell them that I am not utterly wrong in that by Passion I mean not the passions: . . .

"Hui Tzu said to Chuang Tzu: 'Are there, then, men who have no passions?' Chuang Tzu replied: 'Certainly.'

"'But if a man has no passions,' argued Hui Tzu, 'what is it that makes him a man?'

"'Tao,' replied Chuang Tzu, 'gives him his expression, and God gives him his form. How should he not be a man?'

"'If, then, he is a man,' said Hui Tzu, 'how can he be without passions?' 'What you mean by passions,' answered Chuang Tzu, 'is not what I mean. By a man without passions I mean one who does not permit good and evil to disturb his internal economy, but rather falls in with whatever happens, as a matter of course, and does not add to the sum of his mortality.'

"The pure men of old slept without dreams, and waked without anxiety. They ate without discrimination, breathing deep breaths. For pure men draw breath from their uttermost depths; the vulgar only from their throats. Out of the crooked, words are retched up like vomit. If men's passions are deep, their divinity is shallow.

"The pure men of old did not know what it was to love life nor to hate death. They did not rejoice in birth, nor strive to put off dissolution. Quickly come and quickly go; . . . no more. They did not forget whence it was they had sprung, neither did they seek to hasten their return thither. Cheerfully they played their allotted parts, waiting patiently for the end. This is what is called not to lead the heart astray from Tao, nor to let the human seek to supplement the divine. And this is what is meant by a pure man."

*   *   *   *   *

This is the gist of what I wished to say to the actors of the Moscow Art Theatre. But on seeing their kind faces and wrinkled brows I had not the heart to add one more wrinkle. I had at least the wit to abstain once more: . . . and I made one more design for an Über-Marionette.

Appendix 2 _____

"HAMLET,"

by Vlas Doroshevich

Mister Craig sat astride a chair, stared out at a point in space and said, as if dropping a large pearl onto a silver platter:

"What is 'Hamlet'? One need only read the title: 'Hamlet!' Not 'Hamlet and Ophelia,' not 'Hamlet and the King.' But simply 'The Tragedy of Hamlet, Prince of Denmark' — that is Hamlet!"

"I can follow that!" said Mr. Nemirovich-Danchenko.

"All the rest is unimportant. Rubbish. More! All the other characters do not even exist!"

"Well, what business have they got existing!" Mr. Nemirovich-Danchenko shrugged.

"Yes, but all the same on the playbill . . ." Mr. Vishnevsky made an attempt at remarking.

"Ah, will you leave off, dear man, with your playbill! A playbill can be set up anyway you please."

"Listen! Listen!" Mr. Stanislavsky gasped in excitement.

"Hamlet is suffering. Hamlet's soul is diseased!" went on Mr. Craig, staring somewhere at a point in space and talking like a lunatic. "Ophelia, the Queen, the King, Polonius are perhaps not quite so. Perhaps they do not quite exist. Perhaps they are ghosts, just like the ghost of his father."

"Naturally, ghosts!" shrugged Mr. Nemirovich-Danchenko.

"A vision. A fantasy. An hallucination of his diseased soul. That's how it ought to be staged. Hamlet alone. All the rest, ghosts! Here one minute, gone the next. No scenery. This way! Only contours. Perhaps there is no Elsinore. Only Hamlet's imagination."

"I think," said Mr. Stanislavsky cautiously, "I think we ought to put in a Great Dane, you know. To indicate that the action takes place in Denmark?"

"A Great Dane?"

Mister Craig stared at him fixedly.

From V. M. Doroshevich, *Rasskazy i ocherki* (Moscow: Moskovskiy rabochiy, 1966), pp. 120-25.

"A Great Dane? No. A play by Shakespeare may be in performance. Salvini may be acting. But once a dog shows up on stage and starts wagging its tail, the audience will forget both Shakespeare and Salvini and watch the dog's tail. No Shakespeare can stand up to a dog's tail."

"Fascinating!" whispered Mr. Vishnevsky.

"I'm a pretty smart director myself, goodness knows! But smarties like this we've never seen!" said Mr. Stanislavsky.

Mr. Kachalov withdrew, all by himself.

He took walks in the cemetery.

He ate lenten fare.

He placed a skull on his writing-desk.

He read the hymnal.

Mr. Nemirovich-Danchenko said:

"Yessirree! Craig's the thing!"

Mr. Vishnevsky decided:

"We'll print the playbill without the cast."

*   *   *

Mr. Craig ran down "Director's Row", clutching at his head and shouting:

"Stop the rehearsal! Hold it! What are they playing?"

"Hamlet, sir!" said Mr. Vishnevsky in terror.

"But that's nothing but a name! They write 'Hamlet' so you play Hamlet? What if it were "The Gardener's Dog," do you play the dog? Maybe there is no Hamlet?!"

"Anything's possible!" said Mr. Nemirovich-Danchenko.

"It's got nothing to do with Hamlet. It's got to do with those around him. Hamlet is their dream. A fantasy. An hallucination. An illusion! They committed foul deeds and they imagined a Hamlet. As retribution!"

"Naturally, that's right!" said Mr. Nemirovich-Danchenko.

"It must be played by them!" shouted Mr. Craig, — "Scenery! What are these dreams of scenery? Vague hints of scenery? Fantasies of scenery? Give me lush, sumptuous scenery. Life itself! A full-length picture! Laertes is departing. There is probably some court lady in love with him. Show it to me! Probably there's some cavalier sighing for Ophelia. Let me see him. Dancing. A feast! And somewhere, way at the back, through all this comes the tiniest hint . . . You know what I mean, a hint?"

"Why, of course, how else: a hint! Quite simple!" said Mr. Nemirovich-Danchenko.

"A hint, their illusion, a nightmare, of Hamlet!"

"Then I guess we can put in the Great Dane?" Mr. Stanislavsky asked hopefully.

Mr. Craig looked at him in excitement.

"A dog? You can even put a cow in the graveyard! The graveyard is beside the point! The Yoricks are beside the point!"

"That's all right then. Thank you!"

Mr. Stanislavsky shook his head with feeling.

Mr. Kachalov began to go to weddings, attend Literary Circles, debate with dentists — in general, began to have a good time.

Mr. Vishnevsky asked those whom he met:

"What kind of animals do they still have in Denmark? I'm asking on Stanislavsky's behalf. I'd like to give him a treat."

Mr. Nemirovich pensively smoothed his beard:

"An unusual man."

Mister Craig even spit.

"Why did I ever start staging this play? Me? 'Hamlet'? Whom do you take me for? This is a real farce! A mockery of common sense! This ought to be played at Saburov's. And even that would be too decent for it!"

"Yes, the play, of course, is not one of the most successful!" agreed Mr. Nemirovich-Danchenko.

"It's stuff and nonsense! Poppycock! Soft-boiled boots! For five acts a man vacillates whether or not to kill Claudius, — and kills Polonius like gulping down an oyster! Where's the logic in it? Your Shakespeare, — if he existed — was a fool! Good grief! Hamlet says 'the undiscovered country from whose bourn no traveller returns' and yet he's just seen the ghost of his father with his own eyes! How is that to be reconciled? How can we show such twaddle to the public?"

"Quite so!" said Mr. Stanislavsky, "but I think that if we put a Great Dane on stage, the dog's appearance will distract the audience from many of the play's inconsistencies."

"Even a hippopotamus won't help! No! You want to perform 'Hamlet' — we'll perform it as a farce! A parody of the tragedy!"

Mr. Vishnevsky said to a general he knew:

"You know, your excellency, this Shakespeare person, well, it seems there wasn't any!"

"What do you mean, my friend?"

"There wasn't any Shakespeare. Today it only looks that way. But he never was!"

Mr. Nemirovich-Danchenko walked along, clutching his beard in his fist.

"A paradoxical gentleman!"

*   *   *

"My friend!" Mister Craig rushed in.

Mr. Nemirovich-Danchenko actually shrieked.

Craig grasped his hand so tightly.

"What a night I had yesterday! What a night! Last night in a dream I held the book of the future. A book which everyone knows! A book which no one reads, because they all think they know it! 'Hamlet'!"

Mister Craig gripped Mr. Nemirovich-Danchenko by the shoulder.

"It's really something! It's like looking at your sister every day and not noticing that she's grown into a beauty! The world's foremost beauty!"

Mister Craig gripped him by the leg.

"I'll be all black-and-blue!" thought Mr. Nemirovich-Danchenko in despair.

"It's really something! That line 'To be or not to be?' How about that? Gives you gooseflesh! Or this one: 'Are you honest, are you fair?' How about that? Is that frightening or is that frightening? No, can you understand that fear?!"

"Who wouldn't understand!" said Mr. Nemirovich-Danchenko, standing further off. "It's Shakespeare!"

"A genius! A genius! Start the rehearsals of 'Hamlet'! At once! This very minute! We will rehearse 'Hamlet' night and day: Without eating or drinking! Let us do nothing, but nothing, our whole lives except perform 'Hamlet.' Non-stop! Play! Play!"

"Was there any mention of the dog?" Mr. Stanislavsky inquired.

"Vladimir Ivanovich, what's the present situation," Mr. Vishnevsky expressed an anxious curiosity, "with Shakespeare? Is there a Shakespeare or not?"

"What a question!" Mr. Nemirovich-Danchenko shrugged, "how could there be a Shakespeare and then suddenly not be one?"

"Well, thank goodness!"

Mr. Vishnevsky sighed in relief:

"Because you know, you get used to a Shakespeare, — and suddenly there isn't one. Honest, it's just like something was missing."

Mr. Stanislavsky's head was spinning.

"A great enthusiast!"

*   *   *

Mister Craig watched Messrs. Nemirovich-Danchenko and Stanislavsky enter his room with profound amazement.

"What can I do for you gentlemen?"

"We're here about 'Hamlet'!" said Mr. Nemirovich-Danchenko.

Mister Craig asked them to repeat it:

"What did you say?"

"Hamlet."

"Hamlet?! What's that? A town, a dish, a racehorse?"

"Hamlet! Shakespeare's play!"

"And who's this, this Shakespeare?"

"Good God! The playwright!"

"Dunno him. Can't recollect him. Never heard of him. Maybe. What did he do, this gent, that you're talking about him?"

"He wrote 'Hamlet.'"

"Well, good for him! All kinds of plays get written!"

"Yes, but you . . . to stage . . . in our theatre . . ."

"Excuse me, gentlemen! Somebody wrote some play. Somebody for some reason wants to perform it. What's all this got to do with me? Excuse me, gentlemen! I am at the moment thinking of something quite different!"

And Mister Craig plunged into profound meditation.

"This man's genius is capricious!" Mr. Nemirovich-Danchenko smoothed his beard.

"Instead of 'Hamlet' let's just put the Great Dane on stage!" Mr. Stanislavsky was inspired. "There's no reason to give up the dog."

But Mr. Vishnevsky even began to weep:

"Good Lord! I've already told the generals, counts and princes I know: 'It's to be Hamlet!'"

NOTES

ABBREVIATIONS

BA   Edward Gordon Craig papers in the Fonds Rondel, Bibliothèque de l'Arsénal, Paris.
EGC   Edward Gordon Craig
Hamlet 1909   Gordon Craig's promptbook for *Hamlet* at the Bibliothèque de l'Arsénal, Paris
MAT   Moscow Art Theatre
MLIA   K. S. Stanislavskiy, *My Life in Art*, tr. J. J. Robbins (Boston: Little, Brown, 1923). [The translation has been compared with the later Russian text, published in Moscow in 1926, and revised and amended accordingly, whenever quoted.]
o.s.   old style (the Julian calendar)
SS   K. S. Stanislavskiy, *Sobranie sochineniy v vos'mi tomakh* (Moscow: Iskusstvo, 1960-61)
Stan   Konstantin Alekseevich Stanislavskiy
Suler   Leopold Antonovich Sulerzhitskiy
Tex   Gordon Craig papers at the Humanities Research Center, University of Texas at Austin.

PREFACE

1. EGC to N. Chushkin (20 June 1935), Tex.
2. D. Tutaev, "Gordon Craig Remembers Stanislavsky: A Great Nurse," *Theatre Arts* 56, 4 (April 1962): 17-19.

CHAPTER 1

1. E. I. Polyakova, *Stanislavskiy* (Moscow: Iskusstvo, 1977), p. 103.
2. Ibid., p. 110.
3. Ibid., p. 115.
4. Ibid., p. 116.
5. I. N. Vinogradskaya, *Zhizn' i tvorchestvo K. S. Stanislavskogo: letopis'* (Moscow: Vserossiyskoe Teatral'noe Obshchestvo, 1971), I, 201.
6. N. Efros, *Moskovskiy Khudozhestvennyy Teatr 1898-1923* (Moscow-Petersburg: Gos. Izd., 1924), p. 119.
7. N. Gourfinkel, *Théâtre russe contemporain* (Paris: La Renaissance du Livre, 1931), pp. 32-34. For a complete reconstruction of the production, see *"Yuliy Tsezar" Rezhissyorskij plan Vl. I. Nemirovich-Danchenko, MKHT 1903 god* (Moscow:

Iskusstvo, 1964). On Stanislavsky's performance as Brutus, see E. I. Polyakova, *Stanislavskiy — aktyor* (Moscow: Iskusstvo, 1972), pp. 203-10.

8. *Mir Iskusstvo* 1903, No. 12, quoted in M. N. Stroeva, *Rezhissyorskie iskaniya Stanislavskogo 1898-1917* (Moscow: Nauka, 1973), p. 118.

9. Letter of August 1903, quoted in Stroeva, p. 119.

10. V. Bryusov, "Nenuzhnaya pravda," *Mir Iskusstva* 4 (1902). See also his essay "Realism and Conventionality in the Theatre," in *Russian Dramatic Theory from Pushkin to the Symbolists*, ed. and tr. L. Senelick (Austin: University of Texas Press, 1981), pp. 171-82.

11. For the abortive production of *The Death of Tintagiles*, see K. L. Rudnitskiy, *Rezhissyor Meyerkhol'd* (Moscow: Nauka, 1969), pp. 50-69; and in English, E. Braun, *The Theatre of Meyerhold* (London: Eyre Methuen, 1979), pp. 38-52.

12. K. S. Stanislavskiy, *Stati, rechi, zametki, dnevniki, vospominaniya 1877-1917* (Moscow: Iskusstvo, 1958), p. 411.

13. Baroness Bila and P. Burton, "The Russian Stage," *Stage Year Book* (London: The Stage, 1909), pp. 131-35. Only State theatres are mentioned.

14. A. Koonen, *Stranitsy zhizni* (Moscow: Iskusstvo, 1975), p. 135.

15. A. A. Mgebrov, *Zhizn' v teatre* (Leningrad: Academia, 1929), I, 284-85.

16. F. Steegmuller, *"Your Isadora": The Love Story of Isadora Duncan & Gordon Craig* (New York: Vintage Books, 1976), p. 286.

17. Translated back from the Russian translation given in *SS*, VII, 721. A series of Isadora Duncan's letters to Stanislavsky were published in Russian in *Inostrannaya literatura* (1956), No. 10.

18. *SS*, VII, 384.

19. Steegmuller, *"Your Isadora,"* p. 293.

20. *The Mask* 1 (6 April 1908): 127.

21. EGC to Stan, 20 April 1908, BA.

22. Stan to EGC, 28 April 1908, telegram BA.

23. EGC to Stan, 2 May 1908, BA. See also Edward Craig, *Gordon Craig The Story of His Life* (New York: Alfred A. Knopf, 1968) p. 245.

24. Stan to EGC, BA.

25. EGC to Stan, 26 May 1908, BA.

26. EGC to Stan, July 1908, BA.

27. EGC to Stan, 10 July 1908, BA.

28. Quoted in Edward Craig, *Gordon Craig*, pp. 246-47.

29. "Shakespeare's Plays," *The Mask* 1, 7 (September 1908): 142-43.

CHAPTER 2

1. *MLIA*, p. 508.

2. *MLIA*, p. 509.

3. EGC's marginal note in his copy of David Magarshack's *Stanislavsky, A Life* (in possession of Edward Craig).

4. Stan to Ilya Sats, *SS*, VII, 430-31.

5. EGC to Will Rothenstein, quoted in *Men and Memories: Recollections of William Rothenstein 1900-1922* (New York: Coward-McCann, 1932), p. 153.

6. Edward Craig, *Gordon Craig*, p. 249. EGC, Daybook for November 1908 - March 1910, p. 9. EGC to Edith Craig, 29 October 1908, BA. D. Tutaev, "Gordon Craig Remembers Stanislavsky: A Great Nurse," *Theatre Arts* 56, (4 April, 1962):

17-18. D. Magarshack, in his *Stanislavsky*, p. 296, basing his account on the memoirs of the actor Leonidov, misdates these events as February 1910.

7. EGC to Stan, BA.

8. Daybook for 1908-1910, p. 6. For Isadora's reaction, see Steegmuller, *"Dear Isadora"* (New York: Vintage Books, 1976).

9. Tutaev, "Gordon Craig Remembers," p. 17. Daybook for 1908-1910, p. 6.

10. Lilina to EGC, BA.

11. A. Koonen, *Stranitsy zhizni* (Moscow: Iskusstvo, 1975), p. 129. This, her autobiography, gives a full account of her career. See also P. Markov, *Teatral'nye portrety* (Moscow: Iskusstvo, 1974), pp. 285-86.

12. Daybook for 1908-1910, p. 15.

13. Rothenstein, *Men and Memories*, pp. 153-54.

14. Tutaev, "Gordon Craig Remembers," p. 18.

15. EGC, "In Germany, Holland, Russia & England," *The Mask*, 1, 11 (January 1909): 222.

16. Daybook for 1908-1910, p. 8.

17. EGC, "In Germany, Holland, Russia & England," *The Mask*, 1, 11 (January 1909): 222.

18. *"To the Realists*. Hold close to the Body — thinking to reveal the soul through such a means," Daybook for 1908-1910, 4 November.

19. *MLIA*, p. 507. I. N. Vinogradskaya, *Zhizn' i tvorchestvo K.S. Stanislavskogo: letopis'* (Moscow: Iskusstvo, 1971), II, 144.

20. For a synoptic account of Roller's ideas, see M. Dietrich, "Twentieth-century Innovations in Stage Design, Stage Machinery and Theatre Architecture in Austria," in *Innovations in Stage and Theatre Design*, ed. F. Hodge (New York: American Society for Theatre Research/Theatre Library Association, 1972), pp. 101-6.

21. "Concerning Hamlet," *The Page* (1898): 1-2.

22. Notes (1904) in copy of T. J. Hogg's *Shelley* owned by EGC, in possession of Edward Craig, p. 27 and flyleaf.

23. Edward Craig, *Gordon Craig*, p. 259.

24. Edward Craig, *Gordon Craig*, p. 101.

25. EGC, *Index to the Story of My Days* (London: Hulton, 1957), p. 157. See also "The First Time I Played 'Hamlet'," *The Listener* (3 January 1957): 19.

26. Edward Craig, "Edward Gordon Craig's Hamlet," *The Private Library*, Second Series, X, 1 (Spring 1977): 35-48.

27. *The Mask* (July 1908).

28. Stan to I. A. Bunin, 20 November 1908, o.s., *SS*, VII, 411.

29. Stan to L. Ya. Gurevich, 5 November 1908, o.s., *SS*, VII, 414.

30. Daybook for 1908-1910, p. 19.

31. The first salary installment of 500 rubles for 15 December 1908 to 15 January 1909 was sent to Craig on 15 January 1909. Letter from Board of MAT to EGC, Tex.

32. *Vecher'* (24 December 1908).

CHAPTER 3

1. N.N. Evreinov, *Vvdenie k monodramu* (St. Petersburg, 1909), p. 8. For an English translation, "Introduction to Monodrama" in *Russian Dramatic Theory from Pushkin to the Symbolists*, ed. and tr. L. Senelick (Austin: University of Texas Press, 1981), pp. 183-99.

2. Evreinov, *Vvdenie*, p. 16.

3. See A. P. Kugel', *Utverzhdenie teatra* (Petersburg: Teatr i iskusstvo, 1923).

4. For a thorough discussion of the theatrical controversies raging at the time, see E. A. Znosko-Borovskiy, *Russkiy teatr nachala XX veka* (Prague: Plamja, 1925); I. Dukor, "Problemy dramaturgii simvolizma," *Literaturnoe nasledstvo* 27-28 (1937): 106-66; and Ju. K. Gerasimov, "Krizis modernistskoj teatral'noj mysli v Rossii (1907-1917)" in *Teatr i dramaturgiya. Trudy Leningradskogo gosudarstvennogo Instituta Teatra, Muzyki i Kinematografii*, 4 (1974), pp. 202-44. In English, consult Vyacheslav Ivanov, "The Theatre of the Future," tr. Stephen Graham, *English Review* 10 (March 1912): 634-50; B. G. Rosenthal, "Theatre as Church; The Vision of the Mystical Anarchists," *Russian History* 4, 2 (1977): 122-41; and J. B. Woodward, "From Brjusov to Ajkhenval'd: Attitudes to the Russian Theatre 1902-1914," *Canadian Slavonic Papers* 7 (1965): 173-88.

5. F. Sologub, "Teatr odnoj voli," *Teatr: kniga o novom teatre* (St. Petersburg: Shipovnik, 1908), p. 185. For a complete translation, see "Theatre of a Single Will," in *Russian Dramatic Theory*, above, 132-48.

6. Znosko-Borovskiy, *Russkiy Teatr*, p. 205.

7. EGC, "Review of Josef Gregor and Rene Fülöp-Miller, *The Russian Theatre*," *Observer* (undated clipping, Harvard Theatre Collection, c. 1930).

8. Ibid. "Stanislavsky's dramatists were of the Kodak school."

9. Draft letter of EGC, 1 February 1909, Tex.

10. EGC to Olga Knipper, 11 January 1909, BA. Harvey Pitcher reproduces an earlier postcard showing Knipper as the Mayor's wife in *The Inspector General* with her note to Craig, "With a nice little kiss from a big ugly woman." H. Pitcher, *Chekhov's Leading Lady* (London: John Murray, 1979), Plate 16.

11. Stan to EGC, telegram 20 January 1909, o.s., quoted by EGC in his letter to the Board of Directors, 7 February 1909, BA.

12. L. A. Sulerzhitskiy, "Kreg na Khudozhestvennom Teatre," in *Moskovskiy Khudozhestvenniy Teatr: Istoricheskiy ocherk zhizni i deyatel'nosti* (Moscow: Rampa i zhizn', 1913), II, 97-98; N. N. Chushkin, "O khudozhnike Egorove i 'Gamlet' v MKhT," *Teatr* 1 (January 1970): 93-97.

13. EGC to the Board of Directors, 7 February 1909, BA.

14. Ibid.

15. EGC to Mariya Lilina, 13 February 1909, Tex.

16. Stan to L. Ya. Gurevich, before 9 February 1909, o.s., *SS* VII, 420.

17. Letter to A. P. Chekhov, in *M. Gorkiy i A. Chekhov, Perepiska, stat'i, "vyskazyvaniya"* (Moscow-Leningrad, 1937) pp. 63-64.

18. Information from one of these "groupies," later an emigrée. For studies of Kachalov, see N. Efros, *V. I. Kachalov (fragment)* (Petersburg: Solntse Rossii, 1919), pp. 81-82 especially; A. R. Kugel', *V. Kachalov. Zhizn' i tvorchestvo* (Moscow-Leningrad: Kinopechat', 1927); and *Vasiliy Ivanovich Kachalov, Sbornik statey, vospominaniya, pisem* (Moscow: Iskusstvo, 1954). Most biographies are based on these sources. (One who did not admire Kachalov's voice of "honeyed velvet" and found it tedious over time was Vsevolod Meyerhold (*Meyerkhol'd: Stat'i, pis'ma, rechi, besedy* [Moscow: Iskusstvo, 1968], II, 378).

19. Chushkin, "Egorov," pp. 94-95.

20. From notes by Suler, in I. N. Vinogradskaya, *Zhizn' i tvorchestvo K.S Stanislavskogo: letopis'* (Moscow: Vserossiyskoe Teatral'noe Obshchestvo, 1971), II, 170.

21. Notes by Suler, in Vinogradskaya, *Zhizn,*, II, 171.

22. Notes by Suler, in Vinogradskaya, *Zhizn'*, II, 172.

23. Ibid.

24. Ibid.

25. Remark of V. M. Sushkevich to N. N. Chushkin, quoted in Vinogradskaya, *Zhizn'*, II, 173.

26. Chushkin, "Egorov," p. 96.

27. Chushkin, "Egorov," p. 97.

CHAPTER 4

1. According to Stanislavsky, "Craig swears, while she shrugs her shoulders and persuades everyone that he is crazy." Stan to K. K. Alekseeva, 10 April 1909, o.s., *SS*, VII, 427. See also F. Steegmuller, *"Your Isadora." The Love Story of Isadora Duncan & Gordon Craig* (New York: Vintage Books, 1976), pp. 307-10.

2. Daybook 1 for November 1908 to March 1910, p. 116-17 (about 8 May 1909).

3. A. Koonen, *Stranitsy zhizni* (Moscow: Iskusstvo, 1975), p. 135.

4. Ibid.

5. *SS*, V, 664.

6. Quoted in A. Tarashevich, "L. A. Sulerzhitskiy," *Teatr* 1 (January 1957).

7. Quoted in *L. A. Sulerzhitskiy: Povesti i rasskazy, stat'i i zametki o teatre, perepiska, vospominaniya o L.A. Sulerzhitskom* (Moscow: Iskusstvo, 1970), p. 5.

8. *SS*, V, 535.

9. See the chapter on Suler in *MLIA*, and E. Polyakova, "Zhizn' i tvorchestva L.A. Sulerzhitskogo" in *L. A. Sulerzhitskiy*, pp. 17-95.

10. *MLIA*, p. 508. N. Petrov, *50 i 500* (Moscow: Vserossiyskoe Teatral'noe Obshchestvo, 1960), p. 61.

11. Daybook 2 for 1910-1911.

12. Edward Craig, *Gordon Craig The Story of His Life* (New York: Alfred A. Knopf, 1968), pp. 257, 270.

13. *Hamlet* 1909, flyleaf S. Lykiardopoulo had been on the staff of the avant-garde journal *The Balance (Vesy)* and was the Russian translator and biographer of Oscar Wilde. S. Bertenson, *Vokrug iskusstva* (Hollywood, Calif., 1937), p. 120.

14. Edward Craig, *Gordon Craig*, pp. 251-52.

15. B. I. Rostotskiy and N. N. Chushkin, "'Gamlet': publikatsiya materialov k postanovke spektaklya v Moskovskom Khudozhestvennom Teatre," *Ezhegodnik MKhT 1944* (Moscow: Izd. Muzeya Moskovskogo Ordenoy Lenina i Trudovogo Krasnogo Znameni Khudozhestvennogo Akademicheskogo Teatra SSR Imeni M. Gorkogo, 1946), I, 65-70.

16. EGC, flyleaves J and S, *Hamlet 1909*. N. Efros, *V. I. Kachalov (fragment)* (Petersburg: Solntse Rossii, 1919), pp. 86-88.

17. Ursula Cox's transcription of the conversation, BA. Presumably she recorded Craig's English remarks verbatim and translated only his German jargon and Stanislavsky's Russian.

18. For Meyerhold's work with Kommissarzhevskaya, see K. L. Rudnitskiy, *Rezhissyor Meyerkhol'd* (Moscow: Nauka, 1969), pp. 70-113, and E. Binevich, "Rasskaz v karikaturakh o V.E. Meyerkhol'de, rezhissyore Teatra V.F. Komissarzhevskoy," in *Tvorcheskoe nasledie V. E. Meyerkhol'de* (Moscow: Vserossiyskoe

Teatral'noe Obshchestvo, 1978), pp. 211-35; in English, E. Braun, *The Theatre of Meyerhold* (London: Eyre Methuen, 1979), pp. 53-84, and L. Senelick, "Vera Kommissarzhevskaya: The Actress as Symbolist Eidolon," *Theatre Journal* (December 1980): 475-87.

19. EGC, "The Russian Theatre To-day," *London Mercury* 32 (October 1935): 529-38.

20. Vs. Meyerkhol'd, "Edward Gordon Craig," in *O teatre* (St. Petersburg, 1913), p. 91.

21. Ursula Cox's transcription, BA. Although her phrasing is occasionally clumsy and unidiomatic, I prefer her on-the-spot recording to the translations of the Russian text that was published in Rostotskiy and Chushkin, "'Gamlet,'" pp. 673-83. These include N. Gourfinkel, "La Mise en scène de Hamlet," *La Revue théâtrale* 12 (printemps 1950): 7-16, which mistakes Jameson as Doctor Johnson; E. K. Ilyin, "Gordon Craig's Mission to Moscow," *Theatre Arts* (May 1954): 78-79, 88-90, full of misinformation and illustrated by photographs of a *different Hamlet* production; and the excerpts in D. Magarshack's *Stanislavsky*.

22. A. P. Chekhov, "'Gamlet' na Pushkinskoy stsene," *Polnoe sobranie sochineniy i pisem v tridtsati tomakh* (Moscow: Nauka, 1979), XVI, 19-21.

23. E. Rowe, *Hamlet A Window on Russia* (New York: New York University Press, 1976) gives a superficial listing of *Hamlet's* appearances in Russian literature and theatre. Preferable accounts of the earlier period are E. J. Simmons, *English Literature and Culture in Russia (1553-1840)* (Cambridge, Mass.: Harvard University Press, 1935); and A. Lirondelle, *Shakespeare en Russie 1748-1840* (Paris: Hachette, 1912).

24. V. G. Belinskiy, "Gamlet, drama Shekspira," *Polnoe sobranie sochineniy* (Moscow: Akademiya Nauka SSSR, 1953-59), II, 257.

25. V. G. Belinskiy, "O Pushkine," *Polnoe sobranie sochineniy*, VII, 313.

26. For a discussion of Irving's Hamlet, see L. Irving, *Henry Irving* (New York: Macmillan, 1952), pp. 242-49, 278; and E. Phillpotts, "Irving as Hamlet," in *We Saw Him Act*, ed. H. A. Saintsbury and C. Palmer (New York: Benjamin Blom, 1969), pp. 83-88.

27. Quoted in A. Brereton, *Henry Irving A Biographical Sketch* (New York: Scribner and Welford, 1884), p. 51.

28. Probably translated by M. Lykiardopoulo, *The Mask*, 3, 1 (January 1910): 41-42.

29. Vl. I. Nemirovich-Danchenko to Stan, between April 4 and April 9, 1909, *Izbrannye pis'ma v dvukh tomakh [1879-1943]* (Moscow: Iskusstvo, 1979), I, 474.

30. *SS*, VII, 429.

31. "Written at 3 in the morning", entry for 4 May, 1909, Daybook for November 1908-March 1910, Tex.

32. EGC, *Hamlet* 1909, notes for Act I, Scene 4.

33. M. P. Lilina to her daughter, 27 April 1909, o.s., in I. N. Vinogradskaya, *Zhizn' i tvorchestvo K.S. Stanislavskogo: letopis'* (Moscow: Vserossiyskoe Teatral'noe Obshchestvo, 1971), II, 185.

34. *SS*, VII, 430-31.

CHAPTER 5

1. Note of EGC in BA, dated 5 August 1930. Edward Craig, *Gordon Craig The Story of His Life* (New York: Alfred A. Knopf, 1968), pp. 251-52.

2. A. Koonen, *Stranitsy zhizni* (Moscow: Iskusstvo, 1975), p. 129; I. N. Vinogradskaya, *Zhizn' i tvorchestvo K. S. Stanislavskogo: letopis'* (Moscow: Vserossiyskoe Teatral'noe Obshchestvo, 1971), II, 187; B. I. Rostotskiy and N. N. Chushkin, "Obrazy Shekspira v tvorchestve V. I. Kachalova," *Vasiliy Ivanovich Kachalov, Sbornik statey, vospominaniya, pisem* (Moscow: Iskusstvo, 1954), p. 241. N. N. Chushkin, *Gamlet-Kachalov: iz stsenicheskoy istorii Gamlet Shekspira* (Moscow: Iskusstvo, 1966), p. 35.

3. Note of 5 May 1909 in Daybook for November 1908 to March 1910, Tex.

4. EGC, *Hamlet* 1909, flyleaf C. *MLIA*, pp. 511-12.

5. Suler's notes on 10 May 1909, o.s., in English, BA. See also *MLIA*, pp. 514-20, Vinogradskaya, II, 188, and L. A. Sulerzhitskiy, "Kreg na Khudozhestvennom Teatre," in *Moskovskiy Khudozhestvenniy Teatr: istoricheskiy ocherk zhizni i deyatel'nosti* (Moscow: Rampa i Zhizn', 1913), II, 97-98.

6. Chushkin, *Gamlet-Kachalov*, p. 323.

7. Sulerzhitskiy, "Kreg," II, 97-98.

8. Information from Edward Craig.

9. EGC, note of 15 May 1909, o.s., BA.

10. EGC, notes for Act II, Scene 2, *Hamlet* 1909.

11. Chushkin, *Gamlet-Kachalov*, pp. 82-83, 85. *Hamlet* 1909.

12. *Hamlet* 1909. Chushkin, *Gamlet-Kachalov*, p. 85.

13. EGC, notes to Act II, Scene 3. *Hamlet* 1909. See Plate IV in *Gordon Craig et le renouvellement du théâtre* (Paris: Bibliothèque nationale, 1962).

14. Note by Suler, quoted in Vinogradskaya, *Zhizn' i tvorchestvo*, II, 190.

15. Rostotskiy and Chushkin, "Obrazy," p. 247.

16. Vinogradskaya, *Zhizn' i tvorchestvo*, II, 190.

17. Edward Craig, *Gordon Craig*, p. 253.

18. Notes on Act III, Scene 1, *Hamlet* 1909.

19. Suler's notes, Chushkin, *Gamlet-Kachalov*, pp. 153-54.

20. O. V. Gzovskaya, *Puti i pereput'ya* (Moscow: Vserossiyskoe Teatral'noe Obshchestvo, 1976), p. 100.

21. Chushkin, *Gamlet-Kachalov*, pp. 153-54.

22. Entry for 3 June 1909, Daybook for November 1908 to March 1910, p. 129, Tex.

23. Vinogradskaya, *Zhizn' i tvorchestvo*, II, 191.

24. Notes for Act 3, Scene 2, *Hamlet* 1909.

25. English transcription of conversation, BA.

26. Entry for 10 June 1909, Daybook for November 1909 to March 1910, p. 139, Tex.

27. Ibid., p. 133.

28. Letter of V. I. Kachalov to L. S. Sanina, 17 July 1909, o.s., quoted in Vinogradskaya, *Zhizn' i tvorchestvo*, II, 191.

29. All quotations from English transcriptions of the discussions, BA.

30. Chushkin, *Gamlet-Kachalov*, p. 13.

31. EGC, *Hamlet* 1909, flyleaf O.

32. Information from Edward Craig. *SS*, VII, 435.

33. EGC to Stan, [June] 1909, BA.

34. Stan to EGC, July 1909, BA. Stan's German may have been in response to a postcard from EGC (22 June) describing a German Hamlet he had seen recently: "sehr gut . . . aber nicht Hamlet oder Shakespeare . . . oder Poesie . . . oder Heiligen

Geist . . . about *Deutschland* und kein influence von Russland von England. Echt Deutsch . . . und *Mein Gott!!!* . . .*!!* sehr gut. Ich war *erstaunt!!!!!*" BA.

35. Quoted in Chushkin, *Gamlet-Kachalov*, p. 48.

36. Stan to Nemirovich-Danchenko, 15 July 1909, *SS*, VII, 441.

37. Letter from EGC to Craig, 28 July 1909, BA.

38. Letter from EGC to Rumyantsev, 9 August 1909; M. P. Lilina to EGC 12/25 August [1909], BA.

39. EGC to Stan., 5 September 1909, BA.

40. EGC to Stan, 11 September 1909, BA.

41. Daybook for November 1909 to March 1910, p. 156, Tex.

42. Sam Hume to EGC, undated, Tex.

43. Ibid.

44. EGC to Stan, 10 October 1909, 30 October 1909, BA.

45. Letter of 30 October 1909, o.s., quoted in Chushkin, *Gamlet-Kachalov*, p. 46.

46. Nemirovich-Danchenko to EGC, 8/19 November 1909, BA.

47. EGC to MAT Board of Directors, December 1909, draft in Daybook for November 1908 to March 1910, p. 205, Tex.

48. EGC, "In Germany, Holland, Russia & England . . . Letter Three," *The Mask*, 3, 1 (January 1910): 64.

49. Ibid.

50. EGC, "The Ghosts in the Tragedies of Shakespeare," *The Mask*, 3, 1 (January 1910): 61.

51. Suler to EGC, 27 December 1909, o.s., BA. In English.

52. EGC to M.P. Lilina, 24 January 1910, translated from the French quotation in *Gordon Craig et le renouvellement du théâtre* (Paris: Bibliothèque nationale, 1962).

53. EGC to Stan, 10 February 1910; Rumyantsev to Stan, 25 January 1910, o.s., BA.

CHAPTER 6

1. N. Petrov, *50 i 500* (Moscow: Vserossiyskoe Teatral'noe Obshchestvo, 1960), p. 59. Edward Craig, *Gordon Craig The Story of His Life* (New York: Alfred A. Knopf, 1968), pp. 255-56. EGC, Daybook 2 March 1910 to December 1911, Tex. *MLIA*, pp. 510-11.

2. Petrov, *50 i 500*, pp. 59-61.

3. K. A. Mardzhanishvili, *Tvorcheskoe nasledie: vospominaniya, stat'i i doklady* (Tbilisi: Zarya Vostoka, 1958), p. 56-57.

4. *MLIA*, p. 512.

5. Quoted in N. Chushkin, *Gamlet-Kachalov: iz stsenicheskoy istorii Gamlet Shekspira* (Moscow: Iskusstvo, 1966), p. 21.

6. Ibid.

7. A. Koonen, *Stranitsy zhizni* (Moscow: Iskusstvo, 1975), p. 130-31.

8. O. V. Gzovskaya, *Puti i pereput'ya, Portrety, Stat'i i vospominaniya ob O. V. Gzovskoy* (Moscow: Vserossiyskoe Teatral'noe Obshchestvo, 1976), p. 286.

9. Ibid.

10. Ibid. EGC, Daybook 2 for March 1910 - December 1911, p. 3, Tex. Petrov, *50 i 500*, p. 62.

11. EGC, Marginal notes in his copy of David Magarshack's *Stanislavsky*, owned by Edward Craig.

12. Mardzhanishvili, *Tvorcheskoe nasledie*, pp. 78-79.

13. Mardzhanishvili, *Tvorcheskoe nasledie*, pp. 79-80.

14. Chushkin, *Gamlet-Kachalov*, p. 13.

15. Chushkin, *Gamlet-Kachalov*, pp. 17-19, 22. EGC, Daybook 2 for March 1910-December 1911, pp. 176-79, Tex.

16. EGC, "'Hamlet' in Moscow. Notes for a Short Address to the Actors of the Moscow Art Theatre," *The Mask* 7, 2 (May 1915), p. 115.

17. EGC, Daybook 2 for March 1910-December 1911, p. 179, Tex.

18. Stan to Isadora Duncan, 20 March 1910, o.s., *SS*, VII, 463-64.

19. Chushkin, *Gamlet-Kachalov*, pp. 22-23.

20. EGC, Notes of Act III, Scene 4 in *Hamlet* 1909, BA.

21. Ibid.

22. EGC, Notes for Act IV, Scene 1 in *Hamlet* 1909, BA.

23. EGC, Flyleaf I, *Hamlet* 1909.

24. A. Koonen, *Stranitsy zhizni*, p. 162.

25. Chushkin, *Gamlet-Kachalov*, pp. 23-24.

26. A. Koonen, *Stranitsy zhizni*, p. 161.

27. EGC, Daybook 2 for March 1910 - December 1911, p. 15, Tex.

28. Chushkin, *Gamlet-Kachalov*, p. 322.

29. EGC, Flyleaf M, *Hamlet* 1909.

30. Suler's notes, quoted in I. N. Vinogradskaya, *Zhizn' i tvorchestvo K. S. Stanislavskogo: letopis'* (Moscow: Vserossiyskoe Teatral'noe Obshchestvo, 1972), II, 190.

31. *MLIA*, pp. 522-23.

32. Mardzhanishvili, *Tvorcheskoe nasledie*, p. 81.

33. Ibid.

34. Ibid.

35. Gzovskaya, *Puti i pereput'ya*, p. 296.

36. Koonen, *Stranitsy zhizni*, pp. 130-31.

37. Ibid.

38. Quoted in Vinogradskaya, *Zhizn' i tvorchestvo*, II, 233.

39. L. A. Sulerzhitskiy, *Povesti i rasskazy, stat'i i zametki o teatre, perepiska, vospominaniya o L. A. Sulerzhitskom* (Moscow: Iskusstvo, 1970), p. 67.

40. EGC, Daybook 2 for March 1910 - December 1911, Tex.

41. EGC, Daybook 2 for March 1910 - December 1911, p. 27, Tex. Flyleaf F, *Hamlet* 1909, BA. Craig finally made these attitudes public in his review of *An Actor Prepares*: "Young men and women without much natural talent respond to his persuasive logic: yet over some of us there creeps the suspicion that here is a stage-manager who is using the curious gift — possessed by the trainer of elephants and seals — created only to be trained by kindness — creatures who after a few years of training acquire a capacity to do clever tricks which seem more extraordinary than they actually are." "Stanislavsky's System," *Drama* 15, 10 (July-September 1937): 159.

42. Edward Craig, *Gordon Craig*, pp. 258-59.

43. Quoted in Chushkin, *Gamlet-Kachalov*, p. 323.

44. L. M. Leonidov to Stan, 23 April 1910, o.s., in Vinogradskaya, *Zhizn' i tvorchestvo*, II, 238.

45. Stan to EGC (in English), 21 June 1910, o.s., BA.

46. Stan to EGC (in English), 21 June 1910, o.s., BA.

47. Ibid. They hoped to get up-to-date lighting instruments from the new D'Annunzio Theatre in Rome. Letter of M. Lykiardopoulo to EGC, undated, BA.

48. M. Lykiardopoulo to EGC (in English) after 8 June 1910, BA.

49. EGC's notes, after 8 June 1910, BA.

50. EGC to M. P. Lilina, undated, BA.

51. Stan to EGC (in English), 21 June 1910, o.s., BA.

52. Stan to EGC (in English), 21 June 1910, o.s., BA.

53. EGC to Stan, 14 July 1910, translated from the French in *Gordon Craig et le renouvellement du théâtre* (Paris: Bibliothèque nationale, 1962).

54. Sulerzhitskiy, *Povesti i rasskazy*, p. 442.

55. Stan to Olga Knipper, 13 July 1910, o.s., *SS*, VII, 466.

56. Stan to O. V. Gzovskaya, 27 July 1910, o.s., *SS*, VII, 468.

57. Ibid., p. 469.

58. Stan to Suler, end of July 1910, o.s., *SS*, VII, 469-70.

59. Suler to Stan, 1 August 1910, o.s., in L. A. Sulerzhitskiy, *Povesti i rasskazy*, p. 457.

60. Nemirovich-Danchenko to M.P. Lilina, 5 August 1910, in V. I. Nemirovich-Danchenko, *Izbrannye pis'ma* (Moscow: Iskusstvo, 1954), p. 291. Telegram of A. A. Stakhovich to Stan, in Vinogradskaya, *Zhizn' i tvorchestvo*, II, 249. Suler to his wife, 10 August 1910, o.s., in Suler, *Povesti i rasskazy*, p. 458.

61. M. Lykiardopoulo to EGC (in English), July 1910, BA. EGC to M. P. Lilina, from the Russian translation in Vinogradskaya, *Zhizn' i tvorchestvo*, II, 249.

62. EGC, Daybook 2, March 1910 - December 1911, Tex. Quoted in Edward Craig, *Gordon Craig*, pp. 260-61.

63. Suler to EGC (in English), 10 August 1910, o.s., BA.

CHAPTER 7

1. M. P. Lilina to Suler, 6 September 1910, o.s. in *SS*, VII, p. 470.

2. O. V. Gzovskaya to Stan, autumn 1910, *SS*, VII, 739.

3. Quoted in N. Chushkin, "Sud'ba aktrisy," in O. V. Gzovskaya, *Puti i pereput'ya. Portrety, Stat'i i vospominaniya ob O. V. Gzovskoy* (Moscow: Vserossiyskoe Teatral'noe Obshchestvo, 1976), p. 290.

4. EGC to Suler, 23 September 1910 (translated into Russian) in L. A. Sulerzhitskiy, *Povesti i rasskazy, stat'i i zametki o teatre, perepiska, vospominaniya o L. A. Sulerzhitskom* (Moscow: Iskusstvo, 1970), p. 464.

5. Suler to EGC, October 1910 (in English), BA.

6. Suler to EGC, [1910] (in English), BA.

7. Suler to EGC (in English, received 17 October 1910), BA.

8. Suler to EGC, 7 November 1910, o.s. (in English), BA.

9. EGC to the MAT Board, 28 November 1910, BA.

10. Stan to Suler, 25 November, o.s., *SS*, VII, 489.

11. Vl. I. Nemirovich-Danchenko to M. V. Dobuzhinskiy, end of October 1910, o.s., in Vl. I. Nemirovich-Danchenko, *Izbrannye pis'ma v dvukh tomakh [1879-1943]* (Moscow: Iskusstvo, 1979), II, 53.

12. EGC to M. Lykiardopoulo, 2 January 1911, BA.

13. EGC to M. P. Lilina, 13 January 1911, BA.

14. EGC to Stan, 29 January 1911, quoted (translation into Russian) in I. N. Vinogradskaya, *Zhizn' i tvorchestvo K. S. Stanislavskogo: letopis'* (Moscow: Vserossiyskoe Teatral'noe Obshchestvo, 1971), II, 268.

15. EGC, Note and sketch dated Paris 1911, BA.

16. Stan to M. P. Lilina, 16 January 1911, *SS*, VII, 498.

17. Stan to Suler, 1-5 February 1911, *SS*, VII, 505-507.

18. Suler to Stan, before the end of February 1911, in Suler, *Povesti i rasskazy*, p. 480.

19. Stan to Suler, 6 February 1911, *SS*, VII, 507-8.

20. EGC to Stan, 11 February 1911, BA.

21. EGC to Stan, February 1911, BA.

22. Stan to Suler, 12 February 1911, *SS*, VII, 511-12.

23. Stan to Suler, 19 February 1911, *SS*, VII, 515.

24. EGC to Stan, 20 February 1911, BA.

25. Suler to Stan, 21 February 1911, in Suler, *Povesti i rasskazy*, pp. 478-79.

26. Stan to O. V. Gzovskaya, 27 February 1911, *SS*, VII, 516.

27. L. M. Friedkina, *Dni i gody Vl. I. Nemirovich-Danchenko* (Moscow: Vserossiyskoe Teatral'noe Obshchestvo, 1962), pp. 270-71.

28. E. Vakhtangov, *Materialy i stat'i* (Moscow: Iskusstvo, 1959), p. 24. In a letter to Suler, from Novgorod-Severskiy, 8 July 1911, o.s., Vakhtangov had voiced his excitement over the project:

> I think of Moscow. I dream of the theatre. Of *Hamlet*. It's already drawing me, drawing me.
> To sit in the stalls and gaze at the grey columns.
> At the gold.
> At the quiet light.
> I will ask the administration to let me sit in on all the rehearsals for *Hamlet*. [Suler, *Povesti i rasskazy*, p. 484.]

29. N. S. Butova to T. L. Shchepkina-Kupernik, 19 March 1911, o.s., in Vinogradskaya, *Zhizn' i tvorchestvo*, II, 279.

30. EGC to MAT Board, EGC to Stan, 30 March 1911, BA.

31. EGC, Daybook 2 March 1910 - December 1911, entry for 4 April 1911, Tex. He annotated this in later years with the comment: "The root trouble was this — I was professional — born of the stage — & Stanislavsky was an amateur but I was unaware of this defect in S: expected him to pick up the cue — But he seemed unable to) . . . Stanislavsky goes out of his way to prove that I left everything vague — What a funny old donkey he was. Stanislavsky failed to understand, Kessler *did*."

32. Vinogradskaya, *Zhizn' i tvorchestvo*, II, 280.

33. N. N. Chushkin, *Gamlet-Kachalov: iz stsenicheskoy istorii Gamlet Shekspira* (Moscow: Iskusstvo, 1966), p. 37.

34. Vinogradskaya, *Zhizn' i tvorchestvo*, II, 280.

35. Chushkin, "Sud'ba aktrisy," in Gzovskaya, *Puti i pereput'ya*, p. 284.

36. Chushkin, *Gamlet-Kachalov*, p. 118.

37. Chushkin, *Gamlet-Kachalov*, p. 119-20.

38. Vinogradskaya, *Zhizn' i tvorchestvo*, II, 281.

39. Gzovskaya, *Puti i pereput'ya*, pp. 98-99, 109.

40. Stan to EGC (in English), 7/20 April 1911, BA.

41. EGC's pencil note on letter, above, BA.

42. EGC to Stan, unsent, BA.

43. EGC to Stan, 19 April/2 May 1911, BA.

44. S. Spiro, "'Gamlet' v Khudozhestvennom teatre," *Russkoe slovo*, 29 April 1911, o.s., quoted in Vinogradskaya, *Zhizn' i tvorchestvo*, II, 284.

45. Vinogradskaya, *Zhizn' i tvorchestvo*, II, 285-86.

46. Vinogradskaya, *Zhizn' i tvorchestvo*, II, 286.
47. Suler to EGC (in English) 10 May 1911, o.s., BA.
48. Suler to EGC (in English) undated, BA.
49. Stan to O. V. Gzovskaya, 20 May 1911, o.s., *SS*, VII, 523.
50. Suler to EGC (in English) undated, BA.

CHAPTER 8

1. W. Rothenstein, *Men and Memories: Recollections 1900-1922* (New York: Coward-McCann, 1932) pp. 204-5. Menu reproduced opposite p. 204.

2. Quoted in E. Rose, *Gordon Craig and the Theatre* (London: Sampson Low, Marston, n.d.), pp. 97-98. The seating-plan of the banquet, owned by Edward Craig.

3. Stan to EGC, before 3 July 1911, o.s., quoted in I. N. Vinogradskaya, *Zhizn' i tvorchestvo K. S. Stanislavskogo: letopis'* (Moscow: Vserossiyskoe Teatral'noe Obshchestvo, 1971), II, 289. Stan to EGC, 16 July 1911, *The Mask* 4 (1911-1912): 88-89.

4. M. F. Lykiardopoulo to Stan, 17 July 1911, in Vinogradskaya, *Zhizn' i tvorchestvo*, II, 289.

5. Vinogradskaya, *Zhizn' i tvorchestvo*, II, 293-94.

6. Vinogradskaya, *Zhizn' i tvorchestvo*, II, 294.

7. E. B. Vakhtangov, *Materialy i stat'i* (Moscow: Iskusstvo, 1959), p. 27.

8. Stan to M. P. Lilina, 4 August 1911, o.s., *SS*, VII, 531-32.

9. Ibid.

10. N. N. Chushkin, *Gamlet-Kachalov, iz stsenicheskoy istorii Gamlet Shekspira* (Moscow: Iskusstvo, 1966), p. 55.

11. Chushkin, *Gamlet-Kachalov*, p. 34. V. Vol'kenshteyn, *Stanislavskiy* (Leningrad: Academia, 1927), p. 65.

12. Vinogradskaya, *Zhizn' i tvorchestvo*, II, 301. L. M. Friedkina, *Dni i gody Vl. I. Nemirovich-Danchenko: Letopis' zhizni i tvorchestva* (Moscow: Vserossiyskoe Teatral'noe Obshchestvo, 1962), p. 183. Chushkin, *Gamlet-Kachalov*, pp. 47-48.

13. Chushkin, *Gamlet-Kachalov*, p. 41.

14. Rose, *Gordon Craig*, p. 99. "Stage Scenery. Mr. Gordon Craig's Invention," *Times* (23 September 1911).

15. W. Poël, "Gordon Craig and Shakespeare," *The Nation* (30 September 1911).

16. Stan to L. Ya. Gurevich, 4 October 1911, o.s., *SS*, VII, 534.

17. N. Petrov, *50 i 500* (Moscow: Vserossiyskoe Teatral'noe Obshchestvo, 1960), p. 95.

18. Vinogradskaya, *Zhizn' i tvorchestvo*, II, 305.

19. M. P. Lilina to EGC, 17 October 1911, o.s.; EGC to Lilina, EGC to Olga Knipper, undated postcards, BA.

20. B. I. Rostotskiy and N. N. Chushkin, "Obrazy Shekspira v tvorchestve V. I. Kachalova," *Vasily Ivanovich Kachalov, Sbornik statey, vospominaniya, pisem* (Moscow: Iskusstvo, 1954), p. 245. Chushkin, *Gamlet-Kachalov*, p. 33.

21. G. V. Gzovskaya, "Vospominaniya o V. I. Kachalova," *Ezhegodnik MKhT 1948* (Moscow: Iskusstvo, 1951), II, 476.

22. Vinogradskaya, *Zhizn' i tvorchestvo*, II, 308.

23. Ibid., pp. 308-9.

24. Ibid., p. 309.

25. Ibid., pp. 309-10. Chushkin, *Gamlet-Kachalov*, p. 31.

26. Vinogradskaya, *Zhizn' i tvorchestvo*, II, 306-7.

27. Ibid., II, 307.

28. "School of the Theatre," London *Daily Chronicle* (11 November 1911).

29. Vinogradskaya, *Zhizn' i tvorchestvo*, II, 308.

30. Ibid., II, 310.

31. Ibid.

32. Ibid., II, 310-11.

33. Ibid., II, 312.

34. A. Koonen, *Stranitsy zhizni* (Moscow: Iskusstvo, 1975), p. 132.

35. Quoted in D. Bablet, *Edward Gordon Craig*, tr. D. Woodward (London: Heinemann, 1966), p. 139.

36. N. S. Butova to T. L. Shchepkina-Kupernik, 25 December 1911, o.s., in Vinogradskaya, *Zhizn' i tvorchestvo*, II, 313.

37. Gzovskaya, "Vospominaniya," *Ezhegodnik MKhT 1948*, II, 476-77. It is possible that Gzovskaya, not the most reliable of memoirists, is confusing the occasion with Craig's blow-up during the New Year's Day dress rehearsal, since no other writer mentions it. However, it accords well with the barring of Craig from the theatre and his subsequent attitude.

38. EGC, Daybook 2 for March 1910 - December 1911, Tex.

39. Ibid.

40. Ibid.

41. M. P. Lilina to EGC, 14 December 1911, o.s., BA.

42. EGC, Daybook 2 for March 1910 - December 1911, Tex.

43. Marginal notes and notes on flyleaves (p. iv) of EGC's copy of D. Magarshack's *Stanislavsky*, 30 March 1951, owned by Edward Craig.

44. Koonen, *Stranitsy zhizni*, pp. 133-34. S. Birman, *Put' aktrisy* (Moscow: Vserossiyskoe Teatral'noe Obshchestvo, 1962), p. 56.

45. V. A. Simov, "Moya rabota nad 'Zhivym trupom,'" *Teatr i Dramaturgiya* 2 (1935): 27-28.

46. Koonen, *Stranitsy zhizni*, p. 132.

47. Ibid.

48. Ibid., p. 133.

49. Marginal notes and notes on flyleaves of EGC's copy of D. Magarshack's *Stanislavsky*, 20 March 1951, owned by Edward Craig.

50. Stan to Suler, 22 December 1911, o.s., in L. A. Sulerzhitskiy, *Povesti i rasskazy, stat'i i zametki o teatre, perepiska, vospominaniya o L. A. Sulerzhitskom* (Moscow: Iskusstvo, 1970), pp. 486-87.

51. Suler to Stan, 23 December 1911, o.s., in Suler, *Povesti i rasskazy*, pp. 487-89. The version published in the *Ezhegodnik MKhT* for 1944 on which David Magarshack based the excerpts in his biography of Stanislavsky suppressed several of the passages most insulting to Stanislavsky and Craig. Suler's shock can be computed when one reads a passage in a letter he had written six months before: "You anger me when you write of Craig, 'I hope he doesn't leave you holding the bag,' because to my mind, this great artist cannot do such a thing — but, unfortunately, we will more likely leave him holding the bag, either by not adopting his idea in its entirety or else by our own inflexibility, we might interfere and exploit him." Letter of 16 June 1911, o.s., to T. L. Sukhotina-Tolstaya, Ibid., p. 483.

52. EGC to Stan, undated [1911], BA. EGC to Olga Knipper, undated, BA.

53. Koonen, *Stranitsy zhizni*, p. 133.

54. *MLIA*, pp. 521-22.

55. Quoted in E. Rose, *Gordon Craig*, p. 102.

56. On June 29, 1935 he wrote to M. P. Lilina, complaining of a number of errors in *My Life in Art*, the vulgarity of the American translation, and, in particular, the story of the screens falling down; he demanded to see the proofs of the chapter about him in any new edition. Lilina replied on September 11, promising that Stan would make the required changes. This was followed on October 22 by a long letter (in English) from Stan, putting the blame for the screens' toppling over wholly on himself and announcing that he would request his publishers to correct errors of fact. But at the same time he affirmed the truthfulness of his account and enclosed an affidavit signed by five stagehands and machinists, who had worked at the MAT for thirty-five years, attesting the various experiments made with the screens and their rehearsal collapse (Letters in BA). Obviously, Stan was so eager to settle the matter that he had a French translation made as well, and followed it with a telegram asking whether the letter had been received. EGC was unsatisfied and drafted a note to Lilina: "The sworn testimony of the workers touches me. It is really sad to see them lined up, as it were, and made to sign a document admitting their error. I absolve them entirely, for I dislike to see the blame put upon such humble men." Pretending to be his own secretary, he wrote to Stan on 7 February 1936, stating that Mr. Craig was away but had laughed over his letter. (Letters at Tex)

The publishers never did correct the mistakes in *My Life in Art* and EGC was right in fearing the dissemination of the story. In a recent American textbook of theatre history, the only detail given about the *Hamlet* production is the story of the screens with the amplified distortion that they fell down on opening night!

57. Koonen, *Stranitsy zhizni*, p. 134.

CHAPTER 9

1. *MLIA*, pp. 513-14.

2. "'Gamlet' v Khudozhestvennom teatre," *Russkie vedomosti* (24 December 1911); Arkhelay, "Ispolnenie 'Gamleta,'" *Russkoe slovo* (24 December 1911): 3 (clippings at University of California, Los Angeles).

3. Arkhelay, "Ispolnenie." F. D. Batyushkov, "Stilirovannyiy Gamlet," *Sovremmenyy Mir* 4 (1912): 254-58, quoted in E. P. Zinner, "Mezhdu dvum'ya revolyutsiyami," in *Shekspir i russkaya kultura* (Moscow: Nauka, 1965), p. 782. V. Bryusov, "Gamlet v Moskovskom Khudozhestvennom Teatre," *Ezhegodnik Imperatorskikh Teatrov* 2 (1912): 48.

4. *MLIA*, p. 515.

5. L. A. Sulerzhitskiy, in *Moskovskiy Khudozhestvenniy Teatr: Istoricheskiy ocherk zhizni i deyatel'nosti* (Moscow: Rampa i Zhizn', 1913), II, 202.

6. S. Birman quoted in N. N. Chushkin, *Gamlet-Kachalov* (Moscow: Iskusstvo, 1966), p. 67.

7. S. Birman, *Put' aktrisy* (Moscow: Vserossiyskoe Teatral'noe obshchestvo, 1962), pp. 54-55.

8. *MLIA*, p. 514. Kaoru Osanai, "Gordon Craig's production of *Hamlet* at the Moscow Art Theatre," ed. A. T. Tsubaki, *Educational Theatre Journal* 20 (December 1968): 590. Chushkin, *Gamlet-Kachalov*, p. 65.

9. A. Koiranskiy, "'Gamlet' na stsene Khudozhestvennogo teatra," *Utro Rossii* (24 December 1911): 3 (clipping at University of California, Los Angeles).

10. N. Ezhov in *Novaya vremya* (30 December 1911), quoted in A. V. Agapitova, "Letopis' zhizni i tvorchestva Vasiliya Ivanovicha Kachalova," *Ezhegodnik MKhT 1948*, II, 732. N. Rossov, "Gamlet' v Khudozhestvennom Teatre," *Teatr i Iskusstvo* 7 (1912): 157.

11. Osanai, *"Hamlet,"* p. 590.

12. Chushkin, *Gamlet-Kachalov*, pp. 68-69.

13. L. Ya. Gurevich, "'Gamlet' v Moskovskom Khudozhestvennom Teatre," *Novaya Zhizn'* 4 (1912): 201.

14. Chushkin, *Gamlet-Kachalov*, p. 65.

15. V. N — skiy, "Postanovka 'Gamleta,'" *Russkoe slovo* (24 December 1911): 3 (clipping at University of California, Los Angeles).

16. Gurevich, "'Gamlet'," p. 204.

17. Ibid.

18. M. M. Morozov, *Shakespeare on the Soviet Stage* (London: Soviet News, 1947), p. 2.

19. N. Efros, "'Gamlet' v Khudozhestvennom Teatre," *Rech'* (24 December 1911).

20. Koiranskiy, "'Gamlet'," plagiarized by P. A. Markov, *Teatral'nye portrety* (Moscow, 1974), p. 199.

21. Koiranskiy, "'Gamlet'."

22. Osanai, *"Hamlet,"* p. 590. *Russkie vedomosti.* A Rostislavov, "Gastrol' Moskovskogo Khudozhestvennogo Teatre v Peterburge," *Teatr i iskusstvo* 16 (1912): 343.

23. N. Efros, *V.I. Kachalov (fragment)* (Petersburg: Solntse Rossii, 1919), pp. 90-91.

24. Rostislavov, "Gastrol'," p. 343.

25. Koiranskiy, "'Gamlet'." A. S. Ivanitskaya, "V Khudozhestvennom Teatre," in *Narodnyy Artist Soyuza SSR K. P. Khokhlov* (Kiev: Mistetstvo, 1968), p. 61.

26. Arkhelay, "Ispolnenie," p. 3.

27. *Russkie vedomosti.*

28. Efros, "'Gamlet'."

29. Rossov, in *Saratovskie vedomosti* (March 1912), quoted in Chushkin, *Gamlet-Kachalov*, p. 87.

30. B. I. Rostotskiy and N. N. Chushkin, "Obrazy Shekspira v tvorchestvo V. I. Kachalova," in *Vasiliy Ivanovich Kachalov, Sbornik statey, vospominaniya, pisem* (Moscow: Iskusstvo, 1954), p. 251. *MLIA*, p. 515.

31. Koiranskiy, "'Gamlet'." Rostotskiy and Chushkin, "Obrazy Shekspira," p. 251. Z. Shadyrskaya in *Novaya zhizn'* (1912), quoted in Chushkin, *Gamlet-Kachalov*, p. 92.

32. V. P. Verigina, *Vospominaniya* (Leningrad: Iskusstvo, 1974), p. 170.

33. Gurevich, "'Gamlet'," p. 201.

34. Rostotskiy and Chushkin, "Obrazy Shekspira," p. 251. Koiranskiy, "'Gamlet'."

35. Edward Craig, *Gordon Craig The Story of His Life* (New York: Albert A. Knopf, 1968), pp. 272-73.

36. *MLIA*, p. 516. Arkhelay, "Ispolnenie," p. 3.

37. Rossov, "'Gamlet,'" p. 158.

38. Osanai, *"Hamlet,"* p. 590. Chushkin, *Gamlet-Kachalov*, p. 329.

39. N. Vil'de, in *Golos Moskvy* (28 December 1911), quoted in Chushkin, *Gamlet-Kachalov*, pp. 130-31.

40. Rostotskiy and Chushkin, "Obrazy Shekspira," p. 250.

41. Osanai, *"Hamlet,"* p. 590.

42. *MLIA*, pp. 516-17. Osanai, *"Hamlet,"* p. 590.

43. Efros, *Kachalov*, p. 86.

44. Chushkin, *Gamlet-Kachalov*, p. 148.

45. Ibid.

46. Chushkin, *Gamlet-Kachalov*, pp. 146-47.

47. Chushkin, *Gamlet-Kachalov*, p. 331. Z. Shadyrskaya in *Novaya Zhizn'* 2 (1912), p. 163, quoted in Rostotskiy and Chushkin, "Obrazy Shekspira," p. 241.

48. Quoted in Chushkin, *Gamlet-Kachalov*, p. 146.

49. Ibid.

50. A. Koonen, *Stranitsy zhizni* (Moscow: Iskusstvo, 1975), p. 133.

51. Efros, *Kachalov*, p. 86. Koiranskiy, "'Gamlet.'"

52. *Russkie vedomosti*.

53. Efros, *Kachalov*, p. 87.

54. E. Beskin, "Moskovskie pis'ma," *Teatr i Iskusstvo* 1 (1912): 11. Rostislavov, "Gastrol,'" p. 343.

55. Rostislavov, "Gastrol,'" p. 343.

56. Gurevich, "'Gamlet,'" p. 202. Arkhelay, "Ispolnenie", p. 3. *Russkoe slovo*, quoted in Sulerzhitsky, "Kreg na Khudozhestvennom Teatre," *Moskovskiy Khudozhestvenniy Teatr*, II, 102.

57. Osanai, *"Hamlet,"* p. 590. O. Gzovskaya, *Puti i pereput'ya* (Moscow: Vserossiyskoe Teatral'noe Obshchestvo, 1976), p. 109.

58. Quoted in Chushkin, *Gamlet-Kachalov*, p. 204.

59. Gzovskaya, *Puti*, p. 108.

60. Efros, "'Gamlet.'"

61. Koiranskiy, "'Gamlet.'" Rostislavov, "Gastrol,'" p. 343.

62. Craig's notes on flyleaves of his copy of D. Magarshack's *Stanislavsky*, owned by Edward Craig. In an interview of 1912, discussing the subterranean chamber concept for the graveyard scene, he "suggested that one might hear, perhaps from the outside the noises on the street, the jingling of bells, etc. and the whole thing was meant to give 'the sensation of the living world outside and the dead world inside.'" J. Cournos, "Gordon Craig interviewed", *Boston Evening Transcript* (6 July 1912).

63. Beskin, "Moskovskie pis'ma," p. 11. Koiranskiy, "Koiranskiy, "'Gamlet.'"

64. Quoted in E. Rose, *Gordon Craig and the Theatre* (London: Sampson Low, Marston, n.d.), p. 101.

65. Arkhelay, "Ispolnenie."

66. Koiranskiy, "'Gamlet.'"

67. Osanai, *"Hamlet,"* p. 590.

68. Arkhelay, "Ispolnenie."

69. *MLIA*, p. 517.

70. Koiranskiy, "'Gamlet.'" Rostislavov, "Gastrol,'" p. 343.

71. O. Sayler, *Inside the Moscow Art Theatre* (New York: Brentano's, 1925), p. 211. *SS*, VII, 732.

CHAPTER 10

1. EGC, Daybook 3 for December 1911-1918, pp. 8-9, Tex. The English translation was by Mikhail Lykiardopoulo.

2. "Replies of the Sphinx to the A[rt] T[heatre] M[oscow]," *Hamlet* 1909, Flyleaf U.

3. Edward Craig, *Gordon Craig The Story of His Life* (New York: Alfred A. Knopf, 1968), p. 271.

4. N. N. Chushkin, *Gamlet-Kachalov: iz stsenicheskoy istorii Gamlet Shekspira* (Moscow: Iskusstvo, 1966), p. 173.

5. A. Koonen, *Stranitsy zhizni* (Moscow: Iskusstvo, 1975), p. 134.

6. Em. Veskin, "'Gamlet' v shirmakh," *Rannee Utro* (28 December 1911), quoted in E. P. Zinner, "Mezhdu dvum'ya revolyutsiyami," in *Shekspir i russkaya kultura* (Moscow: Nauka, 1965), p. 783.

7. N. Vil'de, in *Golos Moskvy*, quoted in Zinner, "Mezhdu dvum'ya revolyutsiyami," p. 779.

8. Em. Beskin, "Moskovskie pis'mi," *Teatr i iskusstvo*, 1 (1912): 10.

9. "Malen'kaya khronika," *Teatr i iskusstvo*, quoted in Zinner, "Mezhdu dvum'ya revolyutsiyami," p. 780.

10. A. Koiranskiy, "'Gamlet' na stsene Khudozhestvennogo Teatra," *Utro Rossii* (24 December 1911): 3 (clipping at University of California, Los Angeles).

11. K. Arabazhin, in *Birzhevye vedomosti* (3 April 1912), quoted in M. N. Stroeva, *Rezhissyorskie iskaniya Stanislavskogo 1898-1977* (Moscow: Nauka, 1973), pp. 284-86. Arabazhin was one of the few critics to get the point that the action was outside time and space, and the setting representative of a vision.

12. N. Efros, "'Gamlet' v Khudozhestvennom teatre," *Rech'* (24 December 1911).

13. L. Gurevich, "'Gamlet' v Moskovskom Khudozhestvennom Teatre," *Novaya Zhizn'* 4 (1912): 201.

14. A. P. Kugel', *V. Kachalov, Zhizn' i tvorchestvo* (Moscow-Leningrad, Kinopechat', 1927), p. 18.

15. Arkhelay, "Ispolnenie 'Gamleta,'" *Russkoe Slovo* (24 December 1911): 3 (clipping at University of California, Los Angeles).

16. Koiranskiy, "'Gamlet.'"

17. Ibid. See also the reviews from *Moskovskie vedomosti* and *Zhatva* quoted in A. S. Ivanitskaya, "V Khudozhestvennom Teatre," *Narodnyy Artist Soyuza SSR K. P. Khokhlov* (Kiev: Mistetstvo, 1968), p. 62, and V. Bryusov, "Gamlet v Moskovskom Khudozhestvennom Teatre," *Ezhegodnik Imperatorskikh Teatrov*, 2 (1912): 57.

18. Quoted in L. A. Sulerzhitskiy, in *Moskovskiy Khudozhestvenniy Teatr: istoricheskiy ocherk zhizni i deyatel'nosti* (Moscow: Rampa i Zhizn', 1913), II, 101-2. Stroeva, *Rezhissyorskie iskanie*, p. 288.

19. EGC, Marginal notes in his copy of David Magarshack's *Stanislavsky*, owned by Edward Craig.

20. Favorable mention of Gzovskaya appears in V. N—skiy, "Postanovka 'Gamleta,'" *Russkoe Slovo* (24 December 1911) and Em. Beskin, "Moskovskie pis'ma," p. 12. Unfavorable mention can be found in Bryusov, "Gamlet," p. 57.

21. EGC, "Which Era? An additional editorial note," *The Mask* 5 (July 1912), tipped in.

22. Quoted in Edward Craig, *Gordon Craig*, p. 272.

23. Translated from the French, quoted in Enid Rose, *Gordon Craig and the Theatre* (London: Sampson Low, Marston, n.d.), p. 101.

24. Quoted in Chushkin, *Gamlet-Kachalov*, p. 37.

25. W. Woroszylski, *The Life of Mayakovsky*, tr. B. Tabori (New York: Orion Press, 1970), pp. 69-70.

26. Quoted in I. N. Vinogradskaya, *Zhizn' i tvorchestvo K. S. Stanislavskogo: letopis'* (Moscow: Vserossiyskoe Teatral'noe Obshchestvo, 1971), II, 316.

27. Lolo, *Zhretsy i zhritsy iskusstva: Slovar' stsenicheskikh deyateley* (Moscow: Rampa i Zhizn', 1910), II, 19.

28. Reproduced in Chushkin, *Gamlet-Kachalov*.

29. Chushkin, *Gamlet-Kachalov*, pp. 171-72.

30. Koonen, *Stranitsy zhizni*, p. 135. EGC, Daybook 3 for December 1911-1918, p. 25. When Stanislavsky began to get nervous at Craig's teasing and threatening to take Koonen to Italy with him, Lilina made a joke of it: "Miss Koonen loves to be surrounded by people and would die of loneliness and nostalgia in your mono-theatre." Instead, Craig gave Koonen a photograph inscribed "To my ideal Ophelia." As to Schuré, a translation of "The Theatre of the Soul" appeared in *The Mask* (January 1912): 171-79.

31. EGC to M. P. Lilina, undated, BA.

32. EGC, "In Germany, Holland, Russia, England and France," *The Mask* 4 (April 1912): 352.

33. Koonen, *Stranitsy zhizni*, p. 136.

34. Entry for 5 April 1912, quoted in Chushkin, *Gamlet-Kachalov*, p. 325.

35. N. Rossov, "'Gamlet' v Khudozhestvennom Teatre," *Teatr i Iskusstvo* 7 (1912): 156; "Kapriz (otkrytoe pis'mo A. P. Kugelyu)," *Teatr i Iskusstvo* 21 (1912): 437-40.

36. A. Serebrov (Tikhonov), *Zvezda* 25 (3 April 1912), quoted in Zinner, "Mezhdu dvum'ya revolyutsiyami," p. 779.

37. A. Rostislavov, "Gastrol' Moskovskogo Khudozhestvennogo Teatra v Peter-burge," *Teatr i Iskusstvo* 16 (1912): 343.

38. Bryusov, "Gamlet," pp. 53-54.

39. A. Benois, *Rech'* (6 April 1912). Quoted in Stroeva, *Rezhissyorskie iskaniya*, p. 288.

40. Bryusov, "Gamlet," p. 56. E. A. Znosko-Borovskiy, *Russkiy teatr nachala XX veka* (Prague: Plamja, 1925), p. 208. Smolenskiy in *Birzhevskie vedomosti* (4 April 1912), quoted in Chushkin, *Gamlet-Kachalov*, pp. 131-32. Beskin, "Moskovskie pis'ma", p. 12.

41. N. N. Evreinov, *P'esy iz repertuara 'Krivogo Zerkala'* (Petrograd: Academia, 1923), pp. 9-32.

42. Stan to I. K. Alekseev, quoted in Vinogradskaya, *Zhizn' i tvorchestvo*, II, 334, 35.

43. Koonen, *Stranitsy zhizni*, p. 138.

44. Stan to V. V. Luzhskiy, September-October 1912, *SS*, VII, 551; Stan to V. V. Luzhskiy, 14 September 1912, o.s., *SS*, VII, 550.

45. M. P. Lilina to EGC, 27 January 1913, o.s., BA.

46. Chushkin, *Gamlet-Kachalov*, p. 334.

47. V.I. Nemirovich-Danchenko to Suler, 8/21 July 1915 in Vl. I. Nemirovich-Danchenko, *Izbrannye pis'ma v dvukh tomakh* (Moscow: Iskusstvo, 1979), II, 150. Reference to "pesthouse," letter to Suler, 24 July 1915 (II, 151). For his work on the 1942 *Hamlet*, see *Vl. I. Nemirovich-Danchenko o tvorchestve aktyora: khrestoma-tiya* (Moscow: Iskusstvo, 1973), pp. 466-82.

CHAPTER 11

1. J[ohn] S[emar], i.e. EGC, "Which Era? An additional editorial note," *The Mask* 5 (July 1912), tipped in.

2. W. Rothenstein, *Men and Memories. Recollections 1900-1922* (New York: Coward-McCann, 1932), p. 154.

3. EGC, *Catalogue of an Exhibition of Drawings and Models for "Hamlet" and Other Plays* (London: Ernest Brown and Phillips, 1912), p. 5.

4. "Mr Craig's designs for 'Hamlet,'" *Times* (10 September 1912).

5. E.S.G., "Plays that Make You Laugh and Think. Mr. Gordon Craig's Ideas about 'Hamlet,'" *Graphic* (14 September 1912).

6. Lugné-Poë to Stan, 3 August 1912, retranslated from the Russian translation in I. N. Vinogradskaya, *Zhizn' i tvorchestvo K. S. Stanislavskogo: letopis'* (Moscow: Vserossiyskoe Teatral'noe Obshchestvo, 1971), II, 343. Lugné-Poë's *Hamlet*, produced in 1913 at the Théâtre Antoine, had a setting by Jean Variot, consisting of a low central arch and flat walls emblazoned with heraldic eagles. The costumes were old-fashoned and traditional, and neither Stanislavsky nor Craig would have approved of a female Hamlet. See Jean Jacquot, *Shakespeare en France* (Paris: Le Temps, 1964), pp. 44, 46, 49.

7. *Teatr i Iskusstvo* No. 2 (1912): 37-40; No. 3 (1912): 60-64; No. 4 (1912): 84-87; No. 38 (1912): p. 722. The attention devoted to Craig and the appearance of his *Art of the Theatre* drove one irate correspondent to complain that Craig was a feeble epigone of Gustav Mahler, Perfall, Roller, Schipchel, Carré and Oscar Bie. E. M. Bezpyatov, "Kreg i ego kniga," *Teatr i Iskusstvo*, 22 (1912): 451-52. For Meyerhold's *Mid-Channel*, see S. Bertenson, *Vokrug Iskusstva* (Hollywood, Calif., 1957), pp. 178-79.

8. For the Boleslawski production, see N. N. Chushkin, *Gamlet-Kachalov: iz stsenicheskoy istorii Gamlet Shekspira* (Moscow: Iskusstvo, 1966), pp. 174-81.

9. Chushkin, *Gamlet-Kachalov*, p. 204. See also the protocols of the Second Moscow Art Theatre *Hamlet* in *Russkiy sovetskiy teatr 1921-1926: dokumenty i materialy*, ed. A. Ya. Trabskiy (Leningrad: Iskusstvo, 1975), pp. 170-76.

10. N. Petrov, *50 i 500* (Moscow: Vserossiyskoe Teatral'noe Obshchestvo, 1960), p. 63.

11. *Russkiy sovetskiy teatra 1921-1926*, p. 226.

12. Chushkin, *Gamlet-Kachalov*, pp. 232-70.

13. Chushkin, *Gamlet-Kachalov*, pp. 212-231. For discussion of this production in English, see M. Gorelik, "The Horses of Hamlet," *Theatre Arts Monthly* (November 1932) and A. Law, "Hamlet at the Vakhtangov," *The Drama Review* (December 1977): 100-10.

14. W. P. Eaton, *Plays & Players* (Cincinnati: Stewart & Kidd, 1916), p. 230.

15. J. Gielgud, "The Hamlet Tradition," in R. Gilder, *John Gielgud's Hamlet* (London: Methuen, 1937), p. 117.

16. *Wendingen* (September-October 1919): 10-13.

17. S. Young, "Hamlet," *New Republic* (22 November 1922), reprinted in *Immortal Shadows* (New York: Hill & Wang, 1958), pp. 13-14.

18. Stan to V. I. Nemirovich-Danchenko (1 February 1923), SS, VIII, 44. Vinogradskaya, *Zhizn' i tvorchestvo*, III, 355.

19. A collateral effect of the Moscow *Hamlet* was that it made the MAT known in the West through Craig's reports. According to Oliver Sayler, "On the Art of the

Theatre" first alerted Europe and America to the "system" and also began the tradition of thrusting Stanislavsky into prominence while neglecting Nemirovich-Danchenko. O. Sayler, *Inside the Moscow Art Theatre* (New York: Brentano's, 1925), pp. 175, 182. Craig was aware of this himself. See note dated 5 August 1930 in *Hamlet* 1909, BA.

20. Gielgud, "The Hamlet Tradition," p. 123.

21. A. Koonen, *Stranitsy zhizni* (Moscow: Iskusstvo, 1975), p. 131.

22. Entry for 21 September 1922. H. Kessler, *In the Twenties. The Diaries of Harry Kessler*, tr. C. Kessler (New York: Holt, Rinehart & Winston, 1971), pp. 194-95. Craig had described the MAT *Hamlet* as a betrayal of his ideas as early as 1915 to Jacques Copeau. "Visites à Gordon Craig, Jaque-Dalcroze et Adolphe Appia," *Revue d'histoire du théâtre* 4 (1963): 360-61.

23. See Note 56, Chapter 8.

24. *The Mask* 10 (1924): 188: "Your book must live because of the sincerity which breathes out of every page of it. You have raised the entire profession of the Theatrical workers to a position it cannot recede from. You have at last made it impossible to retreat."

25. EGC, Daybook 8, p. 21, Tex.

26. EGC, papers on Moscow visit of 1935; Daybook 8, Tex.

27. Chushkin, *Gamlet-Kachalov*, pp. 14-15, 24-26.

28. Stan to EGC, 22 October 1935, Tex.

29. EGC, "Stanislavsky's system," *Drama* 15, 10 (July-September 1937): 161.

30. EGC, marginal notes and commentary July 10, 1951, in his copy of David Magarshack's *Stanislavsky*, owned by Edward Craig.

31. D. Tutaev, "Gordon Craig Remembers Stanislavsky: A Great Nurse," *Theatre Arts* 46, 4 (April 1962): 19.

32. Kessler, *In the Twenties*, p. 194.

33. Quoted in Vinogradskaya, *Zhizn' i tvorchestvo*, II, 316.

34. G. Kozintsev, *King Lear: The Space of Tragedy. The Diary of a Film Director*, tr. M. Mackintosh (London: Heinemann, 1976), pp. 156-57.

35. "Better method, better outcome," Boston *Transcript* (10 February 1923).

36. L. A. Sulerzhitskiy, "Kreg na Khudozhestvennom Teatre," in *Moskovskiy Khudozehstvenniy Teatr: istoricheskiy ocherk zhizni i deyatel'nosti* (Moscow: Rampa i Zhizn', 1913), II, 102.

BIBLIOGRAPHY

MANUSCRIPT AND ARCHIVAL MATERIALS

Autograph correspondence of Craig, Stanislavskiy, Sulerzhitskiy, Lilina, Knipper, Lykiardopoulo, Rumyantsev et al. Bibliothèque de l'Arsénal, Paris.

Autograph correspondence of Craig, Stanislavskiy, Lilina, Sam Hume, Nikolay Chushkin et al. Humanities Research Center, University of Texas at Austin.

Daybooks of Edward Gordon Craig for 1909-1912. Humanities Research Center, University of Texas at Austin.

Hamlet 1909. Shakespeare's text interleaved and interlineated with Gordon Craig's commentary and notes. Bibliothèque de l'Arsénal, Paris.

Notebooks containing the English text of conversations between Craig, Stanislavskiy and Sulerzhitskiy, transcribed by Ursula Cox and Mikhail Lykiardopoulo, relative to *Hamlet*, Act I, Scenes 2 and 3, Act III, Scenes 2, 3, 4, and Act IV, Scenes 1, 2, 3, 5, 6. Bibliothèque de l'Arsénal, Paris.

Stanislavsky a Life by David Magarshack, with pencil notes and marginal glosses by Edward Gordon Craig. Edward Craig Collection, Bledlow, England.

SELECT BIBLIOGRAPHY OF PRINTED WORKS

Agapitova, A. V. "Letopis' zhizni i tvorchestva Vasiliya Ivanovicha Kachalova," *Ezhegodnik MKhT 1948* Tom II (Moscow: Iskusstvo, 1951).

Arkhelay, "Ispolnenie 'Gamleta,'" *Russkoe Slovo* (24 December 1911): 3.

Arnott, Brian. *Edward Gordon Craig & Hamlet* (Ottawa: National Gallery of Canada, 1975).

Ashevskiy, Pyotr. "Chestvovanie Gordona Krega," *Russkoe Slovo* (24 December 1911): 3.

Bablet, Denis. *Edward Gordon Craig* (Paris: L'Arche, 1962).

Beskin, Em. "Moskovskie pis'ma," *Teatr i Iskusstvo* 1 (1912): 10-12.

Bezpyatov, Evgeniy M. "Kreg i ego kniga," *Teatr i Iskusstvo* 22 (1912): 451-52.

Bibliothèque Nationale, Paris. *Gordon Craig et la renouvellement du théâtre* (Paris: Bibliothèque nationale, 1962).

Birman, Serafina. *Put' aktrisy* (Moscow: Vserossiyskoe Teatral'noe Obshchestvo, 1962).

Bryusov, Valeriy. "Gamlet v Moskovskom Khudozhestvennom Teatre," *Ezhegodnik Imperatorskikh Teatrov*, Vyp. II (1912): 43-58.

Chushkin, N. N. *Gamlet-Kachalov: iz stsenicheskoy istorii Gamlet Shekspira* (Moscow: Iskusstvo, 1966).

_____. "O khudozhnike Egorove i 'Gamlet' v MKhT," *Teatr* 1 (January 1970): 93-97.

Craig, Edward. "Edward Gordon Craig's Hamlet," *The Private Library* Second series, 10, 1 (Spring 1977): 35-48.

_____. *Gordon Craig The Story of His Life* (New York: Alfred A. Knopf, 1968).

Craig, Edward Gordon. *Catalogue of an Exhibition of Drawings and Models for "Hamlet" and Other Plays* (London: Ernest Brown and Phillips, 1912).

_____. "The First Time I Played 'Hamlet,'" *The Listener* (3 January 1957): 19.

_____. "The Ghosts in the Tragedies of Shakespeare," *The Mask* 3, 1 (January 1910): 61-66.

_____. "'Hamlet' in Moscow. Notes for a Short Address to the Actors of the Moscow Art Theatre," *The Mask* 7, 2 (May 1915): 109-15.

_____. "In Germany, Holland, Russia & England. A Series of Letters," *The Mask* 1, 11 (January 1909): 221-22; 3, 1 (January 1910): 34-35; 4, (April 1912): 352-54.

_____. *Index to the Story of My Days* (London: Hulton, 1957).

_____. *On the Art of the Theatre* (New York: Theatre Arts Books, 1957).

_____. Review of *My Life in Art*, *The Mask* 10 (1924): 188.

_____. "Shakespeare's Plays," *The Mask* 1, 7 (September 1908): 142-44.

Doroshevich, V. M. *Rasskazy i ocherki* (Moscow: Moskovskiy Rabochiy, 1966).

Efros, Nikolay. *Moskovskiy Khudozhestvennyy Teatr 1898-1923* (Moscow-Petersburg: Gosudarstvennoe izdatel'stvo, 1924).

_____. *V. I. Kachalov (fragment)* (Petersburg: Solntse Rossii, 1919).

Evreinov, Nikolay N. *P'esy iz repertuara 'Krivogo Zerkala'* (Petrograd: Academia, 1923).

Freidkina, L. M. *Dni i gody Vl. I. Nemirovich-Danchenko: Letopis' zhizni i tvorchestva* (Moscow: Vserossiyskoe Teatral'noe Obshchestvo, 1962).

Gielgud, John. "The Hamlet Tradition" in *John Gielgud's Hamlet* by Rosamund Gilder (London: Methuen, 1937).

Gourfinkel, Nina. *Constantin Stanislavsky* (Paris: L'Arche, n.d.).

_____. "La Mise en scène de Hamlet," *La Revue théâtrale* 12 (printemps 1950): 7-16.

_____. "Repenser Stanislavski," *Revue d'histoire du théâtre* (avril-juin 1971-1972): 103-28.

Gregor, Joseph. "Edward Gordon Craigs Hamlet," *Phaidros* (Vienna): Folge 2 (1946): 153-75.

Gurevich, Lyubov. "'Gamlet' v Moskovskom Khudozhestvennom Teatre," *Novaya Zhizn'* 4 (1912): 190-204.

Gzovskaya, Olga V. *Puti i pereput'ya. Portrety. Stat'i i vospominaniya ob O. V. Gzovskoy* (Moscow: Vserossiyskoe Teatral'noe Obshchestvo, 1976).

_____. "Vospominaniya o V. I. Kachalova," *Ezhegodnik MKhT 1948* Tom II (Moscow: Iskusstvo, 1951).

Ilyin, Eugene K. "Gordon Craig's Mission to Moscow," *Theatre Arts* (May 1954): 78-79, 88, 90.

_____. "How Stanislavsky and Gordon Craig produced *Hamlet*," *Plays and Players* 4, 6 (March 1957): 6-7, 21.

Ivanitskaya, A. S. "V Khudozhestvennom Teatre," in *Narodnyy Artist Soyuza SSR K. P. Khokhlov* (Kiev: Mistetstvo, 1968).

Kessler, Harry. *In the Twenties. The Diaries of Harry Kessler.* Translated by Charles Kessler (New York: Holt, Rinehart and Winston, 1971).

Koiranskiy, Aleksandr. "'Gamlet' na stsene Khudozhestvennogo Teatra," *Utro Rossii* (24 December 1911): 3.

Koonen, Alisa. *Stranitsy zhizni* (Moscow: Iskusstvo, 1975).

Kozintsev, Grigori. *King Lear: The Space of Tragedy. The Diary of a Film Director.* Translated by Mary Mackintosh (London: Heinemann, 1976).

Kugel', A. R. *V. Kachalov. Zhizn' i tvorchestvo* (Moscow-Leningrad: Kinopechat', 1927).

Levin, D. "Nabroski," *Rech'* (20 April 1912).

Lolo. *Zhretsy i zhritsy iskusstva: Slovar' stsenicheskikh deyateley* (Moscow: Rampa i Zhizn', 1910).

Magarshack, David. *Stanislavsky, A Life* (London: Macgibbon & Kee, 1953).

Mardzhanishvili, K. A. *Tvorcheskoe nasledie: vospominaniya, stat'i i doklady* (Tbilisi: Zarya Vostoka, 1958).

Markov, Pavel A. *Teatral'nye portrety* (Moscow: Iskusstvo, 1974).

Marotti, Ferruccio. "L'Amleto di Gordon Craig al Teatro d'arte di Mosca," *Terzo Programma Quaderni Trimestrale* 3 (Rome: Edizioni della Radiotelevisione italiana, 1964).

Morozov, M. M. *Shakespeare on the Soviet Stage.* Translated by David Magarshack (London: Soviet News, 1947).

Nash, George. *Edward Gordon Craig 1872-1966* (London: Her Majesty's Stationery Office, 1967).

Nemirovich-Danchenko, Vladimir I. *Izbrannye pis'ma* (Moscow: Iskusstvo, 1954).

_____. *Izbrannye pis'ma v dvukh tomakh (1879-1943)* (Moscow: Iskusstvo, 1979).

_____. "Moscow," *The Mask* 3, 1 (January 1910): 41-42.

N—skiy, V. "Postanovka 'Gamleta,'" *Russkoe Slovo* (24 December 1911): 3.

Osanai, Kaoru. "Gordon Craig's Production of *Hamlet* at the Moscow Art Theatre," edited by A. T. Tsubaki, *Educational Theatre Journal* XX (December 1968): 586-93.

Petrov, Nikolay. *50 i 500* (Moscow: Vserossiyskoe Teatral'noe Obshchestvo, 1960).

Pitcher, Harvey. *Chekhov's Leading Lady: a Portrait of the Actress Olga Knipper* (London: John Murray, 1979).

Podgorniy, Vl. "Iz pisem I.A. Satsa," *Il'ya Sats* (Moscow-Petrograd: Gos. Izd., 1923).

Poël, William. "Gordon Craig and Shakespeare," *The Nation* (30 September 1911).

Polyakova, Elena I. *Stanislavskiy* (Moscow: Iskusstvo, 1977).

_____. *Stanislavskiy — aktyor* (Moscow: Iskusstvo, 1972).

Rose, Enid. *Gordon Craig and the Theatre* (London: Sampson Low, Marston, n.d.).

Rossov, N. "'Gamlet' v Khudozhestvennom Teatre," *Teatr i Iskusstvo* 7 (1912): 155-59.

_____. "Kapriz (otkrytoe pis'mo A. P. Kugelyu)," *Teatr i Iskusstvo* 21 (1912): 437-40.

Rostislavov, A. "Gastrol' Moskovskogo Khudozhestvennogo Teatra v Peterburge," *Teatr i Iskusstvo* 16 (1912): 341-44.

Rostotskiy, B. I., and N. N. Chushkin. "'Gamlet': publikatsiya materialov k postanovke spektaklya v Moskovskom Khudozhestvennom Teatre," *Ezhegodnik MKhT 1944*, Tom I (Moscow: Izd. Muzeya Moskovskogo Ordenoy Lenina i Trudovogo Krasnogo Znameni Khudozhestvennogo Akademicheskogo Teatra SSR Imeni M. Gorkogo, 1946).

_____. "Obrazy Shekspira v tvorchestve V. I. Kachalova," *Vasiliy Ivanovich Kachalov, Sbornik statey, vospominaniya, pisem* (Moscow: Iskusstvo, 1954).

Rothenstein, William. *Men and Memories: Recollections 1900-1912* (New York: Coward-McCann, 1932).

Sayler, Oliver. *Inside the Moscow Art Theatre* (New York: Brentano's, 1925).

Stanislavskiy, K. S. *My Life in Art.* Translated by J. J. Robbins (Boston: Little, Brown, 1924).

_____. *Sobranie sochineniy v vos'mi tomakh* (Moscow: Iskusstvo, 1960-1961).

_____. *Stati, rechi, zametki, dnevniki, vospominaniya 1877-1917* (Moscow: Iskusstvo, 1958).

Stark, Eduard. "Oshibka Gordona Krega," *Teatr i Iskusstvo* 17-18 (1912): 363-65, 380-83.

Steegmuller, Francis. *"Your Isadora." The Love Story of Isadora Duncan & Gordon Craig* (New York: Vintage Books, 1976).

Stroeva, M. N. *Rezhissyorskie iskaniya Stanislavskogo 1898-1917* (Moscow: Nauka, 1973).

Sulerzhitskiy, L. A. "Kreg na Khudozhestvennom Teatre," *Moskovskiy Khudozhestvenniy Teatr: istoricheskiy ocherk zhizni i deyatel'nosti* (Moscow: Rampa i Zhizn', 1913). Tom II, 97-102.

_____. *Povesti i rasskazy, stat'i i zametki o teatre, perepiska, vospominaniya o L. A. Sulerzhitskom* (Moscow: Iskusstvo, 1970).

Tutaev, David. "Gordon Craig Remembers Stanislavsky: A Great Nurse," *Theatre Arts* 46, 4 (April 1962): 17-19.

Vakhtangov, Evgeniy B. *Zapiski, pis'ma, stat'i* (Moscow-Leningrad: Iskusstvo, 1939).

Verigina, Valentina P. *Vospominaniya* (Leningrad: Iskusstvo, 1974).

Vinogradskaya, I. N. *Zhizn' i tvorchestvo K. S. Stanislavskogo: letopis'.* 4 vols. (Moscow: Vserossiyskoe Teatral'noe Obshchestvo, 1971-1976).

Woroszylski, Wiktor. *The Life of Mayakovsky.* Translated by Boleslaw Tabori (New York: Orion Press, 1970).

Zinner, E. P. "Mezhdu dvum'ya revolyutsiyami," in *Shekspir i russkaya kultura*, ed. M. P. Alekseeva (Moscow: Nauka, 1965).

Znosko-Borovskiy, Evgeniy A. *Russkiy teatr nachala XX veka* (Prague: Plamja, 1925).

INDEX

About the Author

LAURENCE SENELICK is Associate Professor of Drama at Tufts University. He is the author of *Russian Dramatic Theory from Pushkin to the Symbolists, British Music Hall 1840-1923,* and *A Cavalcade of Clowns* as well as the translator of Chekhov's *The Cherry Orchard* and *The Seagull.*

Contributions in Drama and Theatre Studies
Series Editor: Joseph Donohue

American Popular Entertainment: Papers and Proceedings of the Conference
on the History of American Popular Entertainment
Myron Matlaw, editor

George Frederick Cooke: Machiavel of the Stage
Don B. Wilmeth

Greek Theatre Practice
J. Michael Walton